D1530856

Grow or Die!

James A. Weber

ARLINGTON HOUSE·PUBLISHERS
NEW ROCHELLE, NEW YORK

HB
3505
W38

Second Printing, July 1977

Manufactured in the United States of America

Library of Congress Cataloging in Publication Data

Weber, James A
  Grow or die!

  Includes bibliographical references and index.
  1. United States—Population. 2. Birth control
—United States. I. Title.
HB3505.W38   301.32′9′73   76–49985
ISBN 0–87000–367–4

To my parents

CONTENTS

PREFACE

Two centuries ago, we, the people, founded the United States of America on the principle of limited government. Today, the government is proposing to operate on the basis of a new principle: limited people.

One of the basic reasons our country was founded was that the king of England, as the Declaration of Independence proclaimed, had "endeavoured to prevent the population of these States." Now, our own political leaders follow in the footsteps of King George III by promoting zero population growth, or ZPG.

In recent years, the American people have been subjected to a seemingly endless barrage of population control propaganda and other "popullution" pap proclaiming the perils of population growth while extolling the benefits of ZPG. Slower economic growth, resource exhaustion, increased pollution, overcrowding, higher crime rates, greater governmental control—you name it, population growth causes it, according to the simplistic siren songs of the ZPGers. Conversely, we are told, a stationary population will usher in a new era of peace, progress, and prosperity.

The curious thing about all of this is not that the population control movement arose; it has, in fact, been doggedly knocking on the door for decades. Rather, what is strange is the absence of any dialogue on the pros and cons of population growth. The ZPGers ran up their flag of "too many people" and even they must have been somewhat shocked at the apparent complete capitulation of their countrymen to the novel notion that fewer equals better.

The ZPGers have been able to present their case with an aura of scientific respectability because they are describing something that has never existed in this country and exists in practically no other country of the world today—

zero population growth. We know what it is like to live with population growth, but we have no experience with zero population growth. Thus the ZPGers have been relatively free to claim any virtue they wish for their ideal of stationary population, for we have no frame of experience from which to judge their utopian pronouncements. And they have claimed just about every virtue possible with such single-minded ideological certainty that any and all opposing viewpoints have appeared to be based either on blind reaction or hopeless optimism.

However, much as the proponents of population control would like to wear the mantle of objective science, it has always been known that the subject of population is an inexact rather than an exact science, and value judgments are inextricably interwoven into any view of the pros and cons of population growth. As Julian L. Simon of the University of Illinois puts it in *Demography,* the publication of the Population Association of America: "In the past decade so many scientists have made it clear that they favor lower birth rates that one can easily come to think that lower birth rates have indeed been shown to be scientifically better for society in every way, though in fact no such finding has been or could be scientifically arrived at because of the value considerations involved."[1]

In addition, facts have a way of catching up with even the most utopian claims. The United States has been experiencing a rapid decline in the rate of population growth for the last two decades. If the ZPGers were right, we should now be on the threshold of a new era of unprecedented plenty.

In fact, the opposite is the case. We are in the throes of an inflationary recession, confronted by suddenly impending resource and pollution problems. The social fabric of the country grows more tenuous every day, while government at all levels flounders and our posture in the world sinks lower. Is this the utopia to which the ZPGers have led us? Or is it simply the inevitable result of a suicidal population theory based on the false and dangerous assumption that fewer is better?

It is time to revisit the subject of population growth. Throughout the history of the United States, it has been the experience of the American people that population growth produces plenty—not poverty. Population growth has continually proved to be a sign of health and well-being for the country and its citizens.

However, there is a paradoxical cycle in human affairs. When a development such as population growth proves beneficial, we tend to shortsightedly accept the benefits while increasingly neglecting or even forgetting the reasons why they occur. The benefits are so obvious that the need for justification is seemingly obviated. But, regardless of how beneficial a development is, lack of a reasoned argument to support it inevitably opens the door for counter-arguments that eventually undermine it, irrespective of the substance and merit of these opposing points of view.

10

The purpose of this book is to rekindle the instinctive appreciation and approval of population growth that has infused the country since its founding by showing how population growth is vital to the continuing health and well-being of the American people.

Grow or Die! is about population growth in the United States. However, since today's world is growing ever smaller and no one nation is an island unto itself, U.S. population growth is discussed where necessary from an overall world as well as national point of view.

I of course take full responsibility for the complete contents of this book. Yet this in no way absolves me from the great debt I owe to the many authors whose views are cited. Any writer can only stand on the shoulders of those who have gone before. I am no exception.

There are very few insights in this book that can be called original. Somewhere at some time someone else has expressed ideas, explored concepts, or stated facts similar if not identical to the ones presented here. What perhaps is original, however, is the book's synthesis of existing knowledge into a unified concept of population growth that is based on factual observations of the real world rather than the Malthusian misconceptions of zero population growth. You, the reader, will be the best judge of this.

My grateful thanks to my wife, Shirley, who has provided unfailing encouragement throughout the writing of this book. My thanks also to our children, Chris and Theresa, who have provided me with the constant inspiration necessary to complete it. It may not appear so, but this book is really about them.

1
A PERSPECTIVE ON AMERICAN POPULATION GROWTH

More people can do more things better. This has been the experience of humankind in the past. There is every reason to believe that it will continue to be the experience of all the peoples of the world in the future.

We have inhabited this earth for many thousands of years. During these millenia, we have grown in numbers to about 4 billion. Yet, throughout this time, particularly in the last several centuries when population growth has been very rapid, people everywhere have generally enjoyed an improving standard of living, or "quality of life."

This is most obvious today in the advanced nations, where even the poor enjoy goods and services that were unavailable to the rich of a century or two ago. But it is also true for the developing countries, where the vast majority of people are not only advanced well beyond the "nasty, brutish, and short" existences of peoples of the past but materially better off than even their parents before them.

This should not come as a surprise, for growth, in fact, is an inexorable law of life. The opposite of growth is not stability but decline and eventual death. In this ever-changing world of ours, we either go up or we go down. There is no such thing as stability, only growth and life or decline and death.

Growth is necessary for development to take place. This is most obvious in children. In their formative years, children physically grow at a faster rate than they will all the rest of their lives. At the same time, their intellectual and emotional capabilities develop at a faster rate than they ever will again.

In adulthood, physical growth eventually stops. Soon thereafter, physical development stops, too. The professional athlete, for example, reaches a peak at about the age of twenty-seven or twenty-eight. From then on, his physical prowess begins to deteriorate, and the athlete relies more on intellectual and emotional growth to develop his capabilities—he plays "smarter" and "cooler," until, finally, his body gives out.

Life's inexorable requirement to grow intellectually and emotionally is no less demanding in adulthood than the imperious demands of physical growth are in childhood. When physical growth and development is stunted in childhood, we call it a tragedy. But it is equally tragic when intellectual and emotional growth and development cease in an adult. Life and growth are, in a real sense, synonymous. One cannot exist without the other.

This applies not only to individual human beings but to human organizations, too. An organization that is growing is one in which there is a dynamism, an adventuresomeness, a dash for development that is readily apparent, while the opposite is the case in an organization whose membership is declining.

What is true of individual human beings and human organizations is equally true of human societies. A human society that is growing in population is one that is developing. Population growth spurs human development; population decline results in developmental deterioration.

The reason for this is not difficult to determine. Yet it is usually totally neglected. It is simply that population growth provides increasing numbers of people, or human resources. And people are our most important resource, our most significant capital, our greatest and most productive investment.

Why are human resources so important? Because, as R. Buckminster Fuller points out, we live in a material world governed by the second law of thermodynamics. This physical law predicts an inexorable loss of energy known as entropy. In effect, the law states that the material world is gradually winding itself down, "running out of gas." It is growth in population, human resources, that enables us to improve our lot in spite of this law. It is the increasing intellectual and physical energy of growing numbers of creative, dynamic, and productive human beings that makes it possible not only to counteract but to transcend the energy loss due to entropy in the material world. Fuller makes this point with ultimate scientific elegance: "You and I are essential functions of the Universe. We are exquisite antientropy."[1]

The positive and dynamic relationship between population growth and human development is amply shown by the history of the world to date. Throughout practically all of human history, world population growth has been extremely slow, so slow, in fact, that population historians usually represent the average annual population growth rate prior to the seventeenth century with a zero.[2]

If zero population growth were such a wonderful thing, this should have been a time of rapid human development. But it was not, for, although population growth was extremely slow, human development was, if anything, even slower. Fire, for example, possibly was the first technological discovery of prehistori Wood was the first fuel. Many millenia later, in the seven-

14

teenth century, firewood still was humankind's major source of energy.

Somewhere in the distant past, people learned how to domesticate animals so they could be used for work and travel. In the seventeenth century, people were still plowing fields behind mules and work horses and riding to town in horse-drawn wagons.

Paper was invented thousands of years ago, and the written message came into being as a way of communications. In the seventeenth century, letters remained virtually the only method of communicating over long distances.

People have always individually hand-fashioned various types of products, ranging from pottery to plows. Until the seventeenth century's Industrial Revolution, these laborious manual methods of producing goods remained the only available method of manufacture.

The seventeenth century was, thus, something of a watershed for humankind in terms of population growth and human development. Prior to the 1600s, population growth was infinitesimally slow and human development was equally imperceptible.

This is not to say that certain societies at certain times did not experience fast population growth and development. Historical evidence suggests, for example, that the great civilizations of Greece and Rome experienced periods of rapid population growth that coincided with their development as world powers, following which there were periods of population decline and subsequent deterioration of these once-powerful empires. But it is to say that, on the average, world population growth and development have been extremely slow since the beginning of human history.

The influence of population growth on human development in the past has thus been nearly imperceptible, due to an infinitesimally slow rate of growth. As demographic historian Josiah Cox Russell comments, discussing historical population trends, the

very nature of population change defines its possibilities as an influence upon history. With rare exceptions, it is a slow, ponderous force. Major diversions in population trend exert influence so slowly that their results are apparent only one or more centuries later as they induce alterations in economic life and intellectual currents which oppose, modify and sometimes overcome the inertia of the last great demographic movement. Thus the very tardiness of the change would allow its causes to escape attention. Population change acts somewhat as a geological disturbance which tilts the land into a different plane. The movement of population, like that of water forced in a new direction, still follows as far as possible the old watercourses and only reluctantly creates another pattern by erosion. Yet even then the outlines of the older system remain, adding complexity and variety to the pattern.[3]

However, in the seventeenth century, the slow pace of population growth and human development radically changed. Average annual world population growth rates increased from near-zero in the mid-seventeenth century to 2 percent at present. And world population increased from about 500 million in 1650 to one billion in 1800, 2 billion in the early 1900s, 3 billion in 1960, and about 4 billion today.

If the ZPGers were right, this rapid growth in population would have brought on unparalleled conditions of world misery. But the exact opposite is the case. Population growth in the last several centuries has been accompanied by a period of human development that has enabled the vast majority of people in the world to enjoy an ever-improving standard of living.

The growth of human population to 4 billion has actually proved to be humankind's most tremendous and splendid achievement. As Professor W. D. Borrie, director of research at the School of Social Sciences of Australian National University, states: ". . . some who observe the present 'population explosion' decry it as if a great shadow of impending doom had spread upon the world; yet the astonishing growth rate of the world today must be accepted as a triumph of man over his environment."[4]

In the seventeenth century, the prime source of heat energy was wood. Today, energy is derived from not only wood but coal, oil, natural gas, water, geothermal sources, nuclear fission, and directly from the sun itself.

Prior to the population growth of the last few centuries, humankind's maximum mode of transportation was the horse. Today, transport methods include cars, trains, buses, and jet planes. Even rocket trips to the moon are not uncommon.

In place of hand-carried, written messages that may take months to deliver, we now instantly communicate with each other via telephone, radio, television, microwave, and satellite transmission. And, instead of laboriously making individual products by hand, we mass-produce them by machine in quantities of thousands or even millions at a time.

All of this would undoubtedly come as a surprise to Thomas Robert Malthus, the famous parson who in 1798 published his essay on the principle of population.[5] The godfather of those who today decry population growth as a "great shadow of impending doom," Malthus viewed population growth from the wrong end of the telescope. He believed that population growth is not a cause but a result of human betterment.

Malthus envisaged the people of his time as living at the bare level of subsistence. It was not population growth that would enable people to progress beyond this subsistence level. It was this subsistence level—that is, the availability of food supplies—that held back and, in effect, determined the population level.

In Malthus' view, any human development or improvement in living standards that occurred happened independently of population. But, when these improvements were made, they caused population to increase because there was more food available and thus fewer deaths due to famines. As a result, the

16

world was reduced to its previous level of subsistence and no overall human development took place.

It was theories such as Malthus' that caused economics to be called the "dismal science." Malthus is the forerunner of the "doom and gloom" school of today.

However, the history of the past few centuries constitutes a complete refutation of Malthus' views. There is no way that Malthusian dogma can be used to explain the rapid population growth and even more rapid rise in living standards that have occurred throughout the world during the past several centuries, especially in advanced countries such as the United States.

Malthus, in fact, used the United States as a textbook example of a country in which population was increasing at a maximum rate. Founded in the eighteenth century, the U.S. began its life at a running gallop, growing in population at the rate of 3 percent a year. "In the United States of America," Malthus wrote, "the population has been found to double itself in twenty-five years."[6] From Malthus' point of view, this surely was a road to eventual ruin. Yet the United States not only survived but prospered, as rapid population growth spurred even faster human development.

In fairness to Malthus, it should be pointed out that population data was extremely limited at the time he expounded his population principle. Today, we have the advantage of not only hindsight but population data of the past that is infinitely more complete than that available to Malthus.

Malthus also wrote at a time that was a turning point in human history. Never before had there been population growth of the magnitude that was occurring in Malthus' day. And never before had human development proceeded at such a rapid pace. It was a time that economic historian R. M. Hartwell refers to as the " 'great discontinuity' which divided a Europe of slow economic growth and mass poverty, in which population and real incomes were rising very slowly or not at all, and were sometimes falling, from the modern Europe of economic growth and widespread wealth, in which population has grown at an almost terrifying speed and in which there has been, also, a sustained growth of real incomes."[7] It is not surprising, therefore, that Malthus had difficulty in perceiving the true nature of the eventful changes taking place around him.

It should also be pointed out that Malthus did, in fact, temper his views with the passage of time, perhaps because it became increasingly apparent to him that people were improving their lot as population increased. He issued no clarion call in defense of population growth, but in the fifth edition of his book, published in 1817 (nineteen years after the first edition) he stated: "From a review of the state of society in former periods, compared with the present, I should certainly say that the evils resulting from the principle of population have rather diminished than increased. . . . [and] it does not seem unreasonable to expect that they will be still further diminished."[8]

17

However, although Malthus' principle of population has long since been abandoned, even to some extent by its author, the philosophical kernel of the principle has inexplicably been retained. Malthus' basic assumption that population growth is a hindrance rather than a help to human development is today the dominant view. And, even in the face of the blatantly contradictory evidence of the past several centuries as well as the more distant past, efforts continue to cut down human populations to fit the procrustean bed of neo-Malthusianism.

In developing countries, the original specter of Malthusianism is raised in the form of mass starvation. In advanced nations, where per capita incomes are higher and farmers are oftentimes paid not to grow food, neo-Malthusianism necessarily takes a more indirect approach. Here in the United States, for example, ZPGers tell us that continuing population growth will result in slower economic progress, faster resource depletion, greater environmental pollution, deteriorating social conditions, and more governmental controls, among other problems. The way to alleviate, if not eliminate, these problems, we are told, is to reduce U.S. population growth so that our population becomes stationary or even declines in the future.

But, based as they are on the faulty assumptions of centuries-old and thoroughly discredited Malthusianism, these views completely misrepresent past American history and present U.S. conditions. Population growth has proved a boon to Americans in the past. And it will be no less vital and necessary in the future if we are to achieve continuing economic progress, more abundant resources, an improved environment, better social conditions, and greater political freedom and independence.

2
U.S. POPULATION GROWTH AND ECONOMIC PROGRESS

Population growth in the United States has resulted in economic progress that is without parallel in world history. Two centuries ago, the United States had 4 million people and was a "developing nation." Today, the United States has well over 200 million people and is a major world economic power.

The positive relationship between population growth and economic progress is shown by the one hundred years between 1870 and 1970, for which we have fairly reliable economic and population data. During this period, our population grew from 39 million to 208 million, or 433 percent. At the same time, the gross national product (GNP) increased more than 3100 percent, or seven times faster.[1] And, from 1890 to 1970, population increased 230 percent, while GNP per capita grew 334 percent, more than three times faster.[2]

Another example of population growth's multiplying effect on economic advancement is the sharp contrast between the historical experience of the United States and that of France, a country that took Malthusian notions to heart and reduced its population growth accordingly. Even before Malthus' time, for example, the Abbé Raynal categorically stated in *Révolution de l'Amérique* (1781) that it would be "foolhardy to determine the future population of the United States. . . . but it will be surprising if as many as ten million men are ever able to find subsistence on these lands. The country will be more or less able to support itself only provided its inhabitants can learn to be content with parsimony and mediocrity."[3]

However, that's not quite the way it worked out. According to Simon Kuznets, Nobel laureate and recognized world authority on the measurement of economic growth, the United States had a population of 16.7 million and a total national product of some $7.9 billion (in 1965 dollars) in 1834–43, when the country still was a "developing nation." At about the same time, France had a population of 33.9 million and a total product of some $8.2 billion. Turn the pages of history and what do we find? By 1965, the United States was a major economic power with a population of 195 million and a GNP of close to $700 billion, while France was a second-rate power with a population of about 49 million and a GNP of about $100 billion.[4] In other words, at the end of one and a quarter centuries of progress, the United States had four times the population and seven times the total product of France.

Nor is the experience of the United States unique among the advanced nations of the world. Kuznets examined sixteen developed nations for which there are adequate records, and his results corroborate the positive effect of population growth on economic progress.[5]

Prior to the seventeenth century, population growth and economic progress were both imperceptibly slow, and people generally had a very low standard of living, according to Kuznets, who estimates, for example, that the population of Europe had been growing at a rate of only about 17 percent per *century*, while per capita economic product grew only 25 to 50 percent per *century*. Over the next several hundred years, however, population began increasing very rapidly. Population growth rates increased from 17 percent per *century* to as much as 19 to 24 percent per *decade* in, for example, the United States, Canada, Australia, and Japan. And, as population grew faster, rates of economic growth became little short of astounding in all of the countries examined by Kuznets. In older European countries, economies grew at the rate of *600* to *2400 percent* per century, compared to previous growth rates per century of only 25 to 50 percent. In the United States, Canada, and Australia, economic growth rates ranged from *2200* to *3400 percent* per century! And Japan achieved an economic growth rate of more than *5000 percent* per century.

Kuznets discovered no direct, one-on-one correlation between population and economic growth rates. That is, some countries with high population growth rates also experienced high rates of economic growth, and some countries with low population growth rates grew economically at a slow rate. But this was not invariably the case, since there were other countries with high population growth rates and relatively low economic growth rates and vice versa. However, *in all cases,* rapid population growth was accompanied by even more rapid economic progress, leading Kuznets to the obvious conclusion that it "appears that population growth, despite pressure on the limited stock of natural resources and manmade capital, has permitted substantial rises in product per capita, particularly in countries with a social framework attuned to modern technology."[6] As Alfred Sauvy, director of the Institut de Demographie at Paris University and past president of the United Nations Commission on Population, puts it, a "stationary or very slowly moving population does not benefit enough from the advantages of growth. There is no historical example of a stationary population having achieved appreciable economic progress. Theoretically, it is not impossible, but in practice, in our period especially, it does not happen."[7]

The neo-Malthusians would have us believe that no positive relationship has existed between population growth and economic progress in the past or that, even if it did exist in the past, it will not hold in the future. But, as economist Elgin Groseclose points out, this view represents a

misconception . . . of the sources of wealth. The basic axiom of economics—both classical and Marxian—is that wealth is the product of labor. The mineral resources of the earth are not wealth until human effort has been exerted, either to discover or extract them. A tree standing in a forest becomes wealth when it has been felled by human labor, sawed, planed, and fashioned into a table, armchair or other useful article. Throughout the ages—until the current era of statistics-worship—population has been regarded as the foremost source of wealth; the prime object of rulers and governments has been to attract and increase the number of their people. Density of population and rising population historically have been the mark of a prosperous, vital civilization.[8]

Neo-Malthusians would also have us believe that economic progress is something that simply "happens" irrespective of growing numbers of people. However, if this is the case, why has economic progress not occurred throughout history? Why has it only occurred in the past during times of population increase?

This view of economic progress as something that simply happens is what internationally known economist and demographer Colin Clark of Australia's Monash University refers to as the cargo-cult mentality.[9] Clark relates how the leaders of cargo cults in New Guinea tell their followers that shiploads of beer, tinned meat, and other good things originate by a supernatural process in the Central Pacific, but are diverted by cunning Australians to their own use. However, the cult leaders say, sufficient prayers, ceremonies, and financial contributions to the cargo cults will make it possible to divert these shiploads for the benefit of the cult followers. Comments Clark: "The belief of some people that wealth somehow originates independently of human efforts, and that all we have to do is to have a smaller population among whom to divide it, is on an intellectual level not much higher than that of the Cargo Cult."

How Population Growth Creates Economic Progress

The positive effects of increasing numbers of people on economic progress are the results of not only population growth per se but also of population redistribution. As the United States grew from a country of four to more than 200

21

million people, there were two major redistributions of population. One was the migration of growing numbers of people to other regions of the country from the original base along the Atlantic seaboard. The other was the migration of people from rural to urban and metropolitan areas.

Population growth has occurred throughout U.S. history. But, at the same time, the annual rate of population growth has gradually declined over the long term, from a high of 3 percent in the early 1800s to 1 percent and even less in some periods. However, this long-term decline in the national population growth rate has been accompanied by increasing population growth rates in regional, urban, and metropolitan areas during various periods in the country's history. Resulting primarily from the redistribution, or migration, of people to areas with greater economic opportunities, these increases in the rates of regional, urban, and metropolitan population growth have served, in effect, as counterpoints to the overall decline in the national population growth rate, while having the same positive although more localized effects on economic progress.

First and foremost among the positive effects of population growth on economic progress is the fact that people are our most important capital and our most productive investment. It is people who come up with new ways of doing things. It is people who invent the tools and equipment to put these new ideas into practice. And it is people who go out and get the job done. There is no other force on earth that can do all of these things—only people. Population growth thus results in a greater capacity for productive economic development.

But, at the same time and perhaps even more important, population growth creates a *need* for economic development. For necessity, it is said, is the mother of invention. And few other factors create as great a need to discard old, outmoded customs and to adopt new, innovative methods than the demographic pressure of increasing numbers of people for whom room must be made at the table.

Imagine for a moment a society that is locked into cumbersome and antiquated ways of doing things because "that's how we've always done them." What would it take to get this society to change its ways and improve its methods of operation? As long as it is "getting along," it will be very difficult to introduce new ideas and methods because they go against custom and tradition. But suppose that the population of this society begins increasing. The society will eventually reach a point at which it will not be able to get along using traditional methods. This will become obvious in terms of a lower standard of living brought on by increasing numbers of people attempting to share a slower-growing or even same-size pie. It is this initial result of population growth in a culturally tradition-bound country that underlies the views of neo-Malthusians who look on population increase as the harbinger of approaching Armageddon.

22

But what the neo-Malthusians apparently fail to see or admit is that people do not stand still in the face of a challenge to their living levels. They react, and in the process of reacting, they develop new ways of doing things that are superior to the old.

This fundamental point has been well expressed by economist Albert O. Hirschman in terms of Duesenberry's "fundamental psychological postulate" that people will resist a lowering of their standard of living.[10] If a community's population increases while all else remains the same, living standards will, of course, drop. However, population pressure on living standards leads to counter-pressure or activity designed to maintain or restore the previous standard of living of the community. And this successful wrestling with new tasks results in a new situation because the activity undertaken by the community to resist a decline in its standard of living causes an increase in its ability to control its environment and to organize itself for development. As a result, the community is better able to exploit opportunities for economic growth and progress beyond its previous standard of living.

This is what basically happened when today's more advanced countries began experiencing very rapid population growth several centuries ago. This initial population growth was unanticipated, and it occurred in highly tradition-bound societies. But, as these societies began to flexibly improve their ways of doing things to satisfy the need for economic development created by population growth, they also began to anticipate continuing population growth and make plans accordingly. And, insofar as they were able correctly to plan for future population growth, living standards continually improved without the need for regressions to spur development. The initial impetus to development created by lower living standards thus was no longer needed as societies began to plan ahead to meet the growing needs of continuing population increases. And so was born the modern advanced economy.

New Knowledge and Technology. Population growth thus simultaneously provides a challenge to human creativity in the form of actual or threatened lower living standards and the opportunity to exercise this creativity more effectively through the medium of increasing numbers of people. The most significant area in which population growth aids economic development is in the creation of new knowledge and technology.

It is estimated that over the last 250 to 300 years, while world population has grown at rates of up to 2 percent a year, the international growth of new scientific knowledge has been booming at an annual, exponential rate of 7 percent.[11] According to Kuznets, such increases in new knowledge can result from population growth in three ways.[12]

First, population growth produces an absolutely larger number of talented people capable of creating new knowledge. Second, there is a "snowballing" effect due to the interdependence of knowledge. Greater knowledge of chemistry, for example, contributes to greater knowledge of physics, and intellectual progress in both of these fields contributes, in turn, to greater knowledge of physiological and biological functions. Third, the increase in new knowledge is further enhanced by the fact that creative effort flourishes best in a dense intellectual atmosphere, which insures the existence of adequately numerous groups in all fields of creative work and provides the possibility of more frequent and intensive intellectual contacts and greater, more productive specialization. It is no coincidence that today's "knowledge explosion" is occurring at a time when nine out of ten scientists who ever lived are still alive.

Thus, population growth helps to create greater economic development by speeding up the creation of new knowledge far beyond the increase in population. Sums up Kuznets, stressing the importance of people as the only carriers of the learning and creative ability that provide the basis for economic progress, insofar as it is "possible to give the new generation the education and other requisites of Homo sapiens, failure to increase means failure to add to the possible carriers of light and knowledge."[13]

But population growth not only accelerates the accumulation of new scientific knowledge by increasing the numbers of people capable of producing it and providing a more fruitful intellectual milieu in which it can be produced. It also results in a younger population that is more open and alive to potential technological applications of new knowledge. For, as James A. Michener comments, youth "doesn't have the restraint of age. That's why prudent societies traditionally have looked to young people for leadership. . . . the great scientific revolution has been the work of young people."[14]

This is a view that is seconded by Edmund S. Phelps of Columbia University's Department of Economics, who states that "technical progress requires people, especially relatively young people, to create it and to implement it. There can be little doubt, I think, that a slowdown of population growth will reduce somewhat the rate of technical progress simply by reducing the sheer number of people engaged in producing technical change. . . . Furthermore, there can be little doubt that, on the average, scientific invention and, to a lesser extent, technical innovation are more likely to come from the relatively young members of the labor force than from the old."[15]

Increased Entrepreneurship. A growing economy requires entrepreneurs —people who are willing to take the risks of investing in the future. Population growth encourages entrepreneurship by creating expanding markets and new business opportunities. "The expectation of a future in which larger markets and wider opportunities will prevail encourages extension of capacity, both personal and material," states Kuznets. "It discourages the stagnation which results when individuals cling to unsatisfactory but 'safe' routine jobs or when entrepreneurs, bankers, the labor force, and other important agents of economic enterprise hesitate to commit themselves to ventures that depart from the 'tried and true.' "[16]

Furthermore, this effect of population growth is particularly significant in today's modern economy. This is because several centuries ago no one really knew what population was doing. At the time of Malthus and before, for example, accurate population statistics were lacking, with the result that there was disagreement even as to whether population was increasing or decreasing, much less at what rate. Today, however, accurate and detailed population statistics are available monthly. And, based on this data, investments may be made today in anticipation of markets that will be created by population growth one, two, five, or even ten years from now. This not only increases the economic effects created by current population trends but, in comparison to the glacial response of human development to slow population increases of the past, greatly foreshortens economic reactions to current rates of population growth.

Population growth also aids entrepreneurs and spurs overall economic development by minimizing the unfavorable effects of investment errors that inevitably occur in any economy. In a stationary population, mistakes such as overinvestment in a particular activity eventually end up as net economic losses to the community. But investment errors can eventually be rectified through an expanding population, thus enabling the community to gain the benefits of even misguided entrepreneurial investments. As Everett Hagen of the Massachusetts Institute of Technology has pointed out, errors in public and private investment are made in every country. But in a country with a rapidly growing population there is a much better prospect of such misplaced investment ultimately being put to good use than in a country with a stationary population.[17]

Greater Savings. A growing population creates proportionally greater savings than a stationary one because it has a greater incentive to save. This is ultimately due to the effect children have on their parents, the effect the young have on the old.

Typically, young single people do not place great emphasis on savings. Even in marriage, a young but childless couple will tend to place greater emphasis on current consumption rather than savings for the future. It is only when children arrive that the need for savings becomes apparent and the incentive to increase income and save more becomes urgent.

This contradicts a common impression that population growth results in a decrease in savings because money that would otherwise have been put in savings is instead spent on children. But, as Kuznets points out, there is little ground for this supposition.[18] Money spent on children may just as well come from reduced expenditures on consumer goods and leisure as savings. Or it may come from increased income produced as a result of the need to save more.

Allen C. Kelley, chairman of the Department of Economics at Duke University, also analyzed the effect of population growth on savings and came to the same basic conclusion that it is incorrect to assume that savings rates decrease as family size increases. Instead, he points out, family size can exert a positive and strong impact on household savings insofar as savings plans are in part motivated by specific target objectives such as providing for children's education or building an estate for future heirs.[19]

Furthermore, it is often forgotten that saving is a two-way street. What goes into savings eventually comes out. Savings are usually put away for purposes such as education, housing, or retirement. Consequently, at some future point, money placed in savings is taken out and "dissavings" occur. Kuznets points out that in a growing population there are more young people putting money into savings than old people taking money out. The result is that there is a continuing rise in total savings. But, in a stationary population, the amount of money being taken out of savings tends to equal the amount of money going into savings, with the result that there is no increase in total savings.[20]

Capsulizing the effect on savings resulting from France's slow population growth, Sauvy comments that a "population without children does not believe in the future and can hardly be expected to have the pioneering spirit. Only an utter misconception of history and international ethics can have led anyone to think that a nation of investors could continue indefinitely."[21]

He cites the period from 1880 to 1914 when the French followed the advice of economist J. B. Say to "accumulate savings rather than children." During this period, France grew 10 percent in population and savings were 10 percent of national income. Britain and Germany, meanwhile, had population increases of 57 percent and savings ranged from 12 to 20 percent of their national incomes, or almost double that of France. Notes Sauvy: "The fewer children the Frenchman had, the less inclined he was to capital venture. Peguy called the father of several children the adventurer of modern times, and this was no joke."[22]

Reduced Per Capita Capital Requirements. Population growth thus speeds economic development by providing proportionally greater amounts of savings for investment purposes. But, at the same time, it makes possible more productive use of savings by reducing capital requirements per person for many types of public and private investments.

In every society, there is an infrastructure whose initial cost is approximately the same regardless of population size. This infrastructure consists of vital necessities such as basic governmental institutions, transportation and communications systems, water and sanitation facilities, and the like. The more people there are, the less it costs per person to develop this infrastructure. As MIT's Hagen has noted, many of a country's "most costly investment requirements such as transport systems have to be constructed to much the same extent regardless of whether they are to serve a small or large population.

26

Consequently, as population grows, many significant overhead costs, both public and private, are spread more widely, thus substantially reducing capital requirements per person."[23]

Increased Economic Flexibility. Economic growth, like any other type of growth, requires changes, and these changes are better effected with a growing rather than stationary population. This is because a growing population contains a larger proportion of younger, more mobile and flexible workers who are better able and more willing to move from region to region, from rural to urban or metropolitan area, and from industry to industry, as economic opportunity beckons. As Kuznets observes, it is the younger groups in the labor force who are "most mobile—in space and within the productive system—since, unlike older workers, they are not committed to family and housing or to established positions. This greater mobility is particularly true of new entrants into the labor force, who naturally veer toward those sectors that are likely to spearhead the country's economic growth, and who are oriented toward these sectors even in their training within the educational system."[24]

Economic growth first of all requires extensive changes in the geographical locations of areas with the greatest economic opportunities or, as Kuznets puts it, the "realization of economic growth potentials is contingent upon a vast internal migration—movement of people from the country to the cities, and within the cities from places of lesser to those of greater economic promise. A substantial rate of population growth means, then, a greater rate of immigration from abroad or a greater rate of internal migration, or both."[25]

Economic growth also involves changes in the relative significance of different industries within the economic structure. These changes require extensive worker mobility in terms of moving between jobs and industries. Thus, as Kuznets sums up, the

> importance of mobility in the distribution of human resources in response to the differential growth possibilities in the economy can easily be underestimated. Modern economic growth is characterized by rapid structural changes, shifts in importance among industries, and in their location within the country's economy. Stickiness in the response of the labor force to such potential changes can be a serious obstacle to economic growth and greater per capita product. If insufficient labor flows to rising economic opportunities, the relative cost of labor and the relative price of the product remain too high to permit expansion of output to the full potential. Conversely, if the labor force in relatively deteriorating economic opportunities remains attached to them, the national level of product per worker and per capita is not likely to rise. A young or otherwise mobile group within the labor force is therefore strategically important. . . . It follows that population growth, in contrast to population stability, may, because of the greater mobility and adjustability of human resources, be conducive to higher per worker (and hence per capita) levels of output; and this may be true, within limits, of greater vs. lesser population increase.[26]

27

Increased Economies of Scale. Adam Smith was the most famous if not the first economist to recognize the benefits resulting from economies of scale, or, as he called it, division of labor. Smith used the example of a pin factory to show that ten men working together, each specializing in a particular aspect of pin manufacture, could produce 4800 pins per man per day, whereas each of the ten men working alone "could not each of them have made twenty, perhaps not one pin, in a day."[27]

Economies of scale are perhaps the most obvious economic benefit of population growth. But what is not so obvious is that economies of scale resulting from both growing size and increasing specialization operate at every level of the economy. Take, for example, the population growth and concentration of people in metropolitan and urban areas. Edwin S. Mills of Princeton University makes the point that

> important advantages of cities derive from both the scale and specialization of economic activity. In terms of absolute numbers of employees in a single plant, economies of large-scale production are most important in manufacturing. Historically, many cities have consisted of a small number of large manufacturing plants, a much larger number of other firms that sell either to the large manufacturers or to the city's residents, and the employees of these firms and their families. But scale economies are not absent outside of manufacturing; and increasingly, nonmanufacturing activities take place in highly specialized firms, many of which require the demand generated by a large city to achieve efficient size. The best example is the service sector, which is the most urbanized of all employment sectors and the most rapidly growing source of employment in cities.[28]

Consequently, it is not just the huge steel mill that profits from a growing scale of operations. Local bus, telephone, and finance companies as well as medical clinics and the supermarket on the corner reap similar economies of scale.

With population growth, there is a steady stream of new as well as existing businesses and industries that are able to attain a volume of operations sufficient to achieve scale economies resulting from increasing specialization. This is because increasing specialization occurs not only within companies but between companies. For example, a company may attempt to internally handle all of its many functions as it grows. However, not all functions can be internally specialized to the same degree. Consequently, there are always a number of functions in any given company that could profit from increased specialization but whose volume is insufficient to achieve it. It is at this point that a new enterprise will come into being with the express purpose of specializing in the performance of one of these functions. The new firm will specialize in performing this one function not only for the company in question but for a number of companies, thereby achieving economies of scale resulting from size and specialization that none of the companies the firm serves could have

28

achieved on its own. These scale economies may be most obvious and measurable in manufacturing operations, but they are just as prevalent in other areas of economic activity.

Population growth also determines the degree to which economies of scale can be achieved through decentralization, or what George Stigler of the University of Chicago calls "localization." For as a company's or industry's market increases, it becomes possible to achieve economies of scale in transportation costs through the establishment of branch plants localized to individual submarkets. As Stigler comments, such "geographical dispersion is a luxury that can be afforded by industries only after they have grown large (so that even the smaller production centers can reap the major gains of specialization)."[29]

The point is that increasing economies of scale resulting from population growth are as prevalent today as they were in Adam Smith's time—if not more so. The development of ultra-high-voltage transmission systems that send electricity anywhere in the country; the growth of national airline service; the development of high-speed trains; expanding telephone voice and data communications; the increasing use of computers and other types of office automation in banking, finance, insurance, and a host of other commercial and governmental activities; the proliferation of restaurant and fast-food chains; expansion in supermarket size; the widespread development of shopping center complexes: all of these are current, ongoing examples of activities in which economies of scale due to growing size and increasing specialization are being realized as a result of population growth. As Stigler sums up, the "division of labor is not a quaint practice of eighteenth-century pin factories; it is a fundamental principle of economic organization."[30]

More Productive Labor Force. Population growth results in a labor force that is economically more productive than a stationary one. There are several reasons for this.

One is that growth results in a labor force of higher economic quality. Harvard's Harvey Leibenstein points out that in a growing labor force there are a greater number of young people who are the primary recipients of human capital in the form of education. Presuming that this educational input includes knowledge of the latest technological developments and the newest methods of operation, the result is an increase in the average economic quality of the labor force that is faster than if the labor force were stationary. For, as Leibenstein explains, if

education or other forms of human capital are given only to the young prior to entry into the work force, and its quantity increases over time, then the greater the rate of population growth, other things equal, the greater the rate at which human capital increases. In a stationary and stable population, the entrants to the labor

29

force equal those that retire for various reasons. In the stationary population, the increase in the economic quality of the labor force would depend only on the rate of increase in the human capital given to each succeeding generation. But in a growing population, the entrants more than replace the retirements and the average economic quality of the population would be higher than in the stationary population.[31]

Another reason why population growth results in a more productive labor force is that it facilitates smoother changes in the direction of economic production by minimizing economic dislocations and structural unemployment. In any economy, some industries grow, some stay the same, and others decline in terms of relative importance to the economy, based on continuing changes in consumer preferences. However, when population is growing, an industry can decline in relative importance yet remain at the same or even a greater level of production due to the fact that its diminishing share is part of an expanding whole. Consequently, the industry can maintain constant or even growing employment in spite of the fact that the proportion of its output to the total economy is becoming less.

The opposite is the case with a stationary population. Here, a decline in the relative importance of an industry results in an absolute decrease in output. As a result, employment must be reduced and jobs eliminated. Because of their greater mobility, younger workers in the industry may be able to find new jobs. But older workers, who in a stationary population are proportionally in much greater numbers, find it more difficult to locate and adapt themselves to new employment situations. The result is economic disruption and increased structural unemployment.

Writing during the depression of the thirties at a time when it was thought that a stationary or even declining population was imminent, economist William B. Reddaway anticipated these problems, stating that "the advent of a stationary or declining population will aggravate the effects of changes in technique, demand or industrial location in throwing people out of their old jobs. The conclusion is inescapable that a declining population will both increase the amount of adjustment which is necessary and reduce the ability of the system to effect it smoothly."[32] As Sauvy points out, in a "growing society, obsolescent sectors can go into a relative decline without any pain; in a stationary population there have to be sacrifices. Expansion is the only way to adjust proportions. A body can only improve through growth."[33]

Population growth makes the structure of occupations more adaptable and progress more possible, Sauvy sums up, because the "quicker the progress the sharper the demographic growth required. . . . What is true of the structure of occupations is true for any distribution of the population. One can change the proportions making up a whole in two ways: by adding or by amputating. Both methods can be used with materials: the painter adds, the sculptor

30

amputates. With a population, amputation always causes suffering and thus encounters difficulties."[34]

Increased Consumer Demand. A growing population creates greater total consumer demand than a stationary one. This is not only because population growth results in an increase in the total number of consumers but because people are likely to sacrifice some leisure time in order to have children, that is, they will work more to increase the spendable income available to support their families.

In addition, with population growth, consumer demand will be more attuned to economic growth, for as Kuznets notes, it is "not only the size of the domestic market but its responsiveness to new products that is important."[35] And, since younger individuals and families are more responsive to new products than older ones because the latter have more firmly established habits and most of their durable consumer goods have already been acquired, Kuznets concludes that it "follows that population increase, accompanied as it usually is by a higher proportion of young units, may also be associated with greater responsiveness of the body of ultimate consumers to new goods—which in turn facilitates modern economic growth and may contribute to a higher product per capita."[36]

Faith in the Future. Population growth both stimulates and reflects faith in the future—an intangible yet absolutely necessary precondition of economic advancement, since every investment in a country's economy has a future-time dimension. Discussing population growth resulting from immigration as well as natural increase (births minus deaths), Kuznets points out that "allowing substantial immigration reflects a faith in the country's power to absorb immigrants and put them to productive use, a faith in the country's future. Having children is also evidence of faith in the future. . . . Granted, in recent decades this faith has an apocalyptic tinge, colored by visions of atomic holocausts and Armageddon. It is a faith, nevertheless, in the country's future, unless or until terminated by such calamities as transcend the limits of planning of a household, a firm, or even a country. Contrariwise, a constant or slowly growing population is implicit evidence of lack of faith in the future."[37]

Thus, the effect of population growth on the implicit view of the future held by entrepreneurs and households, says Kuznets, can "hardly be denied— particularly for entrepreneurs, for whom there is an economic rationale in being more venturesome, more forward-looking, under such conditions than when the view of the future is pessimistic. Greater venturesomeness, greater willingness to build for the future, is likely to contribute to more vigorous growth of both total and per capita product."[38]

31

The Malthusian Argument against Population Growth

Despite the abundant evidence accumulated over two centuries demonstrating the positive effects of population growth on economic advancement, the Malthusian position that population growth is a detriment to, rather than a determinant of, economic progress continues to be advanced. Perhaps the most comprehensive statement of this viewpoint appears in the report of the Commission on Population Growth and the American Future.

The commission, established by the federal government, flatly states at the outset of its report that

in the brief history of this nation, we have always assumed that progress and "the good life" are connected with population growth. In fact, population growth has frequently been regarded as a measure of our progress. If that were ever the case, it is not now.[39]

The commission was well aware of the discrepancy between this conclusion and the experience of the American people. In a later section of its report with the demeaning title of "The Growth Mystique," the admission is made that

periods of rapid population growth in this country have generally been periods of rapid economic expansion as well. It is not surprising, therefore, that we associate growth with economic progress.[40]

The commission attempts to explain away this positive relationship between population growth and economic progress by suggesting that it was primarily due to immigration rather than to natural increase resulting from more births than deaths:

The historical association of population growth with economic expansion would be an erroneous guide to the formulation of population policy for the future. This connection reflects in large part the fact that periods of rapid economic expansion attracted immigrants to our shores and thus quickened population growth as a result. Additions to population through immigration are far more stimulating to economic growth than are additions by natural increase. This is because, while babies remain dependent for many years before beginning to contribute to output, many immigrants are of working age and thus become immediately productive.[41]

But this explanation simply does not hold water. Immigration has certainly played an important role in the economic development of the United States, but to credit it as the major reason for the country's economic advancement is absurd. The share of total population growth due to natural increase was 80 percent from 1810 to 1860, 67 percent from 1860 to 1910, and 90 percent from 1910 to 1960.[42] Meanwhile, since 1810 immigration has contributed only

32

about 18 percent of total population growth per decade. This represents an important contribution, but in no way can it be used to explain "in large part" the historical association between population growth and economic advancement.

However, sweeping past this contradiction, the commission arrives at the conclusion that "we have looked for, and have not found, any convincing argument for continued national population growth. The health of our economy does not depend on it. The vitality of business does not depend on it. The welfare of the average person certainly does not depend on it."[43]

The commission goes on to investigate the economic effects resulting from two different populations, one growing at a zero population growth or two-child-per-family rate and the other growing at a three-child-per-family rate. According to the commission, its research indicates that "in the year 2000, per capita income may be as much as 15 per cent higher under the 2-child than under the 3-child population growth rate."[44]

The main reason advanced by the commission for this conclusion is that "people of working age will constitute a larger fraction of the population under conditions of slower population growth."[45] The commission believes this to be the case for two reasons. First, the population growing at the two-child-per-family rate would have proportionally fewer dependent children and proportionally more working-age people; thus, income per person would be increased. Second, it is anticipated that with lower birth rates the percentage of women in the labor force versus women at home would rise somewhat faster than it would otherwise, further increasing the ratio between workers and dependents. In short, the commission's conclusion of higher per capita income with slower population growth is based on the simple notion that, as the commission somewhat crassly puts it, there would be more workers and earners and "fewer mouths to feed."[46]

However, as population growth slows down, the proportion of aged dependents increases at the same time that the proportion of youthful dependents declines. The commission recognizes this, but states that "because of higher death rates at these ages, the increase in aged dependency offsets only part of the decline in youth dependency, and the overall result is still a major drop in total dependency and an increase in income available per person in the population."[47]

The commission reaches this conclusion by assuming that the costs of supporting young and old dependents are the same. However, this is decidedly *not* the case. It clearly costs less to support a child than an elderly person. There are obvious economies of scale in housing, clothing, and food in raising a child that are not available to a retired person or even a retired couple. In addition, the consumption requirements of a child are less than those of an adult.

As was pointed out by Duke University's Allen Kelley—who prepared the lead article in the commission's economic research report—the commission's dependency argument focuses on the high resource costs to society of a young population due to high birth rates. But the argument is a two-edged sword. A low birth rate—for example, zero population growth—will yield an older population whose resource costs, *in precisely the same theoretical framework,* also represent a social dependence. And these resource costs, Kelley notes, could "dramatically increase in the future if serious attention is directed to the acute social problem of poverty of the elderly, a cohort whose high consumption standards are increasingly being frustrated by rising medical costs, taxes and inflation."[48]

Consequently, whatever increase in per capita income might be achieved as a result of a reduction in the proportion of young dependents in the slower-growing population would be relatively small and temporary due to the increasing support costs resulting from a growing proportion of older dependents. By the year 2000, these increasing costs of aged dependents might not only cancel out the small increase but begin to cause a *decrease* in per capita income. As Kelley sums up, it is possible that a "continuing decline in birth rates will exert a small impact . . . in the coming decades; around the turn of the century, the changing age structure could even exert a negative influence. . . ."[49]

Neither is it realistic to assign an economic value of zero, as the commission does, to the services of a woman acting as a housewife and mother simply because she does not work in an outside-the-home job where she receives a paycheck from an employer. Admittedly, work in the home does not normally enter into the computation of GNP or per capita income. But this is due to the difficulty of measurement and the absence of a money exchange, not a lack of economic value. As a housewife and mother, a woman provides services in the home whose quality and value would be quite difficult and expensive to match in the form of a hired housekeeper. In addition, society is becoming increasingly aware of the costs of parental neglect from the standpoint of crime and social maladjustment among youth.

But the most serious criticism of the commission's conclusions is that they give short shrift to or simply ignore the many positive effects of population growth on economic progress. In comparing two-child and three-child population growth rates, for example, the commission assumes that: (1) "technological options available to both societies would be the same,"[50] (2) aggregate savings values are "independent of changes in population,"[51] and (3) "there are no further economies of scale to be realized."[52]

Although the commission is completely unable to find any beneficial effects of population growth, it does recognize that some problems might result from slower population growth. But the commission has a ready answer—actually the same answer—for each problem.[53] The commission observes, for example, that investment problems might be caused by slower population growth. But they are not of considerable concern, the commission maintains, becau. "the extent that a problem did exist, it was felt that monetary and fiscal policies could effectively deal with it." The commission also notes that "fears were expressed that because aggregate demand, at least in the long run, is dependent on population, a slower population growth rate will lead to some economic slack and possibly to unemployment." And it adds that "the slowing pace of aggregate economic activity might reduce, say, the rate of implementation of new ideas and hence have a negative impact on per capita income."

However, the commission asserts, if the government made "sensible use of its monetary and fiscal policy tools, there is no necessary reason to believe that the long-run slower growth of aggregate demand that would follow from slower population growth should lead to slower growth in per capita income." Furthermore, the commission declares that "on balance, it would seem that the commission was correct in concluding that unemployment would not be a serious consequence of slower population growth. In essence, an unemployment problem can be solved by wise fiscal and monetary policies."

In other words, as long as "sensible" and "wise" monetary and fiscal policies are alive and well and living in Washington, slowing population growth will not result in (1) reduced investment, (2) lower consumer demand, (3) increasing unemployment, and (4) slower growth in per capita income.

But monetary and fiscal policies, sensible, wise, or otherwise, are not tools for solving problems caused by slowing population growth. They constitute a political reaction to the problems and, insofar as "monetary and fiscal policy management" is simply a code word for inflation, they only serve to cover up and, in the end, exacerbate the severity of the problems.

The relationship between slowing population growth and economic problems was noted by no less an authority than the originator of monetary and fiscal policy management, J. M. Keynes. During the twenties, Keynes was an enthusiastic Malthusian and a leading proponent of reduced population growth. However, in the midst of the Great Depression of the thirties, when the annual U.S. population growth rate had drastically dropped to an all-time low of 0.6 percent, Keynes apparently had second thoughts, for he issued this foreboding warning: "in the final summing up, therefore, I do not depart from the old Malthusian conclusion. I only wish to warn you that the chaining up of the one devil (population growth) may, if we are careless, only serve to loose another still fiercer and more intractable."[54]

Keynes' "fiercer and more intractable" devil of the thirties was unemployment resulting from falling consumer demand and declining capital investment. Updating Keynes' devil to the seventies, we can add the more basic economic problem of inflation, which has been induced by the same kinds of fiscal and monetary policies advocated by the commission as a solution to the problems caused by slowing population growth. In today's Welfare State, inflation is not a solution to the problems caused by a declining rate of population growth but a major problem resulting from the population decline. This is because even as the American population experiences declining growth it finds itself confronted with a growing "overhead" in terms of governmental welfare programs, which increase completely independently of the downward population trend. The pressure on government thus becomes irresistible to use monetary and fiscal policies to reduce the burden of rising per capita welfare costs through "cheaper money": inflation. But inflation does not solve the problems caused by slowing population growth; it only aggravates them and makes them more difficult to solve.

Summing up, there have been two periods in U.S. history when the decline in the rate of population growth has been short-term and sharp rather than long-term and gradual. One of these periods was during the twenties and early thirties, when the annual population growth rate plunged from near 2 percent to 0.6 percent. According to the neo-Malthusian views of zero-population-growth enthusiasts such as the Commission on Population Growth and the American Future, this should have ushered in an era of bustling economic advancement and rapidly rising per capita income due to the fact there were more workers and earners and, in the commission's words, "fewer mouths to feed." It, of course, did nothing of the sort, ushering in the Great Depression instead.

The other period of rapid decline in the rate of population growth began in 1957, when the annual population growth rate was 1.8 percent. It has proceeded to a low close to 0.7 percent. If the ZPGers were correct in their negative view of the effect of population growth on economic progress, we should all be basking in plenty by now. But, of course, the exact opposite is the case. We are struggling with an inflationary recession—some would say depression—that periodically shows signs of disappearing, only to reappear with greater force and fury than before.

By contrast, the period from the mid-thirties to the mid-fifties was a time of rapid increase in the population growth rate, from 0.6 to 1.8 percent. If we are to believe in the antipopulation growth position, this rapid population increase should have plunged us into economic problems of all sorts. But the fifties are recalled today not with horror but fondness as a time of booming and practically inflation-free prosperity.

Contrary to the findings of the Commission on Population Growth and the American Future and other zero population growth advocates, population growth has in the past and will continue in the future to be the major factor promoting economic progress in the United States. Population growth provides a stimulus to economic advancement for which there is no comparable substitute, and this is as true today as it has been for the past two centuries of U.S. history.

Conclusion

"An increase in population enables . . . a society to extend its power in any chosen direction. New uses will be found for the surplus product, additional tracts will be cultivated, and new fields opened in manufactures and commerce. Increased division of labour will lead to even more remarkable improvements in methods and productivity. In the U.S.A., the growth of population stimulated agriculture; in England it stimulated manufactures and commerce. In both cases growth in numbers has been the source of wealth and abundance. . . . 'A dense and increasing population on a limited territory, instead of bringing with it any danger of scarcity, is not only an immediate cause of greater abundance to the nation where it exists, but a principle of prosperity and civilization to every part of the world.' "[55]

These views were expressed more than 150 years ago by A. H. Everett, an American critic of Thomas Malthus' population growth misconceptions, in a book called *New Ideas on Population with Remarks on the Theories of Malthus and Godwin*. Suffice it to say that Everett proved to be a better student of the effects of population growth than Malthus.

In a creative and dynamic society such as the United States, people solve more problems than they make. More people do more things better. This is the ultimate source of improving living standards and economic progress. It is increasing capabilities resulting from growth in numbers of people that promote material advancement, not the other way around. As economist Ludwig von Mises put it, production "is a spiritual, intellectual, and ideological phenomenon. It is the method that man, directed by reason, employs for the best possible removal of uneasiness. What distinguishes our conditions from those of our ancestors who lived one thousand or twenty thousand years ago is not something material but something spiritual. The material changes are the outcome of spiritual changes."[56]

Population growth is a boon to, rather than the bane of, economic progress. And in the future, the rate of U.S. population growth will be more important and have a more immediate impact on the country's economic advancement than ever before. This is because the gradually declining rate of population growth that has occurred throughout the country's history has been offset to some extent in the past by contrapuntal increases in the regional population growth rates of urban and metropolitan areas. But fast rates of regional population growth in general and urbanization in particular have about run their course, leaving it more and more for national population growth per se to provide the impetus for economic advancement in the future.

Furthermore, as the population-induced reasons for today's economic problems become more apparent and a greater awareness of the economic importance of population growth becomes more prevalent, people and businesses will be quicker to react to changes in the direction of the population growth rate.

This is not to say that there are no disadvantages to population growth. To increase population obviously requires that an "investment" be made in more children, more new people. And, as with any future-oriented investment, this means that a sacrifice involving more work or less consumption or both must be made today in the interests of achieving greater population growth tomorrow. Conversely, if all children below working age suddenly vanished today, we could all immediately enjoy the "advantage" of consuming more and working less tomorrow, although the achievement of such an "advantage" would obviously be shortsighted as well as short-lived.

However, whether or not an investment in more children is really a "disadvantage" depends ultimately not on economic analysis but on the values of the people having the children. For children can increase our total welfare in ways not measurable by economists. Children provide us with what economists call "psychological income" or "welfare effects," which in many ways can provide personal rewards far greater than and not comparable to purely economic compensations. Consequently, whether children are a joy to have or a burden to bear, or both, is ultimately a question that must be answered on the basis of value judgments (not economic calculations) made by parents in terms of their desire to have children and their interest in investing in the welfare of future generations.

Nor is it possible, with our present knowledge, to predict with any degree of certainty what specific economic growth rate will result from any given rate of population growth. As Kuznets puts it, we "have no tested, or even approximate, empirical coefficients with which to weigh the various positive and negative aspects of population growth. While we may be able to distinguish the advantages and disadvantages, we rarely know the character of the function that relates them to different magnitudes of population growth."[57]

It is also true that the rate of population growth does on occasion react to economic conditions or business cycles. However, these reactions are temporary and minor, for, as reported by Dudley Kirk, Morrison Professor of Population Studies at Stanford University's Food Research Institute, demographic and economic data "do not confirm the view that *major* changes in fertility are a function of business cycles. In other words, while the deviations from trend of fertility rates seem to move in the same direction as the trend deviations of economic indicators, the former series exhibits a distinctive character of its own, describing a trend in many respects quite independent of economic conditions. The surface waves are indeed much influenced by economic fluctuations, but the underlying tide appears to be an independent and surprisingly stable force."[58]

Summing up, population growth is not an automatic and immediate panacea for today's economic problems. Every facet of a country's life—its economic structure, sociology, politics, culture, in short, its basic life-view—is involved in determining how effectively population growth is translated into economic progress. However, as Sauvy observes, one "point is certain. Other factors cannot suppress the creative effect of demographic pressure nor, especially, the depressive influence of demographic decay. . . . Demographic stagnation brings a country to a moral and material crisis that is never foreseen in economic analysis."[59]

3
U.S. POPULATION GROWTH AND RESOURCE DEVELOPMENT

Population growth in the United States has spurred continuing resource development and an expanding resource base. As the country has grown from 4 million to more than 200 million people, resources have become more rather than less abundant.

This undoubtedly would also come as a surprise to Malthus, who viewed the capacity of the earth to support its human population as relatively fixed. And it is a development that is ignored if not denied by today's neo-Malthusians, who prefer to preach that we are rapidly "running out" of resources due to population growth.

However, increasing resource abundance is a result of population growth because, just as population growth promotes economic progress, so also it spurs resource development. The correlation between rising per capita income and increasing resource availability is, in fact, one of the most direct in the social sciences. Population growth increases supplies of the most important resource of all: people. It is the increasing knowledge, technology, investment capabilities, economies of scale, and per capita income produced by growing numbers of people that make it possible to expand the resource base.

The positive results of this interaction between population growth and resource development are shown by the record of resource consumption in the past. For at least a century—the period for which we have reasonably usable statistics—the average per capita increase in consumption of all raw materials has been growing at the rate of about one-third of one percent a year, according to Joseph L. Fisher, former president of Resources for the Future, Inc. As Fisher points out, in the "sense that the per capita consumption of most of these raw materials has been going up over many years, raw materials have

41

nut become scarcer. They have become more plentiful."[1]

This increasing abundance is further demonstrated by the fact that we have been able to obtain a growing amount of resources with less labor and at no increase in cost. If resources were becoming scarcer, the effort involved in obtaining them and their costs would increase over time. But the opposite is the case. As Fisher states, we have, over the long run, become more efficient in developing resources. The ratio of employment to output in the resource industries has been going down, meaning we are getting more resources for less effort. And, over the past century, costs of resource products have in most cases remained comparable to the general level of costs in the overall economy, indicating that growing resource abundance has been achieved without creating problems of economic scarcity.[2]

Population growth has thus stimulated an expansion of resources that has been more than adequate to provide for increasing per capita resource consumption. For, as Melvin Kranzberg of the Department of Social Sciences at the Georgia Institute of Technology states, the "history of technology during the last two centuries is the story of an expanding natural-resource base."[3] In the words of Ronald K. Ridker of Resources for the Future, past generations have "opened up a road toward technological accomplishments that, in retrospect, seems to dwarf any drain on resources."[4] Dr. Karl Brandt put it this way when he was director of the Food Research Institute of Stanford University: "The only genuine resources on this earth from which wealth can flow in ever-increasing volume are the intelligence, the skill, the creative mind, the determination to manage and work of people."[5] Or, as the authors of *The Next Hundred Years* conclude, focusing on the ultimate importance of growing human knowledge in resource development, it "appears that the critical limiting factor as far as the world's resources are concerned is not materials, energy or food, but brainpower."[6]

How Population Growth Spurs Resource Development

The earth is truly an immense place with unimaginably vast resources. These resources are, of course, fixed and finite. But, currently, this does not mean much. No one at this time knows or can even begin to comprehend the ultimate limits of our natural resources.

As the United Nations' Symposium on Population, Resources and Environment found, the "problem is ignorance of the factors determining such ultimate limits. The mineral and energy reserves ultimately available to man are unknown. Also unknown are how much new land can be made suitable for agriculture, the extent to which additional fresh water supplies can be developed. . . ."[7]

Regardless of what we do, there is no way we are going to be able to expand

42

these ultimate limits, whatever they may be. When we talk about expanding resources, we do not mean that the ultimate limits of resources are being or can be extended. What the concept of expanding resources means is that human knowledge of the earth's resources and human capabilities to effectively make use of them are increasing. Increasing resources therefore are not a function of resources per se—that is, the resources themselves are not increasing—but of improvements in human knowledge and technology that make increasing amounts of the earth's resources available to us. And population growth advances resource development by increasing the human resources of knowledge, technology, capital, and labor necessary to expand the available supply.

The relationship between population growth and resource development is thus dynamic rather than static. Those who preach that we are running out of resources envision a static, unchanging society in which population grows while available resources remain the same. Of course, if society does not respond to the need for additional resources created by population growth, then resources will become scarcer and it is possible that we will eventually "run out."

But this is *not* what happens in the real world, nor is it what has happened in the United States during the past several centuries. Instead, the United States has responded to the need for increasing resources in a variety of different ways, stimulated by the increasing human resources of knowledge, technology, capital, and labor provided by population growth.

Development of New Resources. Perhaps the most important way in which resources are expanded is through the discovery and development of new resources not previously known or used. For example, in times prior to the seventeenth century when population growth proceeded at a snail's pace, wood, water, and wind were the primary sources of energy. In the seventeenth century population began growing rapidly, promoting the discovery of a variety of new power sources such as coal, oil, natural gas, and geothermal, nuclear, and solar energy, all of which previously had been unknown or little used due to lack of population growth sufficient for their development.

Each of these resources is different, but all of them share one thing in common: they can be used to produce useful energy. Taken all together and allowing for the possibility of the development of other new resources in the future (such as controlled nuclear fusion), the total availability of energy is, as James Boyd, former executive director of the National Commission on Materials Policy, points out, "so enormous that the possibility of running out of energy materials in any conceivable time-frame is preposterous."[8]

Expansion of Existing Resources. The next most important method of enlarging resources is the expansion of resources already in use. This involves not only finding new resource deposits but developing new ways of economically and efficiently obtaining resources of lower quality or grade from known deposits. Even though resource consumption has been increasing for several centuries, the possibilities of finding new supplies of existing resources in the future remain practically unlimited. In the case of minerals, for example, the United Nations Symposium on Population, Resources and Environment points out that "on a global basis the sheer physical availability of minerals will not pose any limit to population growth. . . . Even today, large parts of the earth have not been explored in the detail necessary for resource discovery purposes. This is especially true of the seabed and in areas more than a few metres below the land surface; but it is also true of significant portions of the exposed land surface itself."[9]

The potential of technology to increase resource supplies by facilitating the economical development of resources of ever-lower grade is equally vast. For example, the average grade of copper ore has decreased from 3 percent to less than 1 percent since 1870. Yet the price of copper in constant dollars has remained fairly stable due to the technological development of more economical methods of mining and extraction.[10] This technological improvement has greatly increased the economical availability of copper because, as the report of the Symposium on Population, Resources and Environment comments, the "average crusted rock is known to contain potentially useful amounts of important minerals and there is a tendency for the quantity of such minerals at a given concentration level to increase as concentration decreases, at least down to very low concentration levels. If the price of a mineral increased or the cost of mining went down sufficiently, it would not be surprising to find that the volume of minable materials increased by factors of hundreds."[11]

In similar fashion, technological improvements in mineral recovery and processing add to the supply of many other minerals by "reducing the costs of exploitation, thus making possible the use of lower grade deposits or deposits which were not previously accessible because of cost considerations."[12] And, since these lower-grade deposits usually contain vastly greater mineral quantities, advancing technology often has "a multiplier effect in expanding the volume of resources. United States reserves of uranium, for example, are currently estimated at some 250,000 short tons, which at the present level of technology may have an energy equivalent slightly above total United States energy consumption in 1960. With a more advanced technology, the present uranium reserves might be equivalent to between 10 and 100 or more times 1960 energy consumption."[13]

Greater Resource Interchangeability. Resources are valued for the properties they provide, that is, energy, strength, durability, and so forth. The property of energy, for example, can be provided by a variety of different resources such as coal, oil, gas, hydro-power and nuclear fission. The properties of strength and durability can be provided by aluminum and plastic as well

44

as steel. The same "interchangeability" is true for practically every other material property desired by the modern world.

Advances in physical science leading to greater resource interchangeability or substitution result in growing material flexibility, which, in effect, extends the resource supply. Modern man, as Boyd says, needs "more than ninety mineral materials produced from the earth to provide him with the properties he needs. He can, however, obtain similar if not comparable properties from more than one element or mineral . . . assuring supplies of properties in such magnitude that they cannot run out in any imaginable period."[14] Or, as Harold J. Barnett and C. Morse point out, "few components of the earth's crust, including farm land, are so specific as to defy economic replacement, or so resistant to technological advance as to be incapable of eventually yielding extractive products at constant or declining cost."[15]

More Efficient Resource Use. More efficient resource use does not increase the supply of resources. But it does reduce resource consumption, having the same effect as an increase in supply.

In the case of land, for example, Hans H. Landsberg, Leonard L. Fischman, and Joseph L. Fisher note in *Resources in America's Future* that "the physical acreage from which crops were harvested in 1960 was nearly identical with that of half a century ago, but the average acre in 1960 yielded some two-thirds more than did the average acre forty years earlier—adding the equivalent of nearly 250 million acres to our land supply."[16]

The outlook for the future in terms of more efficient use of land for food production is no less positive. Says Marion Clawson, director of the Land Use and Management Studies Program at Resources for the Future:

> At present, and for the next decade or two at least, American agriculture has a large unused productive potential. If prices were more favorable than at present, and seemed likely to remain so, and if markets would absorb everything that could be produced, farmers could materially step up their output—a 50 per cent increase in 10 years is wholly possible. This estimate does not depend upon any new and striking technological change but rather upon fuller use of presently known means of production. . . . By increasing agricultural output and by shifting to more cereals and less meat in the national diet, the country can feed 10, or 20, or even more times its present population, by the time population reaches such a level—if it ever does. The ultimate food productive capacity is so far above the present level that there is nothing to be gained from trying to estimate just how large it is.[17]

Another way that resources are used more efficiently is through the adoption of entirely new technology that makes it possible to do more with less. This is what R. Buckminster Fuller refers to as "ephemeralization," citing the example of a one-quarter-ton communications satellite that out-performs 100,000 tons of transoceanic cable.[18]

Increased Resource Reuse. Reuse or recovery of previously used materials is another method of extending the supply of resources. Currently, such reuse plays an important role in total consumption, amounting to as much as 40 percent in the case of metals such as copper and lead, according to Frank Austin Smith of the Center for Environment and Man.

However, from the standpoint of reuse, the term *consumption* is actually a misnomer, since hardly anything is consumed in the sense that it is no longer present on earth after use. Leonard L. Fischman and Hans H. Landsberg, for example, observe that "except for the negligible amounts shot off into space, the resources of this earth are never finally 'consumed.' They may be widely dissipated, into the air, seas, or over the surface of the earth; they may be changed in chemical, or even in elemental form; they may temporarily be retired from availability while they remain part of an increasing stock of things in use. But the vast bulk of the mineral wealth of the earth, once used, remains as much a part of the earth's resources as if it had never been mined."[20]

John D. Morgan, Jr., assistant director of Mineral Position Analysis in the U.S. Bureau of Mines, points out that most new copper, for example, is "really not 'consumed' at all but instead it is converted into copper wire, copper tubing, brass and alloys from which useful articles having a long life are fabricated. Most of the copper tubing, the copper wiring, the brass hardware, etc., in use now was reported as 'consumed' many years ago. But it is estimated that the pool of copper in use in the United States is probably of the order of four hundred pounds per person." And this is twenty times the reported new copper consumption of about twenty pounds per person.[21]

The degree to which society reuses existing resources rather than using new, virgin resources is, of course, a function of the relative costs and profitability of these two methods of resource development. However, the potential for profitable resource recovery is large and, as Frank Austin Smith notes, the "economic system already contains a solid technological base for materials recovery, as well as an industrial structure and specialized marketing organizations that are at least partially attuned to exploiting these potentials." Smith sums up that "the existence of substantial unexploited material recovery opportunities, though presently beyond the margin of profitability, provides a considerable element of flexibility to the future of the system. As such, it provides a capability to absorb at least some future shocks over a relatively long period of time, as and if they occur, thus allowing considerably more time and resources to discover what the future world resource and population picture may hold forth."[22]

Perhaps V.E. McKelvey, director of the U.S. Geological Survey, has best described the various processes by which resources have been created in the past and will continue to be created in the future. Writing in *Summary of United States Mineral Resources,* McKelvey states:

Personally, I am confident that for millenia to come we can continue to develop the mineral supplies needed to maintain a high level of living for those who now enjoy it and raise it for the impoverished people of our own country and the world. My reasons for thinking so are that there is a visible undeveloped potential of substantial proportions in each of the processes by which we create resources and that our experience justifies the belief that these processes have dimensions beyond our knowledge and even beyond our imagination at any given time.

Setting aside the unimaginable, I will mention some examples of the believeable. I am sure all geologists would agree that minable undiscovered deposits remain in explored as well as unexplored areas and that progress in our knowledge of regional geology and in exploration will lead to the discovery of many of them. With respect to unexplored areas, the mineral potential of the continental margins and ocean basins deserves particular emphasis, for the technology that will give us access to it is clearly now in sight.

For many critical minerals, we already know of substantial paramarginal and submarginal resources that experience tells us should be brought within economic reach by technological advance.

The process of substituting an abundant for a scarce material has also been pursued successfully, thus far not out of need but out of economic opportunity, and plainly has much potential as a means of enlarging usable resources.

Extending our supplies by increasing the efficiency of recovery and use of raw materials has also been significant. For example, a unit weight of today's steel provides 43 per cent more structural support than it did only 10 years ago, reducing proportionately the amount required for a given purpose. Similarly, we make as much electric power from 1 ton of coal now as we were able to make from 7 tons around the turn of the century.

Our rising awareness of pollution and its effects surely will force us to pay even more attention to increasing the efficiency of mineral recovery and use as a means of reducing the release of contaminants to the environment. For similar reasons, we are likely to pursue more diligently processes of recovery, re-use, and recycling of mineral materials than we have in the past.[23]

The Availability of Resources in the Future

No one knows the ultimate extent of the world's resources for two reasons. First, the total resources of the earth are so huge as to defy the imagination. In fact, it is entirely possible that we never will even approach, much less determine, the resource limits of the world. Second, and more important from a practical point of view, there is no present economic justification for spending the time and money necessary to attempt to determine the world's ultimate resources—assuming they are knowable—when we have no need for them in the immediate foreseeable future. Rather, the path that resource development has followed in the past and will continue to follow in the future is to bring new resources into use as they are needed. In effect, the pace of resource demand is what determines the path of resource development.

To meet resource demand, resource development follows a two-step approach. First, science discovers new resources. Second, technology makes these resources economically available for use. In the case of solar energy, for example, science has discovered that the sun's rays can be used to produce useful energy on earth. This is an energy source of vast potential. Technology is being developed to transform solar energy from a potential to an actual energy source that is competitive in cost with other sources of energy and is thus economically available for use.

This process of transforming potential, presently unusable resources into actual, economically available reserves is dynamic and ongoing rather than static and unchanging. For example, as reserves of minerals are used in response to demand, additional potential resources are converted into reserves to replenish the reserve supply.

Reserves, of course, are of great current concern because, as Donald A. Brobst and Walden P. Pratt of the U.S. Department of the Interior point out, they "are the only part of the total resource that is *immediately available.*" Thus, reserve estimates for most minerals are generally available and undergoing constant revision. However, current reserves usually are only "a small part of the total resource. The remainder of the total—the *potential resources*—are by far the most important for the longer term. . . ."

Brobst and Pratt warn that the distinction between potential resources and reserves must be kept in mind at all times, for

potential resources are *not* reserves. . . . No matter how optimistic an outlook is engendered by estimates of vast resources, such resources cannot be mined, much less used, until they have been converted into the category of reserves, whether by discovery (of undiscovered resources of minable quality), or by improvements in technology (for recovering identified subeconomic resources), or by both. For nearly all minerals, the estimates of potential resources indicate quantities that may become available *only if we vigorously pursue geologic and technologic research* to discover new mineral deposits in regions and geologic environments that are known to be favorable, to discover new favorable regions and environments, to discover new kinds of mineral deposits not previously recognized, to improve existing exploration techniques and develop new ones, and to improve extractive technology for processing low-grade ores that are not now economically recoverable.

Resource estimates are therefore only estimates, not measurements; and they "present an optimistic outlook for many commodities *only in the context that they represent a potential, not a reality.*" Yet, as Brobst and Pratt state, each of the geologic and technologic research approaches enumerated above "has in fact resulted in the conversion of potential resources into minable reserves. Indeed the events of the last 20 years are the best reason for optimism," they conclude, citing the phoenixlike rejuvenation of the lead district in southeast Missouri as the perfect example of a potential resource converted to a reserve.

In 1952, U.S. recoverable reserves of lead were estimated to be 7.1 million tons, of which only about one million tons were called "proved" reserves. A significant part of this reserve was located in southeast Missouri. According to the Paley report issued by the President's Materials Policy Commission in 1952: "The poor discovery record of the past few decades provides little basis for optimism that the equivalent of the southeast Missouri district can be expected to turn up in the future; the major hope lies in the development of some new methods of prospecting, as, for example, methods that would indicate the probability of deposits in the absence of surface outcrops."

Within only a few years after this report was published, drilling on the west side of the southeast Missouri district resulted in the discovery of large, unexposed deposits of lead ore known as the Vibernum Trend. By 1970, six mines were operating, and the reserves of lead in Missouri alone had increased to 30 million tons.[24]

It is from the standpoint of not only reserves but potential resources, then, that total resource availability must be evaluated. Reserves are known resources that can be economically made available for use with existing technology. Potential resources are either resources that have been identified but cannot be economically obtained with present technology or resources that have not as yet been discovered but are believed to exist. The former can be converted into reserves by either improvements in technology that lower the costs of obtaining the resource or increases in price that make the resource economically available with existing technology. The latter are converted into reserves through exploration and technological development.

It is also important to distinguish between domestic and foreign resources. Whether domestic or foreign sources are developed for any particular resource is normally a question of geologic availability and economic feasibility. For example, even though a resource may be geologically available domestically, it may be obtained from a foreign source because it is more economical to do so. In other cases, resources may be imported because there is no other choice due to the fact that they have limited or no geologic availability in this country.

There is another factor involved when resources are obtained from a foreign source. This is the possibility that supply may be interrupted for military, political, trade, or other reasons independent of geology and economics. This is an increasingly important factor, since although 85 percent of U.S. annual mineral needs measured in dollar value still come from this country's own mineral deposits, imports have been growing in recent years.

What follows is an evaluation of the total resources available to the United States in the future from both domestic and foreign sources in the four major resource categories of energy, nonfuel minerals, land, and water.

49

Energy. Energy can be obtained from a variety of different sources, and the United States is fortunately blessed with potentially huge and varied supplies. As the final report of the National Commission on Materials Policy states, the nation

> possesses vast quantities of coal (even low-sulfur coal), oil, natural gas, and other energy materials. Although developed reserves of energy source materials are insufficient to meet demand, undeveloped resources are, in general, sufficient to meet projected demands. The Nation is concerned less with the size of reserves than with the lead time and costs of developing them.[25]

Between now and the year 2000, the United States will draw most of its energy from four major sources. These sources and their current contribution to energy consumption are petroleum, 46 percent; natural gas, 32 percent; coal, 17 percent; and nuclear power, 1 percent.[26]

Petroleum. The United States currently uses about 6 billion barrels of petroleum, or oil, a year. It is estimated that, from 1968 through the year 2000, the country will use a minimum cumulative total of 195 billion barrels.[27] Present domestic oil reserves are estimated at 62 billion barrels, or only 32 percent of this minimum anticipated demand. But U.S. Geological Survey estimates of potential oil resources range from 50 to 127 billion barrels,[28] while other estimates vary from 165 billion to 2900 billion barrels, many times the expected cumulative demand through 2000.[29]

We presently produce only about two-thirds of our oil consumption while importing the rest. But this is due to reasons of economics rather than any absolute shortage of domestic oil resources. However, with rising international oil prices and increasing threats to national security, steps are now being taken to further develop domestic oil resources, including construction of the trans-Alaska pipeline to bring oil down from the Alaskan North Slope, accelerated development of oil resources in the outer continental shelf off the shores of the country, and testing of methods to extract oil from vast shale deposits in Colorado and Utah, which are estimated to contain 1.8 trillion barrels. Until at least the turn of the century, therefore, U.S. domestic oil resources will be ample to meet demand, even if imports should eventually be completely phased out, which is not likely to be the case.

Natural gas. The United States currently consumes about 23 trillion cubic feet of natural gas a year. It is estimated that minimum cumulative demand through 2000 will be 860 trillion cubic feet.[30]

Present domestic reserves of natural gas are 439 trillion cubic feet, or only about half of anticipated demand. But U.S. Geological Survey estimates of potential gas resources are in the range of 322 to 655 trillion cubic feet,[31] while the Colorado School of Mines estimates potential resources at 1.2 quadrillion cubic feet.[32] These estimates indicate a potential gas supply at least equal to and probably well in excess of anticipated demand through the turn of the century. Imports currently account for only about 4 percent of total domestic use and thus are not a significant factor in the current consumption picture.

Coal. U.S. coal resources are larger than the combined resources of petroleum and natural gas. Domestic production of coal in 1974 was 606 million short tons, of which 62 million short tons were exported. It is estimated that minimum cumulative demand through 2000 will be 27 billion short tons.[33] This demand is dwarfed by coal reserves of 197 billion short tons and potential resources in the thousands of billions of tons.[34] These coal resources are valuable not only as a practically inexhaustible direct source of energy but as a potential source for the manufacture of synthetic natural gas, which can be used to supplement naturally occurring gas supplies.

Nuclear power. The development of technology to split the atom has provided a new energy source with a potential many times that of fossil fuels such as oil, natural gas, and coal. In the early seventies, nuclear energy produced only one percent of the nation's electric power requirements. But, according to the U.S. Geological Survey, it is expected to provide about 21 percent in 1980, 38 percent in 1990, and 60 percent in 2000.[35]

Nuclear energy is presently produced from uranium in converter reactors by means of a process called fission. In 1974, the United States produced and used 11,000 to 12,000 tons of uranium ore, 96 percent of which was utilized in the generation of electricity. It is estimated by the U.S. Geological Survey that minimum cumulative demand for uranium ore through 2000 will be 2.4 million tons. Domestic reserves of uranium ore add up to about 273,000 tons, which can supply requirements only into the early 1980s. Potential resources are estimated at 6 million tons, more than twice the anticipated demand. But development of these resources will require major technological improvements.

Another potential source of nuclear energy is thorium. Considerable work has been done in the development of reactors fueled by thorium, with the furthest advanced to date being the high-temperature gas-cooled reactor. Assuming the development of economically attractive thorium reactors by 1980, domestic reserves of thorium are equivalent to 50 percent of the maximum anticipated cumulative demand of 27,500 tons of refined metal through 2000.

Potential resources are many times this cumulative demand. For example, the Conway Granite of New Hampshire contains an average of two ounces of thorium per short ton of rock. The energy released by nuclear fission of the thorium contained in just one cubic yard of this rock would be equivalent in fossil-fuel energy to about 300 short tons of coal or 1500 barrels of crude oil. If the entire Conway Granite area of 300 square miles were quarried to a depth of only 110 yards and the thorium used in nuclear reactors, the fossil-fuel equivalent of the energy produced would be about 30 trillion tons of coal— 165 times the coal reserves of the United States—or 150 trillion barrels of

51

crude oil, more than 3900 times our proved crude oil reserves.[37]

Another highly probable technological development that is a possibility for the early 1980s is the use of breeder in place of converter reactors. Converter reactors use only about 1.5 percent of the potential energy in uranium, while breeder reactors convert about 80 percent of the uranium energy. The development of breeder reactors thus will be of immense significance in expanding the supply of energy available from uranium. As M. King Hubbert, a research geophysicist with the U.S. Geological Survey, points out, the "energy potentially obtainable by breeder reactors from rocks occurring at minable depths in the United States and containing 50 grams or more of uranium and thorium combined per metric ton is hundreds of thousands of times larger than that of all of the fossil fuels combined."[38]

Further in the future, the development of controlled thermonuclear fusion using deuterium as fuel is a distinct possibility. An isotope of hydrogen, deuterium is superabundant and easily can be extracted from the earth's oceans. According to Hubbert, if only one percent of the deuterium were withdrawn from the oceans and used for fusion, the energy released would amount to about 500,000 times the energy of the world's initial supply of fossil fuels.[39]

Other energy sources. Direct use of solar radiation is today just beginning to appear on the power scene, yet it represents perhaps the largest total energy resource of all. The thermal power produced by the sun and intercepted by the earth's diametral plane is 100,000 times greater than the world's present, installed electric power capacity.[40] And this thermal power will remain nearly constant over the anticipated 5-billion-year life of the sun.

Solar energy is currently being used on a very limited scale for heating houses. However, the potential for harnessing the sun's energy is so huge that development will assuredly be given increasing priority in the future. As Chauncey Starr, dean of UCLA's School of Engineering and Applied Science notes, the "enormous magnitude of the solar radiation that reaches the land surface of the earth is so much greater than any of the foreseeable needs that it represents an inviting technological target. . . . If only a few per cent of the land area of the U.S. could be used to absorb solar radiation effectively (at, say, a little better than 10 per cent efficiency), we would meet most of our energy needs in the year 2000."[41]

Water power in the form of hydroelectric dams currently accounts for about 4 percent of total energy consumption. This will increase in the future, but it is doubtful that these increases will be significant in terms of total energy demands because most of the best hydroelectric sites in the country are already occupied. However, new developments in hydro-power, such as the use of the rolling motion of ocean waves at sea or the temperature differentials in deep bodies of ocean water to generate power, could change this picture.

Wind power is another source of energy that is not expected to contribute

52

greatly to the satisfaction of future energy needs. This is due not to lack of wind energy but its variability. If methods could be devised to store wind energy for later use—and work is proceeding in this direction—it could contribute significantly to future energy production. The National Aeronautics and Space Administration, for example, estimates that technological breakthroughs could enable wind power to produce the equivalent of the current electric consumption of the United States by 2000.[42]

Exploitation of geothermal energy is a relatively new development in the United States. But experts state that this energy, which is obtained from vast underground pools of hot water and steam, could fulfill all U.S. electrical needs by 2000. The possibility of using the enormous reserves of energy stored in hot, dry rocks deep in the crust of the earth is also being investigated.

Hydrogen, burned chemically like fossil fuels, is another energy source that is relatively new on the scene. Yet it, too, could become a major source of energy in the future. As Alvin M. Weinberg, director of the U.S. Atomic Energy Commission's (now the Energy Research and Development Administration) Oak Ridge National Laboratory, says, hydrogen "is the fuel that put man on the moon, and within 50 to 100 years it will probably start to emerge as the earth's leading secondary source of energy."[43]

The United States thus has a large variety of present and potential energy resources that can meet our needs in the long as well as near term. Our current energy "crisis" thus is not, as Ronald K. Ridker points out, a "result of an overall domestic shortage of energy sources, given our immense reserves of coal and nuclear materials" but rather a result of "inappropriate policies, compounded by the need to adjust energy production to environmental needs."

For example, banning the use of coal with sulfur content and restricting strip mining operations places limits on coal supplies. Environment-related delays in the construction and operation of nuclear power plants further exacerbates energy problems. Meanwhile, price controls on natural gas increase use and discourage development of new supplies, thus insuring an eventual shortage. And pollution-related modifications of automobile engines increase gasoline consumption, while environmentalist protests against off-shore drilling and shale oil processing retard the development of petroleum resources.

Our current "crisis" is man-made rather than a result of any absolute shortage of energy resources. As Freeman J. Dyson, a professor in the School of Natural Sciences of the Institute for Advanced Studies, sums it up, we are

fortunate in having such a variety of energy resources at [our] disposal. In the very long run we shall need energy that is absolutely pollution-free; we shall have sunlight. In the fairly long run, we shall need energy that is inexhaustible and moderately clean; we shall have deuterium. In the short run we shall need energy that is readily usable and abundant; we shall have uranium. Right now we need energy that

53

is cheap and convenient; we have coal and oil. Nature has been kinder to us than we had any right to expect.[44]

Nonfuel Minerals. Known reserves and potential resources of nonfuel minerals in the United States and the world as a whole are more than adequate to supply our needs through 2000. As Vincent E. McKelvey, director of the U.S. Geological Survey, puts it, "ample raw materials are indeed there in the ground—they are geologically available. Innovative application of old geologic theory and the creation of new concepts of ore-formation can be expected to lead to the discovery of minable deposits, and past experience tells us that research and exploration can be counted on to discover some kinds of deposits and some ore environments that we do not know about now . . . provided we are both aggressive and imaginative in our pursuit of research and exploration."[45]

U.S. reserves adequate. There is a long list of nonfuel minerals whose U.S. reserves alone, not even considering potential resources, are approximately equal to or greater than probable U.S. cumulative primary demand through 2000, according to the National Commission on Materials Policy.[46] These include arsenic, barium, beryllium, boron, bromine, calcium, chlorine, clay, construction stone, diatomite, feldspar, gallium, hafnium, kyanite, lithium, magnesium, mica, molybdenum, nitrogen, peat, pumice, rare earths, rhenium, sodium, sand and gravel, scandium, talc, titanium, and zirconium.

U.S. potential resources adequate. Current U.S. reserves of another group of minerals are inadequate, but potential U.S. resources are more than adequate to meet U.S. probable cumulative primary demand through 2000. This group includes aluminum, cobalt, copper, gold, graphite, gypsum, iodine, iron, lead, limestone and dolomite, manganese, nickel, niobium, phosphorous, platinum, potassium, silicon, silver, strontium, sulfur, tantalum, vanadium, and zinc.[47] Many of these minerals are currently imported, with import percentages ranging from 18 percent in the case of copper to 100 percent in the case of strontium. However, potential U.S. resources are large enough that reserves could be developed domestically if necessary, with expanded exploration and improved technology.

World reserves adequate. There are a number of minor metals for which it is difficult to even predict future demand due to their small usage. But, even considering the variability of possible demand, few of these minor metals—including antimony, bismuth, cadmium, cesium, germanium, indium and mercury—seem to be in short supply from the standpoint of world reserves.[48]

A major metal, chromium, for which the United States has no reserves and only small potential resources, has sufficient world reserves to meet anticipated demand through 2000. The bulk of these reserves are in the Republic of South Africa, Rhodesia, and the USSR. There is, of course, always a possibility that imports might be interrupted, but as Fischman and Landsberg state, there is little that the United States can do to increase its long-range security with regard to chromium by developing different current supply sources abroad; we already have a number of minor supplying countries, and the bulk of the reserves are in South Africa and Rhodesia. There are a variety of other actions possible. One of these—stockpiling—is a long-standing but basically short-term measure tailored to meet a specified contingency. Over the longer haul, substitution, increased secondary recovery, and development of technology to permit resort to lowgrade domestic ores are additional approaches. Research and development have been carried on in all of these aspects, and the principal requirement is that such research and development be kept sufficiently up-to-date to permit minimum-cost satisfaction of emergency requirements in the event of interruption of foreign supplies and exhaustion of stockpiles. In the meantime, the continued import of chromium and its incorporation in products is, of course, building up an "above-ground" stock that will enter the scrap cycle and, in time, add to supplies and security.[49]

World potential resources adequate. The United States imports virtually 100 percent of its primary tin requirements—of which about 90 percent comes from Malaysia and Thailand—while relying on secondary sources of reclaimed tin (containers, other used products, et cetera) for close to 25 percent of total tin consumption. U.S. tin reserves are miniscule, and potential U.S. tin resources are currently insignificant, although there is at least a possibility of finding tin deposits in new, unexplored geologic environments.

Current world reserves of 4.9 million short tons of tin are also inadequate to meet world demand through the turn of the century. However, the U.S. Bureau of Mines considers this reserve figure conservative and judges that the reserve figure is more nearly 7 million short tons (assuming a modest price increase and the inclusion of omitted smaller sources). An additional 8 million short tons is credited to lower-grade resources by the U.S. Geological Survey. Assuming all of these resources were to become minable at a cost not radically higher than historical levels, they would just about cover cumulative world demand through 2000.[50]

World potential resources inadequate. Tungsten is a mineral which most authorities agree could present a serious shortage problem in the future. Yet, even here, data is insufficient to support firm conclusions. McKelvey, for example, states that there is a possibility of the discovery of major new resources of tungsten in the United States.[51] And Fischman and Landsberg point out that, while adequate tungsten supplies cannot be foreseen with any degree of confidence, supply difficulties need not become a significant stricture either on United States or world welfare if they are compensated for by such other actions as greater recovery, increased material substitution, and switches to other methods of operation that do not involve the use of tungsten, for example, substituting fluorescent for incandescent lights.[52]

Based on the best knowledge currently available, nonfuel mineral resources are adequate to meet the needs of the United States through the turn of the century. Beyond this, predictions become increasingly speculative because no one can accurately anticipate what mineral needs may be and because there is no current economic justification for attempting to find out what minerals may be available. As Wilfred Beckerman, head of the Department of Political Economy at University College, London, puts it, the world is "rarely likely to know, at any moment of time, how much 'total' reserves it has, since it never needs to know this. It needs only to find enough reserves to supply foreseeable demands at reasonable costs."[53]

Perhaps the best that can be said is that, in Beckerman's words,

new reserves are found, on the whole, as they are needed. . . . In fact, given the natural concentrations of the key metals in the earth's crust, as indicated by a large number of random samples, the total natural occurrence of most metals in the top mile of the earth's crust has been estimated to be about a million times as great as present known reserves. Since the latter amount to about a hundred years' supplies this means we have enough to last about one hundred million years. Even though it may be impossible at present to mine to a depth of one mile at every point in the earth's crust, by the time we reach the year A.D. 100,000,000 I am sure we will think up something.[54]

Land. The United States is blessed by a large supply of usable, productive land. As Marion Clawson of Resources for the Future states, the "people of the United States are extremely fortunate in their land heritage. Our total land surface per person is almost exactly the same as the world average. But our land is on the average vastly more productive than that for the world as a whole. Not more than 10 to 15 per cent can reasonably be classed as wasteland; even the deserts, tundra, and mountain tops often have some value for wildlife, mineral production, watershed, or other purposes."[55]

Land is relatively fixed in terms of its physical area. But, from the standpoint of its ultimate potential to support human populations, it is not. First of all, land provides a fairly limitless three-dimensional, rather than simply a relatively fixed two-dimensional, potential. Land can be used vertically both above and below ground as well as horizontally along its surface. Second, the ultimate capability of land to produce renewable resources such as crops and timber is unknown. Furthermore, land is, in many instances, replaceable. The use of fertilizer to increase crop production, for example, in effect takes the place of land that otherwise would have to be put into production to achieve the same crop increase. Thus, as Clawson says, our concern is "not really with the acreage of land, but with the products and services of land. These depend not only on the area and the characteristics of the land, but also upon the inputs of labor, capital, management, and technology into various productive processes. The volume, variety, and scope of these inputs has risen greatly over the years, and promises to rise more in the decades ahead. As a result, the

56

products and services of land are not in danger of running out, and the total land situation of the United States is relatively comfortable."[56]

The United States has close to 2.3 billion acres of land, including Alaska and Hawaii. There are more than ten acres, the equivalent of nine football fields, for each man, woman, and child in the country.

According to the Economic Research Service of the U.S. Department of Agriculture, demands on our land resources have increased greatly over the last two decades. Population has grown by a third, while the total output of goods and services has risen even more, as is reflected by improvements in the standard of living. However, despite these demands, the total land-use pattern has remained virtually unchanged since 1950 and, for that matter, since the beginning of this century. Cropland still comprises about a fifth of our total land area, grassland pasture and range about a fourth, forest land about a third, and wasteland an eighth.

Land for urban uses has approximately doubled since 1950, but still takes only 1.5 percent of the country's total land area. Land for transportation purposes, which comprises about one percent of the total, is up only slightly because many new roads have been built on existing rights-of-way and some roads have been abandoned. In response to greatly increased demand, land designated as recreation and wildlife areas has tripled and now accounts for about 4 percent of our land resources. This increase is largely due to a reclassification of some public forest or wilderness, while the land cover itself remains unchanged. Total land available for recreation, including land available on a shared basis, comprises a high proportion of the country's total area.[57]

Cropland. The nation's cropland resources total 472 million acres, or 21 percent of our total land area. Of this, the total acreage required for crop production in 1973 totalled 354 million acres, with the rest either being used for pasture or remaining idle.

During the last two decades, cropland actually used for growing crops decreased from a record high of 387 million acres in 1949 to 335 million acres in 1964, remained near this relatively low level through 1972, and then increased sharply to 354 million acres in 1973 as farmers were encouraged to expand production to supply domestic and export demands. Overall, the cutback in cropland used for crops came about because of great increases in cropland productivity. From 1949 to 1969, population increased a third, while output per crop acre increased more than half and total crop production rose 41 percent. Thus, output per person actually gained even though there was a cutback of 14 percent in cropland.[58]

Looking to the long-term future, the Department of Agriculture's Economic Research Service predicts a further decrease in the amount of cropland required for crops to about 300 million acres, due to continuing effects on crop yields of technological advances such as more efficient farm organization; improved machinery; increased use of agricultural chemicals such as fertilizers, pesticides, and ration additives; improved crop species and management; more irrigation; and regional shifts in crop production to more productive areas of the country.[59] In addition, wholly new methods of agriculture such as closed agricultural systems involving the hydroponic production of food with chemicals and artificial lights in enclosed areas may increasingly come into use. As Ronald Ridker says, "protection from pests would be accomplished mechanically rather than chemically, no nutrients would be lost to land or air, and use of land would be minimal. For special crops, where water, land, or distribution costs are especially high, this method of production is proving to be commercially viable even now. If the price of good agricultural land increases very greatly—this method of production may become sufficiently important to release substantial quantities of cropland for other purposes."[60]

Pasture and rangeland. Livestock graze on 890 million acres, or 39 percent of the total land area of the country. This represents a decrease of 13 percent in land area grazed in the last two decades, despite a 46 percent increase in cattle numbers. Most of the decrease can be attributed to a reduction in areas of low forage productivity such as woodland.

In the future, it is anticipated that total acreage required for grazing will decline slightly, with continued increases in per capita meat consumption being achieved by improving pasture and range productivity, more fully utilizing land now available for grazing, and increasing more productive pasture acreage by converting woodland and idle farmland to pasture. Other means of carrying increasing numbers of beef cattle may also be used: greater substitution of feed grains for range or pasture forage, new livestock management practices to increase weight gains of cattle being grazed, and further research to maintain high range and pasture productivity. The possibility of improving livestock breeds and feeding efficiency through research is another important means of increasing beef production without large-scale conversion of land to pasture.[61]

Forests. A third, or 754 million acres, of the country's total land area is in forests. About a sixth of this area is in Alaska, where little timber is harvested for wood products. Of the 633 million acres of forest land in the forty-eight contiguous states, almost 80 percent, or 493 million acres, is commercially productive.

In the future, it is anticipated that the acreage of total forestland will decline as forestland is converted to urban areas, highways, airports, reservoirs, parks, wilderness areas, and cropland. Unless steps are taken to raise forest productivity, there will be problems in meeting the nation's need for timber.[62]

However, there is great potential for increasing forest productivity. Marion Clawson notes, for example, that forests may be on the verge of a biological revolution. In the last few decades, the field of forest genetics has been growing rapidly. Superior trees have been selected from natural stands, their seed has been saved, planted, and their progeny thereby increased. This is similar to what has been done within agriculture, but the process is much slower for trees than for farm crops because the forest cycle is so long. It takes 40 years or more for almost all species grown in the United States, although some seed may be produced earlier. However, forest genetics is now moving into hybridization on a larger scale, and already has produced some superior varieties, which will be multiplied in the years ahead. The development of new and vastly more productive strains of trees might greatly change the picture, as far as output in relation to standing volume is concerned.[63]

Other steps that can be taken in raising forest productivity to meet future needs include reducing losses from fire, insects and disease; increasing salvage of dead timber; improving timber utilization, fertilization and forestation; and developing better access and logging methods.

Urban and related land uses. By the year 2000, urban and related land uses are expected to increase by about 20 million acres, to a total of 80 million acres. Included in these uses are residential, commercial, industrial, and transportation applications for metropolitan area expansion and outlying land uses required to support this expansion. Interstate highways and airports are required to meet emerging transportation needs.

Only a part of the land required for urban and related intensive land uses has been taken from operating farms. At the same time, agricultural land-use adjustments have, on the whole, greatly exceeded shifts of land to nonagricultural uses. Whether future conversion of rural lands will have a noticeable impact on agricultural production will depend on the use and quality of land that is converted.[64] On the other hand, most urban areas have a sizable amount of land—up to as much as 30 percent—that is unused or not used to its full potential. Utilization of this land presently contained within urban areas would reduce the need for expansion. In addition, just as building upward frees space below, technological advances in tunneling will increasingly make possible use of the underground for urban facilities such as highways and power plants, leaving additional space aboveground for residential and recreational development.

Recreational and other public land uses. There are currently 319 million acres of public land available for public recreation. However, not all of the public recreation area is uniformly available for recreational use. Limited-use recreation sites, such as reservoirs and wildlife preserves, which serve a variety of purposes other than recreation, account for a high proportion of the total lands available for public recreation. Thus, only 81 of the 319 million acres are specifically designated as national and state parks or recreation, wildlife, wilderness, and primitive areas.

More land will be required in the future for recreation, parks, and wilderness areas. To some extent, these requirements may be met by reclassification and reservation of public lands now in other uses or by multiple shared uses of land with acquisition of additional land amounting to about 20 million acres.

Public installations and facilities include national defense areas (23 million acres), federal atomic development and test areas (2 million acres), and state-owned land (2 million acres). These land uses are expected to grow in the future, but at a moderate rate.

The general outlook for land is one of sufficient supply to meet demand. The figures cited above for land uses actually add up to more than 2.3 billion acres, the total land area of the United States. But, when adjustments are made to take account of various shared land uses such as forest preserves and recreational areas, the picture is one of land adequacy through the turn of the century.

Water. According to the Agriculture Department's Economic Research Service, a comparison of national requirements and supplies indicates that the United States will have an adequate water supply through 2000, although there are and will continue to be severe localized problems. Problems of water quality and quantity could constrain growth of the regional economies in several parts of the country. Water quality problems are serious in parts of the Northeast and in some areas of the West; limited water supplies are a threat in the West and Southwest. However, these potential problem areas can be alleviated somewhat by treating waste water properly, recycling water in industrial plants, supplementing existing supplies through desalinization, and building additional storage and treatment facilities.[66]

Furthermore, as Ridker observes, there are "considerable possibilities for using water more prudently. Most water is used either free of cost or on a flat fee basis that provides no incentive for conservation. Yet in the largest areas of use—for irrigation and cooling—substantial possibilities are present to reduce withdrawals without serious welfare losses. Finding equitable means to increase prices or otherwise ration major users would not be easy, but certainly could be done if the need arises."[67]

The United States has sufficient supplies of the four basic resources of energy, nonfuel minerals, land, and water to meet its needs through the year 2000. A number of these resources will not become economically available for use without continuing research and development efforts. But, given a strong resource and development program, the United States need not fear "running out" of resources.

The Argument against Resource Adequacy

Significant advances in knowledge and technology and large infusions of capital and labor will be required to insure resource adequacy in the future. In no way should the problems that must be solved be minimized.However, it is one thing to call attention to the fact that continuing efforts must be made to achieve an assured flow of future resources. It is something else to proclaim that resources are "running out" and society will cease to exist unless population growth is stopped.

The more strident proponents of this view gaze into their crystal balls and predict imminent catastrophe within a decade or two. The more sophisticated process huge amounts of data through a computer and come out with the year 2040 for the blow-up. But, in all cases, the analysis is basically the same: infinite population growth, finite resources, BOOM!

There is, of course, a long and undistinguished history of predictions forecasting resource exhaustion. For example, as Wilfred Beckerman relates, "just over a hundred years ago, a distinguished occupant of my chair in Political Economy at University College London, the great economist Stanley Jevons, predicted an inevitable shortage of coal within a short space of time. But, although coal demand has since increased far more than Jevons anticipated, known coal reserves are now estimated at about 600 years' supply."[68]

In 1908, President Theodore Roosevelt was alarmed about a supposed exhaustion of mineral resources in the United States. He called for a survey, which soon turned up many more reserves. Another survey carried out in 1944 gave estimates of available reserves that, had they been correct, would have meant that by 1973 half of the products on the list would have already been exhausted. In particular, the United States would have already run out of tin, nickel, zinc, lead, and manganese. But, in fact, more deposits were found in the United States during the 1950s than during the previous twenty-five years.[67]

It is in light of these previous ill-founded predictions of imminent resource exhaustion that current claims that resources are running out should be evaluated. Perhaps the most vocal proponent of the resources-are-running-out view today is Preston Cloud, professor of biogeology at the University of California, Santa Barbara. States Cloud:

Nothing can increase infinitely on a finite earth. It is evident, moreover, if one equates quality of life with the variety and flexibility of options available, that the quality of human existence over much of the earth is threatened where it is not already nullified. In the author's view, the number of men, not only in the world at large but even in the United States, already exceeds the optimum. Yet, populations will continue to increase until the numbers of men come under the restraints of nature or of human will. It is the central thesis of this paper that food and raw

61

materials place ultimate limits on the size of populations; that the latter must come into balance with the ecosystem at lower levels if acceptable quality is to be preserved. Since, at current rates of population growth, such limits will be reached within the next thirty to one hundred years, it is essential to human welfare that we move as rapidly as possible toward zero population growth.[70]

However, we have seen that, although the resources of the earth are theoretically finite, their ultimate limits are actually unknown. As the World Bank says, *we do not know* the true extent of the resources that exist in, and can ultimately be recovered from, the earth. Nor will we know in the next two years or ten years. The reason why we do not know the absolute limits of the resources we have is simple and does not even require recourse to elaborate arguments about the wonders of technology. We do not know because no one has as yet found it *necessary* to know and therefore went about taking an accurate inventory."[71]

Thus, to say that resources are finite is to state a truism that adds little to the discussion. The real question is: How finite? As B. Delworth Gardner, head of the Department of Economics at Utah State University, puts it, since "in a physical sense the resources of the earth are indisputably finite, any positive rate of net consumption of non-renewable resources will ultimately deplete these resources and end human life as we know it on this planet. [But] this conclusion is not an hypothesis; it is a tautology. It is true by definition. The interesting question, however, is not *whether* mankind will run out of natural resources given positive rates of consumption, but *when*."

In an attempt to answer this question, Cloud uses copper as an illustration. Copper, he states, is

a metal that is neither abundant nor in immediate jeopardy. Its abundance in the earth's crust averages about 55 parts per million, and the total mass of the crust is roughly 2.5×10^{19} tons. That suggests about 1.4×10^{15} tons of copper in the entire crust of the earth—under continents and ocean basins alike—which is a lot of copper. However, of that amount, probably no more than a billion or two tons is recoverable under likely circumstances. Of this possibly recoverable copper, about 210 million tons is represented by ore reserves now known. Thus, even with new discoveries and the working of lower grades of ore, an increase in copper eventually mined to as much as ten times current reserves is unlikely. If we then allow for increasing population and for expected end-of-century demands, it becomes clear that a limit must be reached within another couple of generations when the continuing availability of copper will depend largely on the recycling of already-mined metal. It is inevitable that the same must ultimately be true of all other metals.[73]

But such a belief in the "inevitability" of resource depletion does not accord with the strong probability of future technological developments, particularly that of extracting elements from ordinary rock with energy furnished by nuclear fusion. For, as Harrison Brown, professor of geochemistry at the California Institute of Technology, states, if we

> look at the earth's crust as a whole, with a copper content of but 55 parts per million, some one million billion tons of copper could, in principle, be made available were we to develop the requisite technology. It will be a very long time indeed before we need to process ores containing as little as 55 parts per million copper—namely, ordinary rock. I am convinced, however, that, if necessary, we in the United States could live quite comfortably off ordinary rock, which could provide us with virtually all of our metals as well as our energy. One ton of average granite, for example, can yield, rather easily, the energy equivalent of fifteen tons of coal in the form of uranium and thorium. In the interim, as prices of ores and metals increase, we will process ore of steadily lessening grade and we will learn how to recover scrap more efficiently.[74]

Cloud is dubious concerning the possibility of recovering minerals from the sea. Writing in 1973, he points out that "sixty-four of ninety naturally occurring elements now known on earth have been detected in seawater," but quickly adds that the metal elements we are likely to have greatest need to extract from seawater offer little promise for direct recovery.[75]

Yet, in a report published the previous year, the World Bank states that

> literally vast quantities of minerals can be obtained from as yet unexploited seabeds, through the mining of so-called manganese nodules. . . . According to some experts, recovering 100 million tons of nodules per annum, which appears to be within reach in 10–20 years, would produce annually manganese, copper, nickel and cobalt in amounts equivalent to 572 per cent, 28 per cent, 320 per cent, and 1,200 per cent of current "free world" consumption, respectively. Reserves are in the order of "hundreds of billions of tons," and a mining rate of 400 million tons per year is possible for a literally unlimited period of time. . . . It is worth noting that $50–$100 million have already been spent or committed, mostly by American companies, for nodule mining; at least a dozen national or multi-national corporations and consortia are actively working on it; and the subject has received earnest attention in at least three international conferences in the last six months. It is a mark of the subject's vast dimensions and ramifications that at one of these conferences the focus was on "how to prevent potential *drastic declines* in mineral prices resulting from nodule mining."[76]

Following in the path of Cloud was *The Limits to Growth,* the report of a study sponsored by the Club of Rome and conducted by an MIT team of systems analysts headed by Professor Dennis L. Meadows. Assuming that current rates of resource usage will continue indefinitely into the future, *The Limits to Growth* concludes reserves will prove inadequate, with the result that sometime in the middle of the next century resource exhaustion will cause a worldwide catastrophe.

But, as the World Bank points out, *The Limits to Growth* group made a number of assumptions about resources that

turn out to be extremely pessimistic on close examination . . . reserve estimates have changed frequently over time and are likely to change again in our own lifetime. Just between 1954 and 1966, in the case of one of the largest resources, iron ore, the reserve estimates have gone up by about 5 times. It is estimated by the U.S. Bureau of Mines that even these reserves can be doubled at a price 30% to 40% higher than the current price. . . . The authors allow for this in their model by the "generous" assumption that reserves could increase by 5 times over the next 100 years, but what appears to be an act of generosity turns out to be an unduly conservative assumption in the light of historical evidence and recent finds.[77]

Furthermore, the assumption of indefinite expansion of current rates of resource consumption is untenable. *The Limits to Growth* extrapolates thirty-year exponential projections of demand prepared by the U.S. Bureau of Mines indefinitely into the future. But, comments the World Bank, "this, of course, is absurd. Even small changes in the assumptions . . . could alter not only the volume but also the composition of future output, with far-reaching implications for resource requirements."[78]

The rate at which the growth of demand for iron ore has slowed down during the course of the century is a striking example of the dangers of simple extrapolation of past trends. Barbara Ward, for example, notes that between 1900 and 1910 the annual increase in the production of iron ore in the United States was 7.8 percent, or a doubling of output every 8.9 years. This, in turn, implies that output now would be 256 times as great as in 1900. In fact, it is only three times as great![79]

Even more significant, when the prophets of doom tell us that resources will be depleted in x number of years, what they are really telling us is that they know when the world is going to end. For, in fact, if resources are actually limited and we are able to determine those limits, then what good will it do to control population growth? We will eventually run out of resources anyway, regardless of what we do. Instant ZPG might delay the blow-up another decade or two, but the end would still come and that would be that.

As Beckerman puts it, one "cannot have it both ways. Either resources are finite in some meaningful sense, in which case even zero growth will fail to save us in the long run, and as long as we go on using up these finite resources we must run out of them some day. Or, resources are not really finite in any meaningful sense, in which case this argument for slowing down growth collapses." Beckerman goes on to note that, in *The Limits to Growth*, this dilemma is avoided by cutting off the computer printout at the year when it becomes clear that even the authors' proposed stationary state would still be untenable on account of exhaustion of what they assume to be a finite supply of resources.[80]

In truth, most resources always appear to be running out, because, while it is a relatively simple mathematical exercise to extend any current rate of resource usage into the future, it is a laborious, time-consuming, and costly undertaking to actually develop new reserves of any particular resource. Even so, although resource-reserve figures thus may appear inadequate at any given point in time, reserves for many resources have generally *increased* over time, as the World Bank notes for:

Iron ore. In 1954, world iron ore resources were estimated at 85 billion gross tons, with an iron content of 42 billion tons. In 1966, reserves were on the order of 250 billion gross tons, and another 200 billion gross tons were identified as "potential ores," leading to a total estimate of about 200 billion tons of metallic iron, or five times larger than the 1954 estimate. (The estimate of iron ore resources used in *The Limits to Growth* is 110 billion tons, or roughly half the 1966 estimate of "reserves and potential ores," which most knowledgeable people agree is extremely conservative.)

Copper. In 1935, world copper reserves were estimated to amount to about 100 million tons. In 1972, reserves were placed at 340 million tons, or roughly 3.5 times more than in 1935.

Bauxite (from which aluminum is extracted). World reserves increased sevenfold between 1950 and 1972, from 1.6 billion to 11.7 billion tons.

Phosphate rock. World reserves increased from 17 billion tons in 1929 to 47 billion tons in 1950 and 104 billion tons in 1972, or sixfold in forty-three years.[81]

Sums up the World Bank:

It is not our intention to dispute that resources, after all, are finite nor to deny that some are more scarce than others. There are problems. But these ought not to be approached without a proper sense of proportion. We should realize that the true magnitude of resource availabilities is *uncertain* rather than proceed on the conviction that they are *definably* finite. Uncertainty calls for taking out reasonable insurance. The *Limits'* [*Limits to Growth*] prescription is a radical one, amounting to nothing less than telling the patient to live without exposing himself to the very risks of life.

If certain resources are likely to become more scarce . . . it is a scientific and intellectual service to humanity to draw attention to those resources and to the time period over which they may vanish with current usage and on present knowledge. Research into these areas is both useful and vital. But it is quite another thing to argue that no amount of research or technological breakthroughs will extend the lifetime of these resources indefinitely. . . . sweeping generalizations about complete disappearance of all nonrenewable resources at a particular point of time in [the] future [are] mere intellectual fantasy.[82]

65

Or, as Herman Kahn, head of the Hudson Institute, puts it:

For a while, I think about two-thirds of the people who seem to have at least the higher educational qualifications have believed that we're running out of food, out of resources, out of energy. None of this seems to be true. Not only not true, but by a very large amount not true. You may have food shortages, or energy shortages, or material shortages for a short period, because you made a mistake, or something happened, but we're talking about shortages like for the next 20 years. To us, it's remarkable how what we might call this neo-Malthusian point of view has been spread around the country, mainly by the educated people, by the experts, which shows you why we're skeptical of both education and expertise.[83]

Perhaps John Stuart Mill best caught the continuing frustration that is inevitably experienced by those who preach that growth must stop because the world is running out of resources. On the one hand, Mill observed that "it must always have been seen, more or less distinctly, by political economists, that the increase of wealth is not boundless; that at the end of what they term the progressive state lies the stationary state, that all progress in wealth is but a postponement of this and that each step in advance is an approach to it." But, on the other hand, Mill pointed out that "we have now been led to recognize that this ultimate goal is at all times near enough to be fully in view; that we are always on the verge of it, and that if we have not reached it long ago, it is because the goal itself flies before us."[84]

What always turns out to be limited is not resources but the perspective and imagination of those who proclaim that resources are running out.

Conclusion

Current knowledge and available technology provide assurance that resources are more than adequate to meet the needs of the United States through the turn of the century. Beyond this, although reasonable confidence can be expressed that resources will continue to be adequate, it becomes increasingly difficult to predict the precise shape that resource adequacy will take because, as Ronald Ridker and Allen Kneese comment, projecting the specifics of technology into the remote future is a "bootless chore. When we are considering events more than a few years or decades ahead, uncertainty mounts and after a while it becomes almost total."[85]

This is not to say that there are no problems to be solved in achieving continuing resource adequacy. There are immense problems that will require great efforts to resolve. Many of these problems are technological. Others are economic and political. But solutions must be and *can be* developed to insure adequate supplies of resources in the future.

Nor is it to say that shortages of particular resources will not occur from time to time. The current "energy crisis" is a case in point. As the World Bank notes, this "is not, of course, an ultimate crisis for the availability of sufficient energy sources to meet demand, but is more a crisis of *policy* on what sources of energy [the United States and other developed countries] should be reliant on, at which prices, and from where these sources should be obtained."[86] However, a shortage still causes problems, regardless of whether it is a result of absolute scarcity or economic and political policies.

Nor is it to say that we do not have an immediate need to take action on resource development for the future. In July, 1975, more than seventy earth scientists held a special White House conference to convey a sense of national urgency in meeting future needs. "Our message is that the problems of supplies of raw materials, energy and water are economic and political—not resource problems," stated James Boyd, the group's spokesman. "The real issue becomes not a lack of resources, but a lack of understanding in the body politic. The body politic has to realize the essence of this problem. Then it must provide the manpower, technology, capital and will. . . ."[87]

But it is to say that the manpower, technology, capital, and will can best be supplied by continuing population growth. For the problems will exist regardless of whether population grows or not. But they can be solved better by increasing through population growth the amount of human resources devoted to them.

Mineral supplies today are a small and falling proportion of our gross national product. Currently, the value of primary minerals consumption, including energy materials, is only about 3 percent of GNP, while the value of nonenergy minerals is only a little more than one percent.[88]

Future population growth will not result in a proportional increase in resource consumption, primarily because of the trend in advanced economies such as the United States to increasingly produce services rather than goods. But population growth will provide proportionally greater inputs of the knowledge, technology, capital, and manpower required to develop resources in the future.

What is needed is a dynamic rather than a static view of population growth in relation to resource development. Population growth increases the knowledge and technology necessary to discover new resources and devise new methods of obtaining them. It spurs economic growth necessary to provide the capital for financing the large investments involved in resource development. It provides the increasing manpower required to actually make resources available for use. Overall, it results in the growing resource abundance that has been achieved in the past and can be expected to continue in the future.

In essence, to say that we are running out of resources means, according to sociologist Ben J. Wattenberg, that "the one key resource—the intellect of man—is running dry. But that is not happening."[89] In fact, as Wattenberg notes, the "wits of man have never quite been so titillated as they are now." For the more we learn, the more we find out how much we do not know, or, as distinguished mathematician Warren Weaver puts it, as science "learns one answer, it is characteristically true that it learns several new questions. It is as though science were working in a great forest of ignorance, making an ever larger circular clearing. But, as that circle becomes larger and larger, the circumference of contact with ignorance also gets larger and larger."[90]

A dynamic view of population growth as a stimulant to resource development is, of course, the opposite of the static view that population growth should be stopped in order to conserve resources for ourselves and future generations. But Harold J. Barnett, formerly with Resources for the Future and now professor of economics at Washington University in St. Louis, points out that

resource conservation may, by curbing research and capital formation, have a perverse effect on future output and welfare. It is by no means necessary to reduce production today in order to increase production tomorrow. If, instead, current production is maintained and consumption is reduced in favor of research and investment, future production will be increased. Higher production today, if it also means more research and investment today, thus will serve the economic interest of future generations better than reservation of resources and lower current production.

[The] premise that the economic heritage will shrink in value unless natural resources are conserved is wrong for a progressive world. The opposite is true. In the United States, for example, over the period for which data exists the economic magnitude of the estate each generation passes on—the income per capita the next generation enjoys—has been approximately double that which it received.

Therefore, resource reservation to protect the economic interest of future generations is unnecessary. There is no need for a future-oriented ethical principle to replace or supplement the economic calculations that lead modern man to accumulate primarily for the benefit of those now living.

The reason, of course, is that the legacy of economically valuable assets which each generation passes on consists only in part of the natural environment. The more important components of the inheritance are knowledge, technology, capital instruments and economic institutions. Far more than natural resources, these are the determinants of real income per capita.

. . . [Even with respect to] natural resource wealth alone, as Edmund Jones remarked at the White House Conference of Governors which dealt with conservation in 1908, we shall add far more to our natural resources by developing our ability to increase them than we can ever do by mere processes of saving.[91]

4

U.S. POPULATION GROWTH AND ENVIRONMENTAL IMPROVEMENT

Population growth in the United States has made possible continuing improvement of our environment. The more than 200 million people who live in the United States today enjoy an incalculably better human environment than the 4 million who inhabited the country two centuries ago.

This view of continuing environmental improvement, of course, flies in the face of current received opinion that the environment has deteriorated as a result of population growth. But this is because it is a view that considers the total human environment from the standpoint of the people living in it, rather than merely selective aspects of that environment in terms of the environment itself.

It may appear absurdly unnecessary to stress the point that we are talking about human environment from the viewpoint of the people living in it. But it is nevertheless true that environmental discussions oftentimes lack this basic perspective. Therefore it is necessary, as Miguel Ozorio de Almeida, special adviser to the foreign minister of Brazil and Brazilian delegate to the 1972 Conference on the Human Environment, puts it, to

ask straight away the basic question: according to whose criteria is the environment to be considered healthy, adequate, pleasant, desirable? If the subject were an anaconda, and if the anaconda had a mind capable of value-judgments, it would probably suggest that the world should be a swampy forest; a dromedary would wish it to be a desert. But what should it be for the human race? Certainly not all desert or all swamp. A first assumption . . . will be that environment is supposed to serve human rather than reptilian, ruminant, pachydermic, or any other interests. There is no doubt that human needs themselves may best be served by a degree of contact

69

with certain types of domesticated or wild animals and plants. Within those limits or degrees, the environmental conditions necessary for them must be preserved. But it is to be understood that the final standards for judging the adequacy of any environmental conditions must be specifically limited by human needs and interests, both in the present and in the foreseeable future. In short, the environment under consideration will have to be considered from a "subjective" stand-point, and the "subject" will have to be "man." "Man," moreover, must be understood to be "homo sapiens" at his most advanced stage of civilization, in a habitat representing adequate conditions of personal security and full satisfaction of his basic needs for food and protection against the weather and any kind of elemental disaster. It is for this "subject" that environment must be preserved or restored.[1]

Man lives in the natural environment, and it is the natural environment that provides us with our basic sustenance in the form of sunlight, air, water, land, and animal and plant life. But the natural environment is not an unmixed blessing, for it also includes such things as hurricanes, tornadoes, floods, tidal waves, earthquakes, volcanos, predatory animals, poisonous plants, plagues, snow and rain storms, and extremes of heat and cold.

Certain environmentalists tell us that we must live in "balance" or "equilibrium" with the natural environment. This may be fine when it comes to enjoying the sunlight, air, and water at Miami Beach, but how is one to live in "balance" with a tornado or below-zero temperatures or a hungry lion on the loose? Reflected here, points out de Almeida, is "a certain misunderstanding that has permeated the whole debate on environmental protection and restoration, even in relatively sophisticated circles—namely that we have to keep or protect environment or ecological 'equilibrium.' In relation to this, we run up against very serious problems. The problem to be solved in fact is not achieving an 'ecological balance,' but, on the contrary, obtaining the most efficient forms of 'long-term ecological imbalance.' The problem is not to exterminate mankind now, in the name of ecological equilibrium, but to prolong our ability to use natural resources for as long as possible."[2]

From the beginning, man has been confronted with this problem of how to create an imbalance between himself and the natural environment. His solution has been to create an environment that transcends the natural environment. The first cave men, for example, undoubtedly did not live in a particularly pleasant natural environment, existing as they did in dank, dark caves that at any time might be invaded by hungry carnivores. Then man discovered fire and placed it at the mouth of his cave. The fire, of course, created smoke, which not only polluted the air but probably gave the cave dwellers coughing fits when the wind blew the wrong way. This pollution might be deemed abhorrent from the airy view of the environmental purist. But it seems safe to assume that early man was willing to trade an occasional mouthful of smoke for the environmental improvements of heat, light, and protection from predatory animals provided by the fire. Far from attempting

70

to stay in balance or equilibrium with their natural environment—which probably would have resulted in their eventual extinction—prehistoric men transcended the natural environment by creating a man-made environment of their own.

Ever since, the total human environment has consisted of not only the natural but the man-made environment. That there is a trade-off between these two environments is obvious. The cave man, for example, obtained heat, light, and protection from animal attack in trade for freedom from smoke. But that the benefits of this trade-off far outweighed the costs is also clear, e.g., the caveman found his new, warm, illuminated and relatively safe man-made environment infinitely preferable to his previous existence in a dank, dark, and dangerous—albeit smoke-free—natural environment.

The modern benefits of such man-made environmental improvements are all around us today. We live in heated, lighted, mostly sewered and oftentimes air conditioned, humidity-controlled and dust-filtered quarters that provide maximum physical comfort and convenience while protecting us from the worst of the natural elements. We travel in cars, buses, trains, and planes that enable us to take this same pleasant environment with us wherever we go. We work in offices and factories that similarly provide a most comfortable and livable environment. We live in relatively good health, free from a host of contagious diseases that plagued peoples of the past. These man-made environmental conditions in which we live today are incomparably better than those of even a century ago.

Nor have these man-made environmental benefits been obtained at the expense of negative trade-offs with the natural environment, that is, trade-offs in which degradation of the natural environment resulting from man-made environmental improvements more than cancelled out the benefits of these improvements. In fact, the opposite is the case, for, as environmental improvements have been made, improvements in the natural environment have also gradually been achieved. As Wilfred Beckerman comments, many people today "clearly do not appreciate what the physical environment was like in the past and how great an improvement in the environment has taken place."[3]

Referring to air pollution in the past, Beckerman cites the experience of Chateaubriand, who, when taking up his post at the French embassy in London in 1822, wrote: "At Blackheath, a common frequented by highwaymen, I found a newly built village. Soon I saw before me the immense skull-cap of smoke which covers the city of London. Plunging into the gulf of black mist, as if into one of the mouths of Tartarus, and crossing the whole town, whose streets I recognized, I arrived at the Embassy in Portland Place."[4]

Until the late eighteenth century, according to *Nature* editor John Maddox, most cities lacked sewerage systems, so that the effluents that are now in some parts of the world dumped into rivers were disposed of by open drains running down the middle of city streets.[5] What this meant in terms of London

71

environmental conditions was related by author Hector Gavin in his *Sanitary Ramblings:*

Immediately facing Pleasant Row is a ditch, filled with slimy mud and putrefying filth, which extends 100 feet. The space between Pleasant Row and the central square is beyond description, filthy, dung-heaps and putrefying garbage, refuse, and manure, fill up the horrid place, which is covered with slimy foetid mud. The east end has likewise its horrid filthy foetid gutter reeking with pestilential effluvia; the southern alley is likewise abominably filthy. . . . I entered one of these houses on the southern side, and found that every individual in a family of seven had been attacked with fever. . . . the privy of this house is close to it, and is full and overflowing, covering the yard with its putrescent filth. . . ."[6]

It is therefore not surprising, as Beckerman points out, that "deaths from typhus alone in England in the mid-nineteenth century were nearly 20,000 a year, and that 60,000 deaths a year were attributed to tuberculosis, not to mention high death rates from numerous other diseases associated with insanitary and unhealthy living conditions."[7]

Furthermore, what was true in distant times was also the case in more recent years. Mathew A. Crenson of Johns Hopkins University, for example, has pointed out that "the available evidence indicates that there has been a general decline in sulfur dioxide pollution during the past 30 or 40 years. In some cities, the sulfur dioxide content of the air today is only one-third or one-fourth of what it was before World War II. In some ways, at least, city air is probably cleaner today than it was 30 or 40 or 50 years ago. The city of tenements . . . was probably a good bit dirtier than today's city."[8]

In 1931 and 1932, the United States Public Health Service conducted measurements in fourteen cities and found that the average concentration of particulates in the air was 510 micrograms per cubic meter. Then, in 1957, the Department of Health, Education and Welfare began an air-monitoring program and discovered an average particulate concentration of only 120 micrograms per cubic meter. Since then, the air-monitoring program has been extended to sixty-four cities, and continuing measurements reveal a yearly decrease in particulates. By 1969, the average concentration was down to 92 micrograms per cubic meter.[9]

According to Harold B. Gotaas, dean of the Technological Institute at Northwestern University, the death rate in 1900 from water-borne typhoid in the United States was thirty-five per 100,000 population, with the levels in some cities running considerably higher. In Chicago, for example, it was ninety per 100,000 people. Today, the death rate from typhoid is below .001 per 100,000 population—roughly 35,000 times less than it was in 1900. Sums up Gotaas: "Today in the United States waterborne disease is a very unusual happening. We drink water from public supplies without concern about health problems [from waterborne disease]. Never in history has the quality or the water supplies for cities been better."[10]

One could go on and on with positive comparisons of the natural environment of today with that of the past. We consider the automobile to be a major polluter of the natural environment, but it is practically insignificant in direct comparison with the horse of past generations. Professor Elliott Montrol points out that a car emits only six grams of pollutant a mile, whereas a horse, over the same distance, emits about 600 grams of solid pollutant and 300 grams of liquid pollutant.[11] If we traveled as many miles by horse as we do today by car, we would be up to our hips in you-know-what! Likewise, our cities are considered to be extremely noisy, yet they are comparatively quiet compared to the din created in cities of the past by the clatter of horses' hooves on cobblestones and the clamorous clanging of streetcars. As Kenneth Mellanby, one of the world's foremost authorities on the scientific characteristics of pollution sums it up, commenting on *The Limits to Growth:* "The authors continue to insist that pollution is a new and exponentially increasing problem, forgetting that . . . *real* damaging pollution has decreased in recent years in most developed countries. . . ."[12]

This, of course, is not to say that we do not continue to confront serious environmental problems, some of which are currently growing. But it is to say that the natural as well as the man-made component of the human environment has gradually improved over the long term and, in many areas, even in the short term as a result of increasingly successful trade-offs between the two.

Thus, the sudden emergence of the so-called environmental crisis may be seen to be due not so much to an overall deterioration in the human environment—although some aspects of this environment are certainly showing increasing degradation at this time—but, as suggested by Anthony Downs, economist-urbanologist board chairman of Chicago's Real Estate Research Corp., to "a marked increase in our aspirations and standards concerning what our environment ought to be like. In my opinion, rising dissatisfaction with the 'system' in the United States does not result primarily from poorer performance by that system. Rather, it stems mainly from a rapid escalation of our aspirations as to what the system's performance ought to be. Nowhere is this phenomenon more striking than in regard to the quality of the environment. . . ."[13]

How Population Growth Aids Environmental Improvement

The natural environment provides our basic sustenance. But it is improvements in the environment created by man—the man-made environment—that have made the greatest contribution to the improved total human environment we enjoy today.

73

Improvements in the man-made environment, in turn, are a result of population growth. This is because population growth stimulates the economic progress, technological advancement, and energy development necessary to create a better overall human environment. There are those, of course, who attack economic progress, technological advancement, and energy development as the "culprits" on the environmental scene, claiming that pollution problems can only be resolved by putting a stop to future growth. But, in the words of Peter F. Drucker, these fervent environmentalists "seem almost perversely determined to sabotage their cause—and our future."[14]

Consider, says Drucker, the "widespread illusion that a clean environment can be obtained by reducing or even abolishing our dependence on 'technology.' The growing pollution crisis does indeed raise fundamental questions about technology—its direction, uses and future. But the relationship between technology and the environment is hardly as simple as much anti-technological rhetoric would have us believe. . . . The truth is that environmental problems require technological solutions—and dozens of them."[15]

What about the belief that we can solve pollution problems by reducing economic growth? It is true, Ducker notes, that "we may be about to de-emphasize the 'production orientation' of the past few hundred years. Indeed, the 'growth sectors' of the developed economies are increasingly education, leisure activities, or health care rather than goods. But, paradoxical as it may sound, the environmental crisis will force us to return to an emphasis on both growth and industrial output—at least for the next decade."[16]

One of the reasons for this, Drucker points out, is that "practically every environmental task demands huge amounts of electrical energy, way beyond anything now available." Another reason, he says, is that, if "there is no expansion of output equal to the additional cost of cleaning up the environment, the cost burden will—indeed, must—be met by cutting the funds available for education, health care, or the inner city, thus depriving the poor. It would be nice if the resources we need could come out of defense spending. But of the six or seven per cent of our national income that now goes for defense, a large part is cost of past wars, that is, veterans' pensions and disability benefits. . . . Even if we could—or should—cut defense spending, the 'peace dividend' would be only one or two per cent of national income, at best."[17]

Nor can the cost of cleaning up the environment be paid for out of "business profits," Drucker states, for "after taxes, the profits of all American businesses in a good year come to sixty or seventy billion dollars. And mining and manufacturing—the most polluting industries—account for less than half of this. But at the lowest estimate, the cleanup bill, even for just the most urgent jobs, will be three or four times as large as all business profits."[18]

So, says Drucker, unless we

74

raise output and productivity fast enough to offset the added environmen
the voters will look to the [health, education and welfare] sector for money. ~~~u,
in their rejection of school budgets across the nation and in their desperate attempts
to cut welfare costs, voters have already begun to do so. That the shift of resources
is likely to be accomplished in large part through inflation—essentially at the
expense of the lower-income groups—will hardly make the environmental cause
more popular with the poor. The only way to avoid these evils is to expand the
economy, probably at a rate of growth on the order of four per cent a year for the
next decade, a higher rate than we have been able to sustain in this country in the
postwar years. This undoubtedly entails very great environmental risks. But the
alternative is likely to mean no environmental action at all, and a rapid public turn
—by no means confined to the "hard hats"—against all environmental concern
whatever.[19]

Walter W. Heller, former chairman of the Council of Economic Advisers,
places the issue in even sharper perspective by contrasting the viewpoint of the
ecologist with that of the economist. "First, in starkest terms," says Heller,
"the ecologist lays down an environmental imperative that requires an end to
economic growth—or sharp curtailment of it—as the price of biological survival. The economist counters with a socioeconomic imperative that requires
the continuation of growth as the price of social survival. Some ecologists see
the arresting of growth as a necessary, though not sufficient, condition for
saving the ecosystem. The economist sees growth as a necessary, though not
sufficient, condition for social progress and stability. To focus differences even
more sharply, the economist tends to regard the *structure* rather than the *fact*
of growth as the root of environmental evil and indeed views growth itself as
one of the prerequisites to success in restoring the environment."[20]

For, as Heller points out, the "point of a no-growth policy would be to
check and reverse the erosion of the environment. But there is nothing inherent
in a no-growth economy that would change our polluting ways. So one has to
posit active and costly steps to restore and protect the environment. This
would require an absolute reduction in material living standards, as conventionally measured, in exchange for a more livable natural environment. Just
to sketch this picture is to raise serious questions of its social, political and
economic feasibility. Short of a believable threat of human extinction, it is hard
to imagine that the public would accept the tight controls, lowered material
living standards, and large income transfers required to create and manage a
stationary state."[21]

Heller maintains that "the evidence to date supports the view that it is less
the *fact* of growth than the *manner* of growth and the *uses* made of growth
that lie at the bottom of U.S. environmental troubles. And elusive as a consensus on the basic growth environment trade-offs may be, it appears that a
consensus on the urgency of changing the forms and uses of growth is already
materializing. As a consequence, the nation already is being confronted with

hard choices and the need for painful institutional changes. I submit that both are hard choices and the painful changes required to restore the environment will come much easier in an atmosphere of growth than of stagnation."[22]

For example, explains Heller, amelioration of environmental problems will require that the

taxpayer must foot huge bills to overcome past neglect as well as to finance future collective waste treatment and preserve open space and wilderness. Producers and consumers will have to bear the brunt of outright bans on ecologically dangerous materials and to pay rent for the use of the environment's waste assimilation services that they have been enjoying largely free of charge. A modest estimate of the demands on the federal budget for an adequate environmental program would raise the present outlay of $5 billion a year to about $15 billion, an increase of some $50 billion over the next five years. Without growth, and given the limits to the congressional will to tax, how could we hope to raise the required revenues?
    Or take the case of agricultural and industrial pollution. Imagine the resistance of producers to the internalizing of external costs in a society without expansion and the profit opportunities that go with it. How could consumers be induced to accept the necessary price increases in a world of fixed incomes? Again, if the only alternative, if the ultimate cost, were biological self-destruction, the answers would be different. But, in the absence of that fate, or because of its extreme remoteness, growth enters as a vital social lubricant and is the best bet for getting people to give up private 'goods' to overcome public 'bads.'[23]

Or, as former Resources for the Future president Joseph L. Fisher puts it, if

we really want to improve the environment, so this argument goes, we have to stop economic growth or at least slow it down considerably. So we have the beginnings of a zero economic growth movement (ZEG). Of course, the consequences of success of such a program would be pretty rough on poor people and on anyone who wants to have more income, goods, services, education, travel, or whatever. Still, one of the culprits causing environmental damage is thought to be economic growth. It seems to me that attempting to stop economic growth is using a blunderbuss approach and that it is much more effective to look at the particular kinds of economic and industrial growth—the technologies, industries, and products— which are associated with pollution and environmental deterioration. For example, at least three-quarters of the water pollution caused by industry comes from five or six industries: pulp and paper, food processing, certain chemicals, steel making, and oil refining. Thus, if one wants to do something about water pollution, these are the industries to zero in on. One might concentrate on stopping their growth or inducing them in some way not to cause so much pollution, to recycle their wastes, or to pay the costs of having someone else clean up after them."[24]

Perhaps one of the most comprehensive investigations of environmental problems in the United States has been performed by Barry Commoner, director of the Center for the Biology of Natural Systems at Washington University in Saint Louis. Echoing the insights of Heller and Fisher that it is the *structure* rather than the *fact* of economic growth and particular kinds of economic and industrial growth rather than economic growth per se that are responsible for pollution, Commoner states: "An analysis of the growth of a broad spectrum of productive activities in the United States economy since 1946 shows that many major environmental problems are primarily results neither of population growth nor of an increase in affluence, but of changing production technology."[25]

Consequently, as Resources for the Future's Ronald G. Ridker points out, it is more effective to zero in on pollution rather than growth because a "direct attack on pollution clearly dominates over a reduction in population or economic growth as a strategy for obtaining a cleaner environment. A brief investigation of other pollution control strategies—for example, a selective reduction in the consumption of commodities which are heavy users of the environment, restrictions on the use of the automobile and zoning—supports this general conclusion."[26]

But Ridker couples this observation with the statement that he "finds no advantages from additional population growth at this stage in United States history." Comparing a U.S. society with continuing population growth to one headed for zero population growth, he states that "the one with continuing population growth would be forced to live with far greater risks and fewer options with which to solve problems in a manner compatible with our current way of life. While a reduction in population growth would be a blessing in these respects, it would hardly be a panacea, at least not within the next half century. During that time period, more direct attacks on problems of . . . environmental depletion will be needed in any case; and, as our studies show, they can generally accomplish far more."[27]

However, Ridker bases his view of population growth on the assumptions that (1) growth in GNP per capita would be greater in the society going towards zero population growth and (2) technological options available to both societies would be the same. But neither of these assumptions are valid from the standpoint of population growth's stimulative effect on economic progress and technological advancement.

It is the society with continuing population growth that will be better able to mount an effective attack on environmental problems because it is people, after all, who must provide the funds necessary for investment in new methods of environmental control. The more people there are, the greater will be economic growth, per capita income, and technological progress. Furthermore, the more people there are, the less it will cost per person to invest in the required new technology. Therefore, population growth will speed pollution control by providing increasing capital funds, improving technology, and decreasing per capita costs.

For, as sociologist Ben Wattenberg observes, the

explosionists say people and the industry needed to support people cause pollution. Ergo: fewer people—less pollution. On the surface, a reasonable enough statement; certainly, population is one of the variables in the pollution problem. Yet, there is something else to be said. People not only cause pollution, but once you have a substantial number of people, it is only people that can solve pollution. Further, the case can be made that *more people* can more easily and quickly solve pollution problems than can fewer people. For example: let us assume that $60 billion per year are necessary for national defense. The cost of defense will not necessarily be higher for a nation of three hundred million than for a nation of two hundred million. Yet the tax revenues to the government would be immensely higher, freeing vast sums of tax money to be used for the very expensive programs that are necessary for air, water, and pollution control. Spreading constant defense costs over a large population base provides proportionately greater amounts for nondefense spending. The same sort of equation can be used for the huge, one-time capital costs of research that must go into any effective, long-range, anti-pollution program. The costs are roughly the same for 200 or 300 million people—but easier to pay by 300 million.[28]

Nor is there any dilemma posed by increasing numbers of people in relation to an improving human environment. The exact opposite is the case. Growing numbers of people are better able to improve their man-made environment while reducing pollution in the natural environment for the basic reason that people provide 100 percent of the funds used to pay environmental control costs, yet they inevitably account for only one form of pollution, namely, human waste, which is one of the easiest and least costly forms of pollution to control. All other forms of pollution are indirect, that is, they are the result of people's economic and social activities, and these activities can be changed so as to effectively control and reduce pollution of the natural environment over time. Thus, increasing numbers of people are better able to improve their human environment because they have greater financial and technological leverage, enabling them to more effectively increase the comfort and convenience of their man-made environment while reducing pollution in the natural environment.

The Prospects for Environmental Improvement

No one would question that growing numbers of people have been able to make substantial improvements in their human environment by creating a better man-made environment of their own. This has been necessary because the natural environment in which people would otherwise have to live is not

78

particularly habitable, much less comfortable or convenient.

However, man-made environmental improvements oftentimes cause pollution of the natural environment, reducing the benefits of the improvements in the man-made environment. It is therefore important to control pollution in the natural environment so as to maximize the benefits resulting from man-made environmental improvements.

But what we call pollution of the natural environment is not solely the result of people's efforts to improve their man-made environment. The natural environment is also a pretty big "polluter" in its own right. For example, the late Dr. William Thomas Pecora, a widely acclaimed expert in mineralogy, petrology, and geochemistry who served as director of the U. S. Geological Survey and as under secretary of the U. S. Department of the Interior, pointed out that

hundreds of volcanic eruptions during historical times have contributed vast amounts of particulate matter and gases into the atmosphere, in addition to devastation of land areas and damage to large biosystems. Recorded eruptions, for example, in the Mediterranean Region, Caribbean Islands, Central America, East Indies, and other places have accounted for many thousands of human fatalities, as well as damage to soil and plant and animal life. From my own calculations three eruptions alone—Krakatoa in 1883, Mt. Katmai in 1912, and Mt. Hekla in 1947—have contributed more particulate matter and may have contributed more combined natural gases to the atmosphere than all of man's activity.[29]

In addition, according to Pecora, it can be calculated that "about 95 per cent of the estimated nine billion tons of chemical compounds annually entering earth's atmosphere are derived from natural sources. Of this amount less than one per cent of the nearly 1.7 billion tons of hydrocarbons are derived from human activity; about one-third of the more than 200 million tons of sulfur compounds are contributed by man; but one per cent of nearly seven billion tons of nitrogen compounds. These data exclude natural emanations from volcanic regions."

Pecora went on to say that "for the land area of the United States 44 million tons of natural chemical compounds are carried down to the earth each year. In a local drainage basin covering 44,000 square miles of Virginia and North Carolina, it was calculated that the 107 thousand tons of mixed solids (calcium, magnesium, sodium, sulfate, carbonate, nitrate) dropped from the air per year is equal to about one-half the annual load carried by the local streams in the drainage basin. The airborne salts, moreover, are enough to account essentially for all the sulfate and nitrate in those streams."[30]

Rain, of course, is looked upon as a purifying phenomenon, and it is, Pecora noted, since the residence time of particulate matter or chemicals in the lower atmosphere is indeed a function of the frequency of rainfall. However, he added, rain itself "is not pure." In the hydrologic cycle the moisture that eventually falls as rain or snow carries with it chemical compounds derived from the ocean and from atmospheric processes. These include such compounds as ammonia, chlorides, sulfates, bicarbonates, nitrates, and hydrocarbons. All are essential to the natural environment, in which they serve as fertilizer to the plant kingdom that sustains all life.[31]

Nor is the ocean any less impure, stated Pecora, describing it as "the major sink for waste products of earth. . . . It has been estimated . . . that 97.3 percent of all the earth's water is contaminated by natural salt and the ocean contains 317 million cubic miles of salt water. Durum et al. (1960) calculate that 225 million tons of salt are carried to the ocean by U.S. rivers each year. More than 50 per cent of this total is contributed by the Mississippi River alone and most of that is from natural sources."[32]

Pecora added that the "so-called toxic metals like mercury, lead, cadmium, zinc, selenium, nickel, chromium, etc., are widely distributed in nature. They occur as chemical components of minerals, ores, soils, rocks, and waters and are natural trace components of the biosystem. Among them mercury is probably the most mobile. The mercury content of the atmosphere and the ocean apparently is derived primarily from degassing the earth's crust. This process probably injects 10 to 100 times as much mercury into the planetary atmosphere as all man's industry combined. . . . In seawater the mercury content ranges widely but is estimated to average 0.15 to 0.25 parts per billion, exclusive of the amount held in sea bed sediments. In recent decades annual world production of newly mined mercury falls in the range of 5,000 to 10,000 metric tons. All the mercury mined by man throughout history would total less than 0.001 percent of that contained in ocean water."[33]

In addition, Pecora pointed out that "nature has made many billions of scars on the surface of the land through normal geologic processes. Dry gulches, badlands, landfalls, alluvial washes are among many landforms so common to the geologist. . . ."[34] Furthermore, "seas exist where land masses once prevailed, and vice versa. Lakes formed and disappeared. Mountains became plains and gorges became broad valleys. . . ."[35] And, although "fish kills reported offshore are frequently cited as a consequence of man's pollution, discolored waters ('Red Tides') and related fish kills are mentioned in the Bible, in the Iliad, by Tacitus, and in logs of navigators of the 16th Century. . . . Geologists have long been interested in the causes of mass mortality and attempts to explain some of the remarkable examples of catastrophic deaths of marine animals, the records of which are preserved in geologic formations. For example at Lompoc, California, Jordan (1920) reports that a Miocene (10 million years ago) catastrophe resulted in death of more than a billion herring, 6 to 8 inches long, over an area of 4 square miles. Similar massive deaths and burial are found in many horizons in the geological record, far back into Paleozoic time, where the record of the past one-half billion years shows extinction of many millions of species from earth."[36]

In describing these processes of the natural environment, Pecora's point was that only by examining man's effect in the light of natural environmental processes is it possible to reach long-term decisions that will stand the test of time. Any philosophy of pollution control must therefore recognize geologic processes as a base line for reference, for, as Pecora summed up, "much concern has arisen over man's alteration of the earth's atmosphere and the potential effect on climate and health. On a planetary basis the pollution of man has been miniscule in comparison to the natural baseline. On a local basis, however, concentrated emissions into the air by man are unacceptably high for reasons of aesthetics, nuisance, or potential damage to the environment, however temporary."[37]

As an example of the natural environmental base line, he cited the fact that "recent press reports on the discovery of mercury in many parts of the environment have created great apprehension and resulted in decrease in the public market for certain commercial fish. New information discloses comparable mercury contents in preserved fish caught many decades and centuries ago, lending credence to the conclusion that mercury ingestion by fish is not primarily from recent marine contamination. . . . In the light of knowledge of the ocean's mercury balance, I am impelled to state that the occasional practice of eating tuna fish sandwiches or fish steaks need not be modified and that apprehension is not justified."

On the other hand, Pecora pointed out the harm that can be caused on a local basis by concentrated emissions of mercury, citing the case at Minamata Bay, Japan, where "human mercury poisoning developed from eating of fish and shellfish contaminated by effluent from a chemical plant that used mercury as a catalyst."

Inasmuch as trace metals such as mercury in toxic amounts place life and health in jeopardy, Pecora believed that controls in use and disposal of wastes containing them are warranted. However, he cautioned that "conservative attitudes should prevail until present quality standards are carefully evaluated against experience and records of the past."[38] For "geologic science demonstrates that nature is a massive polluter of the environment. In comparison, man's activity is of little consequence on a planetary scale in some issues, but may be of serious consequence in a local context. Conservation ethic requires a better understanding of the natural base line before rigorous actions are taken out of apprehension and ignorance. Science and research are needed more than ever to provide guidance to courses of national action aimed at fulfilling human needs. As the most intelligent species on earth, man can certainly provide for himself and yet prudently protect the total ecosystem from unnecessary and unacceptable degradation."[39]

An important corollary to Pecora's concept of the natural environmental base line is that, if substances which we consider pollutants are already present in the natural environment and we have successfully lived with them in the past, then man-made emissions of these pollutants do not necessarily constitute pollution unless they are in sufficiently greater concentrations to cause harm. For example, carbon monoxide produced by the internal combustion engine is considered a pollutant. Yet, according to Wilfred Beckerman, there "is now, apparently, reason to believe that carbon monoxide produced by natural processes far exceeds that generated by man-made combustion (as has long been known to be the case with sulfur dioxide, a major form of air pollutant which is produced naturally by volcanoes and rotting vegetation)."[40]

Therefore, a car driving through a forest will emit carbon monoxide, but no pollution results because no harm is done. Conversely, at a busy city intersection with thousands of cars passing hourly, carbon monoxide concentrations may become a serious pollution problem because levels of the gas are both high and harmful. Clearly, then, as Beckerman says, the "term 'pollution' should only be used when it is intended to imply that some harm is being done, not merely that some physical change is taking place. As one eminent scientist puts it, 'A pollutant is a substance in the wrong place in a concentration which is harmful.' "[41]

Thus, no single emission of a pollutant may be sufficient to cause harm, but an accumulation of all emissions may prove harmful, as in the case of the busy traffic intersection. But, although this possibility should be recognized and anticipated, it must still be investigated rather than assumed. In the case of carbon monoxide, for example, Beckerman points out that "it is true that about 200 to 300 million tons of carbon monoxide are put into the air every year; mainly from motor-cars and trucks, i.e., not by natural processes. At this rate the concentration of it in the atmosphere should have doubled over the last five years, in the same way that the concentration of carbon dioxide is rising. But, as a matter of fact, the average concentration of carbon monoxide has not changed over 20 years. . . . For the world as a whole it appears that there is some mechanism, not fully understood yet by scientists, which keeps the carbon monoxide in check. Some scientists think that it is eaten up by certain bacteria in the soil; others think that it is depleted in chemical sinks through reaction with atmospheric materials."[42]

Another corollary of the natural environmental base line concept is that, if we have been able to successfully live with substances in the natural environment that normally are considered pollutants, there would appear to be little benefit, much less feasibility, in reducing them to zero in the future. Rather, the question is how much more of the substance can be added to the environment before harmful effects result? Or, to put it another way, what is the optimum trade-off between the benefits of using the substance and its possible harmful effects in the natural environment?

The situation is somewhat different for a man-made substance that is not found in the natural environment. Yet, because a substance is man-made does not mean that it cannot be absorbed by the natural environment without

82

harmful effects, since it necessarily must be made from components that e̱ ̱st in the natural environment.

A further corollary is that, since we are in most cases interested in determining the relative effect of various substances on the natural environment rather than achieving an absolute ban of these substances, economical and effective pollution control must involve exact-as-possible measurements of the benefits derived from using any particular substance in comparison with the environmental costs resulting from its use in order to attain an optimally beneficial trade-off.

A final corollary is that, since changes are constantly taking place in the types and forms of pollutants being emitted, the capabilities of measuring the pollution caused by these pollutants, the technology available for controlling pollution, and the economic, social, and political incentives for achieving a cleaner environment, environmental improvement proceeds along a jagged rather than a straight line. Even as environmental conditions may be generally improving overall, some aspects of the environment may be getting worse as others are getting better.

Basically, there are five ways to achieve environmental improvement. The first is simply to stop doing something that is harmful to the environment. An example would be the case of the buffalo, which in years past was threatened with extinction. There is no way to save the buffalo as part of the natural environment except to cease indiscriminate slaughtering of the animal. This does not mean that buffalo may not be hunted, because oftentimes it is necessary to remove some animals in order to prevent overgrazing and thus protect the rest of the buffalo population. But it does mean hunting for the sake of hunting must be eliminated.

Second, a substitution can be made. In years past, hydrogen cyanide, the most poisonous of gases, was widely used in fumigating against bedbugs and for ridding ancient buildings of deathwatch beetles.[43] However, the risks were too great, so other, less dangerous pest control chemicals are used today.

Third, a pollutant can simply be prevented from escaping into the environment and be disposed of under controlled conditions. For example, various types of filters, precipitators, and scrubbers are used to remove particulate matter from smokestack emissions.

Fourth, the pollutant can be recycled. Many manufacturing plants, for example, use solvents that when emitted to the air following use can create pollution problems. But a solvent recovery system makes possible reuse in manufacturing processes of 95 percent of the solvents, not only reducing the possibility of pollution but providing economic justification for the solvent recovery system. Likewise, sludge resulting from water purification at municipal sanitation plants is reused as farm fertilizer.

Finally, a change in process can be used to eliminate pollutants. For example, the usual method of removing skins from potatoes in the food processing industry is to soften them in lye and then use large volumes of water to literally wash the peels from the potatoes. But, when the waste water is discharged, the peels cause water pollution. An experimental plant is now using a new process in which peels are heated and mechanically removed, eliminating the water pollution that previously resulted when peels were washed away. An added benefit is that peel wastes that previously added to pollution can now be used for mixed cattle feeds.[44]

Below is a summary of current trends resulting from the increasing use of environmental improvement techniques such as the above to prevent and/or control air, water, and noise pollution; solid, agricultural, and chemical wastes; nuclear radiation; and degradation of land, wildlife, and wilderness.

Air Quality. During 1974, the U. S. Environmental Protection Agency (EPA) completed a major evaluation of data on nationwide trends in air quality and emissions over the period 1940–72. The EPA reported that "some improvements in the nation's urban air quality have been achieved in recent years. Occurrences of poor air quality are still commonly observed, however, and worsening trends have been noted in some areas."[45]

Particulate matter. According to the Council on Environmental Quality, during the 1960s, average ambient levels of total suspended particulates (TSP) declined on the order of 25 percent. This was the case both for average annual and maximum daily concentrations. The composite TSP average for urban stations in the National Air Surveillance Network (NASN) decreased from approximately 110 micrograms per cubic meter in 1960 to 82 in 1972. These results occurred despite a reported increase of 15 percent over the past three decades in "controllable," that is, man-made, nationwide TSP emissions. However, some of this reported emission increase may be due to refinements in measuring techniques. And estimated fluctuations in "uncontrollable," or natural, emissions such as those resulting from forest and agricultural fires have been of greater magnitude than reported controllable increases. Techniques to control particulate emissions have included shifts in fuel use from coal to oil or gas, wider use of technologies such as filtering, scrubbing, and electrostatic precipitation to reduce stack emissions, restrictions on open burning of solid waste, and siting of power plants and other industrial sources of particulate in outlying areas away from center-city locations.[46]

Sulfur oxides. Ambient sulfur dioxide levels in urban air have reportedly declined more than 50 percent since the mid-1960s, according to composite 1964–72 data on average annual and maximum daily concentrations at thirty-two urban NASN sites. This decline occurred in spite of increased nationwide emissions from 1940 to 1970, from about 22 to 33 million tons of sulfur dioxide per year. Much of this increase was due to steam electric-power plants. But, since 1970, nationwide increases have been reduced somewhat by regulated changes in the types and sulfur content of fuels used by power plants, factories, and other stationary sources. Installation of stack controls has also contributed to reducing sulfur dioxide emissions. The apparent discrepancy between rising emissions and decreasing ambient measurements probably reflects in part the siting of new power plants and other large industrial facilities in outlying areas away from center-city NASN monitoring sites, as well as the increased use of natural gas and fuel oil rather than coal by small urban stationary sources.[47]

Major transportation pollutants. The principal air pollutants produced by the automobile and other forms of transportation are carbon monoxide (CO), hydrocarbons (HC), and oxides of nitrogen (NO_x). A recent EPA study of five cities reported that ambient carbon monoxide levels generally declined between 1962 and 1971, despite an estimate that total controllable emissions of CO more than doubled between 1940 and 1970. However, these results must be evaluated in light of the facts that measurements of ambient urban CO levels were limited to one site per city; the levels fluctuate considerably with the time of day, local traffic conditions and season; and man's emissions of CO appear to be an order of magnitude less than the CO produced by the earth's natural sources, including photosynthesis, decomposition of organic matter, atmospheric oxidization of methane, forest fires, and other processes.

Available ambient air quality data regarding HC, NO_x, and total oxidants are less satisfactory for characterizing nationwide trends than the data on other major pollutants. But it is estimated that total nationwide controllable HC emissions roughly doubled between 1940 and 1970. These HC emissions were produced not only by motor vehicles, but also by refineries, petroleum storage and processing facilities, solvent vapors, and other sources. And it is estimated that, over the past three decades, total nationwide NO_x emissions have quadrupled, with emissions from stationary sources contributing progressively increasing proportions.[48]

However, in recent years, emission controls on new cars have resulted in progressive reductions in emissions. For example, 1975 cars cut CO by 83 percent, HC by 90 percent, and NO_x by 48 percent in comparison to cars produced in 1967, the last year in which auto emissions were uncontrolled. As a result, the total volume of pollutants generated by all cars—including those remaining from before 1967—is nearly 50 percent below precontrol levels. Furthermore, as old cars are scrapped for new ones, emissions will continue to be reduced. Thus, by 1980, the total volume of pollutants generated by all cars will be about 45 percent below 1975 levels and 70 percent below 1967 levels. To put it another way, total CO, HC and NO_x emissions for all cars on the road will be reduced to levels existing in 1924, 1936, and 1965, respectively.[49]

The Council on Environmental Quality points out that there are important gaps in our knowledge about air quality, which "involve both the methods by which we measure it and also the information base on which we rely to set protective standards." The council also notes that the "need for improvements

85

is not limited to the major pollutants toward which most monitoring is presently addressed. . . . we need to improve our abilities to characterize ambient sulfates and other chemicals associated with fine particulate matter, including toxic substances such as lead, zinc, mercury, cadmium, and organic carcinogens. Also needed are improvements in the knowledge base by which protective standards are developed. Although the present national ambient air quality standards are based on the results of a considerable amount of research, these standards have necessarily relied upon a number of assumptions and educated conjectures."

Summing up, the council states that

> the limitations of our knowledge about the effects of air pollution, as well as other difficulties in obtaining accurate, representative measurements of ambient air quality and emissions, affect not only the confidence with which protective ambient air quality standards are designated, but also our abilities to interpret the significance of trends observed. Although we have evidence that some air quality improvements have occurred in recent years, there also is an understandable and appropriate tendency to stress new problems and areas of uncertainty as they are recognized and investigated. At the same time, the fact should not thereby be obscured that the considerable efforts and resources that have been devoted to air pollution control in recent years have achieved some improvements in our nation's air quality, especially in comparison with what might have occurred in the absence of such controls.[50]

Water Quality. The *1974 National Water Quality Inventory Report,* the first attempt of its kind at a systematic nationwide inventory, provided mixed results regarding trends in water quality. For oxygen demand and coliform bacteria, progress was evident. Dissolved oxygen levels reportedly improved in 61 percent of water-quality reaches (water locations) studied, and oxygen-demand levels were reduced in 74 percent, while bacterial counts were lower in up to 75 percent. On the other hand, disturbing trends continued with regard to nutrients. Up to 84 percent of reaches exceeded phosphorus and phosphate reference levels associated with potential eutrophication, and up to 54 percent of the reaches showed increased phosphorus levels. Nitrate levels also increased in 74 percent of the reaches examined.

Other pollutants with high but generally improving levels were phenols (industrial compounds that can affect fish palatability and cause taste and odor problems in drinking water) and suspended solids (which interfere with some aquatic life processes). Limited data on metals and pesticides, however, gave cause for concern.

According to the Council on Environmental Quality, these indications of trends should be interpreted with caution, but the findings with regard to increased nutrients were clear enough to indicate that this difficult problem required increased attention.[51]

More recent data appear to indicate some promising results from the reduction of certain types of nutrients, such as point-source phosphate loadings. For example, total and soluble phosphorus levels measured in the Detroit River near its entrance to Lake Erie have decreased dramatically since the late 1960s, reflecting reduced loadings from municipal treatment plants. As a result of this and other improvements, muskies, walleye, pike, salmon, bass, and rainbow trout are being caught in a waterway that was too dirty for gamefish only a few years ago. Furthermore, where the Detroit River empties into Lake Erie, another turning point seems to be in the making, though it is too soon to tell for sure. In Lake Erie, which has oftentimes been declared "dead," scientists say they have noticed that the size of the lake bottom suffocating each summer from oxygen starvation is getting slightly smaller, though it still amounts to almost 4000 square miles, or 87 percent of the lake's central basin.[52]

The developments in the Detroit River are indicative of a general improvement that is currently taking place in all of the Great Lakes. For the "astonishing recovery of this once-dying link between Lakes Huron and Erie has more than local significance. It has signalled a giant turnaround in the Great Lakes, sending ripples of hope throughout the country. For if these lakes, comprising the largest area of fresh water in the world, can be cleaned up, it can happen anywhere."[53] Or, as columnist Jerald terHorst says, it "will take additional huge sums and continued determination to bring the Great Lakes back after generations of contamination and misuse. But the encouraging thing is that the situation isn't getting worse—it's getting better."[54]

As a result of growth, the amount of oxygen-demanding organic matter pollutants discharged by municipal sewage treatment plants has remained constant since 1957, even though sewage receiving some form of primary treatment involving removal of suspended solids has more than doubled. However, these discharges will be reduced in the future because, in 1977, treatment plants will be required to provide secondary treatment that removes dissolved solids remaining in the water. And, in 1983, the plants will be required to provide the "best practicable waste treatment technology," which, in many cases, will mean tertiary treatment for the removal of pollution-causing nutrients such as phosphates and nitrates.[55] Looking further into the future, the technological capability exists today for sewage to be completely reused by converting it into pure water, chemicals, and energy at less cost than current treatment processes.[56] Industrial sources of pollution will also be required to meet increasingly stringent standards between now and the early 1980s. At the same time, water pollution resulting from urban storm-water runoff will receive increasing priority.[57]

Noise Control. According to the Environmental Protection Agency, 16 million people are presently exposed to aircraft noise levels with effects ranging from moderate to very severe. Only 10 percent of the existing fleet of 2000 commercial aircraft now meet Federal Aviation Administration noise regulations applicable to new aircraft, but retrofit procedures with currently available technology could permit existing aircraft to meet this level. Furthermore, technology is available to permit even lower noise emissions from new aircraft.

Proposed noise reduction standards for trucks can be met by functioning mufflers, tires with low noise levels, and some minor adjustments. Regulations to reduce noise from trains would require the use of mufflers, elimination of excessive flat spots on wheels, and proper locomotive maintenance. Other standards are being applied in highway planning and design and product design.[58]

Solid Waste Control. Solid wastes are a major potential source of resource recovery. In the past, it has been absence of markets rather than technology that has been the barrier to increased resource recovery from solid wastes. However, the recent rise in the price of energy has radically changed the situation and created markets where none existed before. The result is that market forces are now activated that promise simultaneously to reduce the problem of disposing of solid wastes, while providing needed resources in the form of energy as well as reusable raw materials.

At least eighteen cities are now actively considering energy recovery systems. Three cities have facilities under construction, and several others are in the advanced planning stage. In addition, at least thirty more cities are evaluating energy recovery systems.

Municipal and industrial solid wastes are also a potential source of reusable materials. Less energy is generally required to reprocess waste materials than to develop virgin materials, when all aspects of acquisition, processing, and transportation are considered. Hence, the rise in energy prices has greatly strengthened the secondary-material market.[59]

As an example of what can be done, Connecticut is in the process of setting up processing plants throughout the state. When the plants are completed, the state hopes to recover 60 percent of its refuse either as material or energy, while reducing air pollution from waste disposal by 70 percent and land consumption required by garbage dumps by 80 percent.[60] Nor is there anything revolutionary in this "cash from trash" approach to the solid waste problem. For example, for fifty years the Dutch in Amsterdam have operated a financially self-supporting "garbage-power" system in which trash is burned to supply 5 percent of the region's electricity, an amount sufficient for an American city the size of Santa Barbara, California.[61]

Agricultural Waste Control. Agricultural wastes are a major contributor to water pollution in the form of animal by-products, fertilizers, and pesticides, which rainstorms wash off along with soil into rivers, lakes, and the ocean.

Livestock annually produce some 2 billion tons of waste, which is equivalent to that produced by a human population of 1.9 billion. As much as 50 percent of this waste may be produced under concentrated feed-lot conditions. Scientists are working today to develop feed-lot management practices that will prevent run-off of these wastes. Another approach is the reuse of animal wastes to fertilize cropland or in the production of an energy resource such as methane gas. Effective control or reuse of feed-lot run-off could greatly reduce the pollution hazard to streams, rivers, and other bodies of water.[62]

Statistics show that in fiscal year 1967 about 14 million tons of plant nutrients were applied to soils in the United States—6 million tons of nitrogen, 4.3 million tons of phosphate, and 3.6 million tons of potash. These figures have led some to the conclusion that plant nutrients applied to the land are the source of the nutrients that cause algae and other water plants to grow and pollute streams and lakes. According to the Department of Agriculture, this is true in some areas. However, where good soil and fertilizer management practices are used, fertilizers from cropland contribute only minor amounts of plant nutrients to water pollution.[63]

Of the more than one billion pounds of pesticides—insecticides, herbicides and fungicides—manufactured annually in the United States, in excess of three-quarters are applied domestically for agricultural and other uses. In 1971, farmers used approximately 494 million pounds of pesticides, 40 percent above 1966 levels.[64] To prevent pollution, some pesticides such as DDT have been banned. Work is proceeding on the development of improved pesticides that degrade faster or do not persist at all in the environment and on better control of pesticide run-off and drift into the air. In addition, research is now being conducted into a number of biological methods of pest control that will not pollute the environment.[65]

Chemical Waste Control. Environmentally safe use and disposal of hazardous residues—toxic chemical, biological, flammable, and explosive wastes—is another aspect of the waste problem. The Environmental Protection Agency estimates that roughly 10 million tons per year of chemical and biological hazardous wastes were generated in 1970, with the total growing at a rate of 5 to 10 percent annually. Much of these wastes, which include substances such as polychlorinated byphenyls (PCBs), asbestos fibers, vinyl chloride gas, and various toxic water pollutants, is currently being dumped, buried, or injected on or into the land. The technology for controlling hazardous waste disposal exists for most of these substances. But adequate treatment and disposal can be ten to forty times more expensive than environmentally unacceptable methods.[66]

Nuclear Radiation Control. The development of nuclear power requires the environmental control of radiation resulting from nuclear power station operation and wastes. According to the National Academy of Sciences (NAS), the average annual whole-body exposure of the U.S. population from all sources of radiation amounts to 182 millirems, of which 102 millirems comes from natural background sources, 73 millirems from medical exposures, 4 millirems from global fallout, and only a small fraction of one millirem from nuclear power plants. The NAS compared the expected exposure to radiation from man-made sources other than medical with the current EPA exposure guide of 170 millirems per year and concluded that this guide is "unnecessarily high" because man-made sources can be expected to result in far lower average radiation exposures than the guide allows.

According to a report prepared by EPA, the overall environmental impact caused by the release of long-lived radioactive materials during normal operation of the nuclear power industry can be relatively small, provided that proper controls are maintained. The Nuclear Regulatory Commission (NRC) recently released the results of a reactor safety study done for the agency by a group of some fifty specialists under the direction of Professor Norman Rasmussen of the Massachusetts Institute of Technology. Findings of the study indicated that the nonnuclear accidents to which society is already exposed are about 10,000 times more likely to produce large numbers of injuries to people than accidents involving nuclear power plants. The study concluded that "the risks to the public associated with nuclear power are very small and the likelihood of reactor accidents is much smaller than many types of non-nuclear accidents with similar consequences."

As nuclear fission becomes a major source of energy in the future, large quantities of radioactive waste will be generated. Much of this waste will have to be effectively isolated from the environment for very long periods of time —as long as a half-million years in the case of plutonium. The NRC has proposed that high-level radioactive wastes be deposited for an interim period in a "Retrievable Surface Storage Facility" pending the development of a suitable method of permanent storage. Radioactive waste designed as "other-than-high-level" would be buried in authorized burial grounds.

A study of possible solutions to the permanent storage of long-lived radioactive wastes was conducted for the NRC by the Battelle Pacific Northwest Laboratory. This comprehensive study analyzes several methods of disposing of long-lived nuclear wastes, including storage in various geologic formations on land, in the seabed, and in ice sheets; disposal in outer space; and elimination by transmutation (nuclear transformation into a less harmful substance). Although the study did not endorse any method, it did examine the relative advantages and disadvantages of each scheme with respect to technical feasibility, development time, costs, and environmental impact. Several of the proposed methods appear to be practical if the associated environmental impacts can be minimized.[67]

Another environmental concern with nuclear power is the thermal effects of waste heat on surrounding waters. But protection of water quality and reduction of environmental effects are assured if proper controls are developed. In fact, there is some evidence that thermal effects, rather than having adverse effects on water biology, will prove beneficial to the production of fish or food crops.[68] And, looking to the future, development of a nuclear breeder reactor will reduce thermal effects, while the advent of controlled fusion power will result in the total elimination of the nuclear waste problem.

Prevention of Land Degradation. Land is threatened by two major forms of degradation: erosion resulting from natural as well as man-made causes and land disruption caused by strip mining. Erosion occurs when rain runs off the ground to rivers, lakes, and the ocean, carrying with it sediment composed of clay, silt, sand, rock, crop residues, and other material that can be transported by flowing water. Erosion from cropland and the banks of streams accounts for a large part of sediment volume. Other contributing factors are construction of forest roads, land made bare by forest fires, over-grazed range land, unprotected road banks, highways, and construction sites.

Proper erosion control is the best way to solve most sediment problems. In nonagricultural areas, sediment can be reduced by covering construction slopes with inexpensive mulch, planting grass, or leaving a natural cover on banks of waterways and protecting trees during construction. On agricultural land, various practices can be followed to reduce erosion by as much as 80 percent or more. And when cropland is converted to pasture or woodland, soil erosion can be reduced by 90 percent or more.[69]

Involving digging up mineral resources such as coal from above ground rather than tunneling down to dig them out from below, strip mining creates great disruptions on the surface of the land. However, a 1974 study by the U.S. Bureau of Mines shows that of the 1.47 million acres used for surface coal mining from 1930 to 1971, 66 percent, or one million acres, had already been reclaimed. And, in 1971, the coal industry actually reclaimed 30 percent more land than it mined. Also in 1971, the entire surface-mining industry reclaimed 80 percent of the land it used. Overall, only a small percentage—0.16 percent, or less than two-tenths of one percent, of the total area of the U.S.—has ever been disturbed by all kinds of strip mining. Of that, almost half has been reclaimed, and the rest is in the process of being reclaimed.[70]

Wildlife Protection. During the past three centuries, approximately 300 species are estimated to have become extinct, worldwide. At least fifty of these known species were higher vertebrate animals native to the United States and its territories. Nearly all of these extinctions are directly or indirectly attributable to human influences, according to the Council on Environmental Quality, which states that, although extinction of species has been a fundamental part of the natural environment as long as life has existed on earth, human activities have greatly accelerated the rate of species extinction.

However, since the development of modern wildlife management in the 1930s, no American wildlife species has been exterminated by sport hunting. On the contrary, wildlife management has restored many depleted or threat-

91

ened species, including the pronghorn sheep, key deer, alligator, sea otter, fur seal, beaver, wild turkey, and trumpeter swan. Furthermore, in recent years, wildlife management techniques have been extended to all animal life and even wild plants.

According to the U.S. Fish and Wildlife Service, approximately one-tenth of nearly 200 species of higher animals—mammals, birds, reptiles, amphibians and fish—one-tenth of 100 species of clams, one-tenth of 200 species of snails, and one-tenth of plant species in the United States are currently endangered. Measures needed to protect these endangered species vary considerably in difficulty and cost. Of the invertebrate shellfish species that presently appear to be threatened, for example, about one-third could be restored by relatively inexpensive means, such as modifying boundaries of designated natural areas. Another one-third are threatened by water pollution, half of which, for instance, could possibly be protected by improved water pollution control efforts in five southern rivers. The remaining one-third would be considerably more difficult to protect because they are threatened by a number of complex factors.[71]

Wilderness Protection. A number of steps have been taken at the federal level in recent years to protect and enlarge all types of park and wilderness areas. Under the "Legacy of Parks" program, 64,000 acres of under-utilized federal properties have been transferred to state and local governments for recreational use, including the 23,000-acre Gateway National Recreation Area near New York City and the 24,000-acre Golden Gate National Recreation Area near San Francisco. The Land and Water Conservation Fund has been used to acquire over 1.3 million acres of land in national parks, recreation areas, historic sites, wildlife refuges, wild and scenic rivers, and national scenic and recreation trails.

In Alaska, proposed legislation would add approximately 63.9 million acres of public lands to the national park and national wildlife refuge system, more than doubling the area presently protected. In addition, 18.8 million acres would be added to the national forest system and 800,000 acres to the national wild and scenic river system.

Under the Wilderness Act of 1964, fifty-four areas in the West were designated as wilderness. Since then, forty more wilderness areas have been designated, eighty are before Congress awaiting designation, and sixty-one are under review for possible designation. A proposed amendment to the Wilderness Act would designate sixteen national forest areas in the East for immediate inclusion in the wilderness system and thirty-seven others to be studied for wilderness suitability.

In 1973, the Forest Service selected 274 roadless areas in national forests, containing a total of 12.3 million acres, for study as potential wilderness areas, and the service is continuing to give consideration for wilderness potential to another 1175 roadless areas. The National Wild and Scenic River System, established in 1968, now includes all or parts of eight rivers, with twenty-seven other rivers designated as potential additions. Another twenty river areas have been proposed for addition by the Bureau of Outdoor Recreation. In addition, two scenic trails have been designated, and another fourteen are being considered as possible additions to the wilderness system.[72]

This brief overview shows that in some cases environmental conditions are getting better, while in other cases they are getting worse. But, in all cases, improved methods and/or better technology is either available or being developed to help create a healthier, cleaner, and more pleasing environment in the future. Thus, as Maddox says, for "all the excitement there has been and which persists about pollution, the fact remains that the essence of the problems with which public administration is concerned is how much money taxpayers are willing to spend for how much improvement in the environment."[73]

According to an estimate made in 1974 by the Council on Environmental Quality, the nation is expected to spend $194.8 billion from 1973 through 1982 for environmental improvement as a result of federal environmental legislation. This estimate was almost one-third higher than the estimate made in 1973, due to a shift in the cost-period analyzed, inflation, and a rise in real costs that accounted for 25 percent of the total increase. Even so, the ratio of each year's estimated pollution abatement cost to projected GNP for that year is only slightly over one percent.

This ratio of pollution control costs to total GNP may increase in the future due to greater environmental needs or a requirement for more expensive control methods. Or it may decrease as a result of technological advancements and more realistic adjustment of environmental standards based on accumulating experience and knowledge. But, in any event, even though it can be expected to remain a small part of the GNP, the cost of pollution control will be a substantial sum, particularly in the case of high-polluting municipalities and industries that will be hard-pressed to find the investment funds required.

These pollution control costs can be more easily paid and pollution problems more quickly and effectively solved with economic progress and technological advancement, for, as Maddox comments, the "truth is that technology and prosperity are not the inherent nuisances of which the environmentalists continually complain but, rather, the means by which a better environment could be created."[74] And these "means" will be more readily available under conditions of not population stagnation but population growth.

The Arguments against Population Growth

Perhaps the most vociferous exponent of the view that population growth is a major, if not *the* major, cause of pollution is Paul Ehrlich, the Stanford

University biologist, author of *The Population Bomb,* and honorary president of Zero Population Growth.

In an article written with John P. Holdren of the University of California, Ehrlich maintains that "each human individual, in the course of obtaining the requisites of existence, has a net negative impact on his environment." The total negative impact of a human society on the environment, or ecosystem, says Ehrlich, is thus equal to population size multiplied times impact per capita.

Ehrlich admits that "improvements in technology can sometimes hold the per capita impact constant or even decrease it, despite increases in per capita consumption." But, in his opinion, this does not justify the belief of "some people" who

have argued that *all* of our environmental impact can be traced to misuse of existing technologies and failure to develop environmentally benign ones. They imply that neither population size nor per capita consumption is important if only the proper technologies are used. The fallacy in this argument is that no technology can completely eliminate the impact of a given amount of consumption. . . . Pollution control and all other means of minimizing per capita environmental impact are also imperfect: Zero release of any contaminant is an unattainable ideal, and attempts to approach it consume great quantities of energy. . . . We may conclude that improving technology to reduce the impact of consumption is worthwhile, but not the entire answer. Under any set of technological conditions, there will be some impact associated with each unit of consumption, and therefore some level of population size and per capita consumption at which the total impact becomes unsustainable. . . . Surely, then, we can anticipate that supplying food, fiber, and metals for a population even larger than today's will have a profound (and destabilizing) effect on the global ecosystem under *any* set of technological assumptions.[75]

The first thing to note about Ehrlich's comments is that they are those of an environmental purist. From this point of view, the pristine natural environment is good and can do no wrong, while human beings are bad and have a net negative impact on the environment.

Elsewhere, for example, Ehrlich tells us that "man's record as a simplifier of ecosystems and plunderer of resources" (note that man is not a user, consumer, or manager, but a "plunderer" of resources) can be traced back to "his probable role in the extinction of many Pleistocene mammals."[76] First of all, it is of course debatable whether these Pleistocene mammals became extinct as a result of man's activities or because "they were unfitted to the changed conditions that came with the passage of geological time."[77] Secondly, it should prove of interest to know that these mammals over whose extinction we are to break out in a rash of guilt included among other beasts the "giant ancestors of the elephants, of the sloths, and of the armadillos."[78] Furthermore, some of these mammals were "fully as weird in form as the reptiles of the

Mesozoic,"[79] which included, among other beasts, carnivorous dinosaurs.[80] Finally, while Ehrlich agonizes over the brutality of man to these mammals of the prehistoric past, he does not tell us that the same natural environment that brought us the wonderful giant armadillo during the Pleistocene Epoch also covered North America from Hudson Bay to the present courses of the Ohio and Missouri rivers with moving ice sheets.[81]

"The role of man on earth is radically different from that of plants and animals," states Hans F. Sennholz, head of the department of economics at Grove City College. "Although man is part of nature, his intelligence permits him to wisely use environmental resources for his best interests. He is like a steward in the use of natural resources who responsibly manages his environment in order to survive. His right to life embodies his right to manage the resources of nature."[82]

One might expect that Ehrlich would have some empathy for Pleistocene man as he fought off giant armadillos on the one hand, while trying to eke out a running existence among moving glaciers on the other hand. But not so. Instead, Ehrlich and other environmental purists see man and environment as antagonists, with man always coming out as the villain. From their point of view, Sennholz says, the issue is "man or environment, that is the choice. As one is not compatible with the other, we are told, the radical ecologists choose the environment. They prefer grass and tree, ant and beast of the forest over man. They would preserve nature undisturbed and in a natural condition, as in a jungle."[83]

But, as Sennholz points out, merely "to preserve nature as man found it when he first set foot on this earth may appear to be easier, indeed, than the wise use of environment for the best interests of man. And yet, mere preservation denies not only the nature of man but also the very laws of nature."[84]

Based on his negative assumption that man is a "simplifier of ecosystems" and "plunderer of resources," Ehrlich denies that man can ultimately use the environment wisely, because "zero release of any contaminant is an unattainable ideal" and therefore there will be "some level of population size and per capita consumption at which the total impact becomes unsustainable." However, in the short run, there is no necessity to reduce pollution to zero. As Jerome Rothenberg of MIT puts it, sometimes

arguments are made in terms of an absolute right to a uniformly high standard of environmental purity. This is very much like requiring that everybody who consumes the services of automobiles must consume a quality equivalent to that of a Cadillac or not at all, or like saying that everybody has the right to a Cadillac-quality automobile. Such a statement would violate the criterion that benefits should be no less than costs, because such a policy would be too expensive to carry out. It would also be morally incongruous, because environmental values are not absolute or infinite but, like all other values, have to be appraised in the context of all the other

95

things human beings find desirable. They are among the commodities which have to be purchased along with automobiles, recreation, clothing, food, television sets and all the others. The goal of public policy, then, is not to *minimize* pollution, but to *optimize* pollution. What we are looking for is not the smallest amount of pollution technically achievable, but the most appropriate amount, the amount that gives us the best compromise between the use of our resources to produce environmental quality.[85]

Furthermore, in the long run, it is theoretically not impossible to devise ways of reducing pollution to, if not zero, at least next to nothing. For example, Barry Commoner envisages such a "zero pollution" system in the area of sewage disposal:

Consider the following simple transformation of the present, ecologically faulty, relationship among soil, agricultural crops, the human population and sewage. Suppose that sewage, instead of being introduced into surface water as it is now, whether directly or following treatment, is instead transported from urban collection systems by pipeline to agricultural areas, where—after appropriate sterilization procedures—it is incorporated into the soil. Such a pipeline would literally reincorporate the urban population into the soil's ecological cycle, restoring the integrity of that cycle, and incidentally removing the need for inorganic nitrogen fertilizer —which also stresses the aquatic cycle. Hence, the urban population is then no longer external to the soil cycle and is therefore incapable either of generating a negative biological stress upon it or of exerting a positive ecological stress on the aquatic ecosystem.[86]

But, even assuming that Ehrlich is theoretically correct that pollution per capita cannot be reduced to zero, this question still remains: At what specific level of population size and per capita consumption will total environmental impact become "unsustainable"? This Ehrlich does not tell us.

Kenneth Boulding, economics professor at the University of Michigan, informs us that the open "cowboy economy" of the past with its "illimitable plains" may have to be replaced in the future with a closed "spaceman" economy in which "the earth has become a single spaceship, without unlimited reservoirs of anything, either for extraction or for pollution. . . ."[87] But he doesn't specify the timetable under which this development is to take place.

Perhaps the most ambitious attempt to establish an approximate date at which time the earth will be unable to sustain further pollution was made by *The Limits to Growth* group.[88] Assuming that the capacity of the earth and its atmosphere to "absorb" pollution is finite, this study uses a computer model to predict that mankind is destined for an environmental catastrophe during the next 100 years unless growth is stopped. But consultants to the World Bank found that if the ratio of pollution generation to capital stock assumed in the *Limits* computer model were to be reduced to three-eights of its value —an adjustment well within the error range of the study's data—the predic-

96

tion of catastrophe would be erased. Furthermore, the *Limits* computer model assumes that there is a limit to the amount of pollution the world can absorb in a year and that this limit is four times the pollution now produced annually. There is absolutely no scientific evidence, according to the World Bank, to support such a conclusion. Moreover, states the bank, the authors do not fully allow for the fact that higher levels of industrial development also increase the options available to take care of the pollution problem by devoting additional resources to it.[89]

One of the most curious parts of the *Limits* computer model, the World Bank goes on to note, is

its treatment of the role of technology. In an age of the most dramatic technological progress, the authors contend that there cannot be a continuation of such rapid progress in the future. And this is merely an assumption, not a proven thesis. The model *assumes* that certain things in this world will grow at exponential rates— population, capital stock, pollution. It *assumes* that certain other things will not grow at an exponential rate—specifically technology . . . to fight pollution. Thus, the *Limits* model builders challenge something basic in human beings—their pride that they have continuously extended the physical limits of this planet through constant innovations and technological progress. Now, how realistic is this? . . . As societies become conscious of pollution problems, will they not find the technology to fight it, as is already becoming apparent? Any model that assumes that certain things will grow at exponential rates and others will not, is inherently unstable. We should not be surprised if it leads to disaster.[90]

The World Bank also points out that "the methodology used in the model further helps us along the road to disaster. There are no costs and prices in the model and no conscious choices made by society—in fact, no real corrective mechanism. There are only physical engineering relationships—not much of economic and social engineering. The world keeps on proceeding in its merry ways—frittering away its resources, populating itself endlessly, accumulating pollution—till one fine morning it hits disaster."[91]

But, concludes the bank, it

is hard to believe that the pollution crisis can sneak up on humanity so insidiously as the model implies. Even a modest level of pollution would mean that even though the world average of persistent pollutants were still quite low and not yet obnoxious to human health, some particular localities would be suffering grievously from pollution. Can we really believe that most of the population of Detroit could succumb to persistent pollutants without the rest of humanity making any adjustments in its producer-consumer behavior? Humanity faces these problems one by one, every year in every era, and keeps making its quiet adjustments. It does not keep accumulating them indefinitely till they make catastrophe inevitable. One does not have to believe in the invisible hand to subscribe to such a view of society. One has merely to believe in human sanity and its instinct for self-preservation.[92]

Nor have other attempts to prove imminent catastrophe from pollution been found to be any less fruitless if not ill-informed. Prominent figures in the scientific world, for example, have on occasion proclaimed that air pollution was leading to a reduction in the world's oxygen supply. Yet scientists of the Environmental Science Service Administration and the National Science Foundation studied the composition of air at seventy-eight sites around the world and found that the amount of oxygen in the air in 1970 was precisely the same as in 1910: 20.946 percent by volume. The conclusion was that not only is oxygen just as plentiful as it ever was, but that "man's burning of coal, oil and gas would not have any appreciable effect on world oxygen supply even if all the known reserves of these fuels were to be consumed."[93]

Another potential "threat" was the possibility that water vapor from supersonic aircraft would reduce the amount of ozone in the atmosphere and increase the amount of ultraviolet light filtering through to the surface of the earth, thus causing skin cancer. But water vapor, John Maddox notes, turned out to be much less destructive than assumed, and the link between ultraviolet light and cancer much less strong than supposed. "As it turns out," he comments, "much more water vapor is carried into the stratosphere by familiar meteorological processes than could ever be left there by supersonic aircraft. Another objection to this tortuous theory was that . . . the dire effects predicted could be avoided if only each person in the United States would wear a hat or carry a parasol one day during his or her lifetime."[94]

A currently proposed calamity is that the climate of the earth may be irreversibly changed by man's activities. On the one hand, dust from industrial activity may accumulate in the stratosphere and prevent significant amounts of solar energy from reaching the surface of the earth, resulting in a reduction in the earth's temperature. On the other hand, carbon dioxide from burning fuel may accumulate in the atmosphere so as to prevent the escape of heat, resulting in a "greenhouse" effect that will raise the temperature of the earth.

Up until the 1930s, the temperature of the earth was increasing. Since then, measurements show that the amount of sunlight reaching the surface of the earth has decreased by about 4 percent. But, as Maddox observes, it is "hard to know what importance to attach to the measurements. . . . Has artificial contamination been more serious than volcanic dust? Have there in any case been fluctuations in the output of energy from the sun? And how is it possible to relate the reduced amount of solar energy, itself comparatively small as a proportion, to the likely course of climate change? Not nearly enough is known about the physical processes involved for meteorologists to be sure of the outcome. This is why there is a need for more vigorously directed programs of research on atmosphere dust. In the meantime, however, the fact that a single natural volcano can produce as much dust in the stratosphere as several years of industrial activity is a sign that the fear of calamity is misplaced."[95]

Ultimately, of course, as Maddox states, the

scale on which industry can be practiced on the surface of the earth will be limited by the amount of heat which is produced. . . . The total amount of waste heat is expected to multiply at least five times between 1970 and 2000, and a century after that, if the pace of growth of energy consumption is somewhat maintained, will amount to 10 per cent or so of the energy received from the sun. Long before then, it is clear, some densely industrialized areas will have created serious problems for themselves. Already large cities such as New York and London generate enough waste heat to influence the local climate—the average temperature on Manhattan is two degrees centigrade higher than in surrounding countryside. But there is no reason why these tendencies should imply calamity, regional or global, or even an intolerable restriction of industrial development. They will, however, create steady pressure to make more economical use of the energy resources of the earth.

What these arguments imply is that the ways in which the atmosphere of the earth might be affected in the foreseeable future by human activities of various kinds are not at present likely sources of disaster. Indeed, the prospect is still remote that industrial activities of any kind could compare in scale with the natural phenomena which have in the past million years or so produced a succession of Ice Ages. To be sure, the uncertainties which abound are a challenge to human understanding but they do not yet constitute a sign that the direction of industrial development should be changed.[96]

Conclusion

Current environmental pollution is a problem due—in some cases, overdue— for correction. Contemporary and new technologies now coming off the drawing boards are fully capable of solving most major pollution problems. The challenge, therefore, is not developing radical new technology, although undoubtedly such technology will be developed in the future, but rather resolving the political and economic questions of who is going to pay how much money under what conditions to achieve what degree of environmental improvement. In John Maddox' words, environmental pollution "is not so much a threat to the global environment and the existence of the human race as a demonstration of the need for the vigorous application of social instruments, laws and taxes, which are as old as society itself."[97]

These "social instruments" can be more vigorously and effectively applied with rather than without population growth, because increasing numbers of people will be better able to achieve the economic progress, increasing flow of technology, and accumulating capital funds necessary for pollution control. For the environmental problems of today are a result of not failure but success in gradually achieving an overall improvement in our human environment. And the way to overcome the problems that success always creates is not to reject it but, as Peter Drucker states, to "build on it."[98]

99

5
U.S. POPULATION GROWTH AND SOCIAL ADVANCEMENT

Social welfare has increased immeasurably for all Americans as the country's population has grown from 4 million to well over 200 million. This has been a consequence of the continuing economic advancement, increasing resource abundance, and improving human environment resulting from population growth.

There are those, of course, who would claim that social welfare has gotten worse rather than better in recent years. But, as Anthony Downs says, although "many social critics hate to admit it, the American 'system' actually serves the majority of citizens rather well in terms of most indicators of well-being. Concerning such things as real income, personal mobility, variety and choice of consumption patterns, longevity, health, leisure time, and quality of housing, most Americans are better off today than they have ever been and extraordinarily better off than most of mankind."[1]

As Downs' comments suggest, there is no one factor that serves to indicate the status of social welfare. Rather, a variety of different indices are required to provide a full picture.

Rising Real Income

Perhaps the key indicator of improving social welfare is growth in real, disposable per capita income—after-tax, per capita income adjusted for inflation. We have no record of what this figure may have been when the country was founded, although a good guess, based on general knowledge of economic conditions at the time, might be somewhere in the neighborhood of one or two hundred dollars. Data for the nineteenth and early twentieth centuries is also incomplete, but there is little doubt that between the Civil War and the First World War, as University of Chicago economist Milton Friedman observes, per capita real income "went up decade after decade at a rate of about 2, 2½, 3% per year."[2] As a result, by 1929 when modern calculations of real, disposable per capita income began, this figure had grown to $1236 in terms of constant 1958 dollars. Between 1929 and 1970, real, disposable per capita income more than doubled to $2595.[3]

It is, of course, true that this vast increase in per capita income (just like GNP, of which it is a function) cannot be directly equated with improvements in social welfare. It has been argued, for example, as Wilfred Beckerman notes, that expenditures on military defense and law and order, which are included in GNP, "do not reflect desirable 'goods,' but are merely 'regrettable necessities' that have to be incurred in order that modern industrial society can operate, and so should not be counted as positive components of welfare. Similarly it has been argued that commuters' transport expenditures should not be included in GNP since these are part of the urbanization costs of economic growth, not positive final benefits enjoyed by the population."[4]

Thus, says Walter Heller, economists "labor under no illusion that GNP is a satisfactory measure of welfare or that it can be turned into one. They would agree with J. Petit-Senn that 'not what we have, but what we enjoy, constitutes our abundance.' "[5] But, as Heller goes on to point out, granting that

rising GNP is a poor index of human betterment is not to deny that one is generally associated with the other. It should require no lengthy demonstration to show that, while a significant part of GNP is illusory in a welfare sense, wide differences and large advances in per capita GNP are associated with significant differences and advances in well-being. In a careful appraisal of the growth-welfare correlation, Robert Lampman found that a 26 percent gain in real GNP per capita from 1947 to 1962 brought with it a 26 percent gain in real GNP per capita private consumption, a distinct improvement in income security, and a significant reduction in poverty. He concluded: 'All things considered, the pattern of growth in the United States in the post-war years yielded benefits to individuals far in excess of the costs it required of them. To that extent, our material progress has had humane content.' "[6]

Furthermore, although GNP includes some things that do not positively contribute to welfare, it excludes other things that do, such as leisure. Adding the value of leisure to GNP after making adjustments for the costs of urban civilization and other factors, A. W. Sametz found that for the period 1869–78 to 1966 total GNP plus leisure was equal to $555 billion compared to $315 billion for GNP alone.[7] "Contrary to the assertions of those who constantly complain that, on account of various omissions, the growth of conventionally measured GNP overstates the 'true' rise in welfare," comments Beckerman, "the above figures show that one of the omissions from GNP, namely leisure, has shown a spectacular rise over the last century, and has hence made an enormous contribution to the rise in economic welfare in the U.S.A."[8]

William Nordhaus and James Tobin prepared a similar but more comprehensive estimate of a welfare-oriented measure of what they called "NNP" (net national product). They concluded that "there is no evidence to support the claim that welfare has grown less rapidly than NNP. Rather, NNP seems to underestimate the gain in welfare, chiefly because of its omission of leisure from consumption. Subject to the limitation of estimates, we conclude that the economic welfare of the average American has been growing at a rate that doubles every 30 years."[9]

This continuing increase in economic welfare is, of course, particularly significant in terms of enabling the poor and disadvantaged to improve their socioeconomic position and thus helping to reduce social problems related to poverty. For example, Heller points out that "between 1959 and 1969 the number of persons below the poverty line fell from 39 million to 24 million, from 22.4 percent to 12.2 percent of a rising population. The improvement came from a 3 percent increase in productivity per year, a drop in unemployment from 6 percent to a 4 percent, shifts of the poor from lower to higher income occupations and regions, and an extraordinary growth in governmental cash transfers, from over $2 billion in 1960 to over $50 billion in 1970. Every one of these factors was in some way the direct outgrowth of or was associated with or facilitated by per capita economic growth."[10]

Conversely, Heller in effect asks, what social problems might have erupted if there had been no per capita economic growth, for "even with the aid of a rise of 55 percent in GNP and 34 percent in real per capita personal income from 1959 to 1969, we have found in the United States that our inroads on these problems have not kept pace with our rising expectations and aspirations. Imagine the tensions between rich and poor, between black and white, between blue-collar and white-collar workers, between old and young, if we had been forced to finance even the minimal demands of the disadvantaged out of a no-growth national income instead of a one-third increase in that income."[11]

Of course, it might be thought that the reduction in poverty cited by Heller has come about primarily as a result of redistribution of income from the rich to the poor. But, despite the "War on Poverty" and other public welfare programs, this is not the case. The lot of low-income people has primarily improved not because they have received larger slices of the economic pie but because the pie has gotten bigger, resulting in the expansion of income for all, rich and poor alike. As the table below shows, the percentage shares of aggregate income received by families ranked by fifths in terms of income have remained remarkably stable over the years between 1947 and 1973. Redistribution has had some effect—for example, the lowest fifth increased its share from 5.1 to 5.5 percent while the share of the highest fifth was reduced from 43.3

to 41.1 percent—but the effect has been minor in comparison to growth in terms of alleviating poverty.[12]

Percent Distribution of Aggregate Income

	1947	1973
Highest fifth	43.3	41.1
Fourth fifth	23.2	24.0
Middle fifth	16.7	17.5
Second fifth	11.8	11.9
Lowest fifth	5.1	5.5

Economic advancement resulting from population growth is therefore playing a vital role in improving social welfare, particularly from the standpoint of alleviating social problems related to poverty such as unemployment, inadequate education, poor health, and high crime rates. Conversely, reduction or elimination of population growth will slow down economic advancement, aggravating these social problems by hindering the development of low-income people.

Upward Social Mobility

Population growth has in the past promoted increasing upward social mobility for several reasons. One is that a society with a growing population provides an increasing number of different types of occupations. This growing occupational diversity not only helps to create greater job choice and thus the potential for increased job satisfaction. It also results in a broadening spectrum of job opportunities, both in newly developing fields and in new specializations within existing fields. Because these job opportunities are new, they hold out a potential for rapid occupational advancement to those who enter them. But, since their newness causes them to be speculative, they primarily appeal and are open to those who are on or close to the bottom rung of the economic ladder, people who do not already have it "made."

Those who entered the new field of data processing in the fifties, for example, were admittedly taking a "flyer" with their careers because there were many who did not think the computer would ever "fly." Today, in retrospect, we can see that data processing opened up tremendous new paths for rapid job advancement, particularly among young people who had everything to gain and relatively little to lose by entering the field and thus effectively bypassing more conventional, established fields in which promotions were fewer and farther between.

Another even more powerful reason for the positive relationship between increasing numbers of people and upward social mobility lies in the relationship between the age distribution of population growth and the hierarchical structure of occupations. A growing population has an age distribution that looks like a triangle or pyramid with a large number of young people at its base tapering up to a decreasing number of older people at its peak. Likewise, the occupational structure also resembles a pyramid with many low-level jobs at its base tapering up to a smaller number of middle-level occupations and even fewer high-level managerial and executive positions at its peak. Thus, under conditions of population growth, the age pyramid of population conforms to the pyramid shape of the occupational structure. As a result, there are proportional opportunities for job advancement along every step of the occupational ladder all the way to the top because the diminishing number of higher-level jobs available is roughly in proportion to the decreasing number of older people competing for the jobs.

However, under conditions of zero population growth, the situation gets out of kilter. This is because the age distribution of a stationary population is more like a square with vertical sides, reflecting the fact that there are as many old as young people in the population. This age distribution square extends beyond the pyramid shape of the occupational structure at its peak, resulting in a growing number of older people competing for a decreasing number of top positions. At the same time, the age distribution square falls short of the occupational pyramid at its base, resulting in a shortage of younger people for lower-level positions. These results are shown in the diagram on page 106.

What the above analysis means for occupational mobility in terms of lack of room at the top for job advancement has been stated by Ansley J. Coale, director of the Office of Population Research at Princeton University, who points out that the age pyramid for a stationary population is "virtually vertical until age 50 because of the small number of deaths under the favorable mortality conditions we have attained. In contrast, the age distribution of the United States to date has always tapered more or less sharply with increasing age. The stationary population with its vertical sides would no longer conform in age composition to the shape of the social structure—to the pyramid of privilege and responsibility. In a growing population, the age pyramid does conform, so there is a rough consonance of shape between diminishing numbers at higher ages and the smaller number of high positions relative to low positions. In a stationary population there would no longer be a reasonable expectation of advancement as a person moves through life."[13]

Under conditions of zero population growth, people are thus stymied in occupational advancement and social mobility. People who normally would advance up the job ladder under condition of population growth are instead forced to remain permanently in lower-level positions because there is not only no room at the top but a shortage of workers at the bottom.

One alternative to this situation would be to expand the number of high-

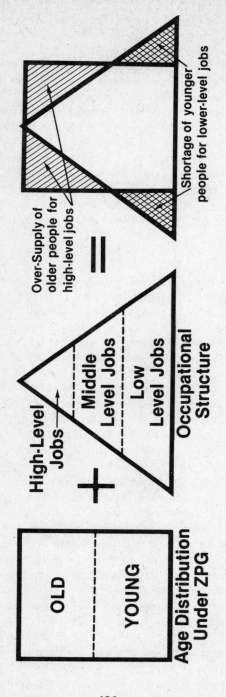

Age Distribution Under ZPG

OLD

YOUNG

+

Occupational Structure

High-Level Jobs

Middle Level Jobs

Low Level Jobs

=

Over-Supply of older people for high-level jobs

Shortage of younger people for lower-level jobs

106

level occupational positions to accommodate the demands of older workers for job advancement. But this would have the effect of creating a top-heavy bureaucracy. Something like this has apparently occurred in the military, where the number of generals, admirals, lieutenant generals, vice admirals, colonels, Navy captains, lieutenant colonels, and commanders has increased since World War II even though the "population" of the armed services during this same period decreased by 10 million.[14] Perhaps this over-staffed chain of command can be justified on the grounds that it insures that sufficient leaders will be available to direct a rapidly growing military force in case of crisis. But in the civilian economy such an enlargement of high positions would constitute nothing more than bureaucratic overkill.

The other alternative would be to pressure older workers into early retirement to make way for the advancement of the younger generation. But this would result in increasingly unbearable burdens on Social Security and public and private pension programs, which already are hard-pressed to maintain some semblance of fiscal integrity in the face of a growing number of older people making claims on funds provided by a diminishing number of younger people.

Adequate Retirement Income

Population growth is vital to the continuing adequacy of Social Security benefits paid to retiring workers. This is because the Social Security program is funded on a "pay-as-you-go" basis, with the money taken in from this year's taxes on workers being immediately paid out to current beneficiaries. There is also a trust fund, or reserve, for emergencies, but its assets do not amount to even one year's benefit payments.[15]

As a result of an increase in the population growth rate in the forties and fifties, there has in recent years been a growing number of young people whose addition to the work force has helped to provide the taxes for Social Security benefits. Even so, the Social Security system is running into increasing difficulty in paying its bills due to reduced income resulting from current high levels of unemployment as well as the fact that benefits in recent years have been not only extended to an ever-widening circle of beneficiaries but indexed to the cost of living.

However, in the early and mid-eighties, the rate of addition of young people to the work force will begin to decline because of the rapid drop in the rate of population growth that began in the late fifties. Furthermore, as the proportion of young people in the work force capable of paying Social Security taxes goes down the proportion of older people entitled to benefits will continue to go up.

Currently, some 92 million workers are providing benefits to 30 million retirees—about a three-to-one ratio. But, based on present trends, this ratio will sink to two to one by the turn of the century, a far cry from the 150-to-one ratio between workers and beneficiaries which existed in 1940, a few years after the Social Security program was adopted.[16] As the American Institute for Economic Research has commented, while "population was increasing during recent decades, the number of employed has greatly enlarged in relation to the number of retired. Now that the rate of population increase has dropped below the replacement rate, a markedly different situation is beginning to develop. Social Security taxes already are a great burden on individuals and business. Moreover, most private pension plans are similarly situated. Many have not even funded their current pension payments, and the amounts required in the future will be astronomical."[17]

One alternative to the future money crunch now confronting the Social Security system is to tax workers more heavily. But, in 1975, workers were already paying up to $824.25 each, more than double what they paid only four years before and more than four times the level of a decade ago. Indeed, more than half of all workers already pay more in Social Security taxes than they do in federal income taxes.[18] Consequently, how long can Social Security taxes continue to be increased before the young either stage a political revolt or go bankrupt?

Another alternative is to pay Social Security benefits from general tax revenues. But this would simply shift rather than alleviate the tax burden; the money would still come out of the same workers' pockets through either increased income taxes or inflation.

Continuing population growth can help to keep the head of the Social Security system above water. But lack of population growth can be expected to have the almost certain effect of substantially diminishing benefits if not eventually bankrupting the program and thus dashing the hopes of millions of people who are depending on the system for a reasonably comfortable retirement.

Health

Modern population growth primarily began as a result of basic medical and sanitary improvements in the seventeenth century. From this beginning, increasing numbers of people have built a continually improving health record in the United States. For example, average life expectancy when the country was founded was probably about thirty-five years. Today, life expectancy has more than doubled. The death rate two centuries ago was in the neighborhood of forty per 1000 population. Now, it is less than ten per thousand.

As recently as 1940, there were forty-seven infant deaths per 1000 live births. Today, there are less than twenty. During the same period, maternal deaths were reduced from 376 to less than 25 per 100,000 live births.[19]

Between 1950 and 1971, national health expenditures increased six times, from $12 billion to $75 billion, while funds invested in medical research grew twenty-five times, from $73 million to $1.8 billion.[20] The number of physicians per 100,000 resident population increased from 149 in 1950 to 171 in 1970.[21] Meanwhile, in terms of access to medical facilities, hospital admissions per 1000 population doubled, from 74 in 1940 to 152 in 1972. But the total days spent in hospitals per 1000 population increased only 50 percent, from 1019 to 1440, because the average length of stay was cut from 13.7 to 9.5 days.[22]

Although there is still a long way to go to further alleviate health problems, particularly in the case of the poor and the elderly, the picture of health over the past several centuries of population growth is one of continuing progress. Moreover, the ability to improve on this health record in the future, particularly in the case of the elderly, will be directly affected by population growth.

This is because a growing population with a predominance of young people not only has more funds for investment in health improvements but is better able to afford the per capita costs of health problems related to death. Currently, the death rate in the United States is 9.4 per 1000 population. This death rate is the equivalent of a life expectancy of 106 years because it reflects population growth of the past in which the proportion of youth has been much greater than that of the elderly. However, as growth slows down and the proportion of elderly in the population increases, the death rate will inevitably increase, not because of any greater across-the-board incidence of death but simply because the elderly will constitute a growing percentage of the total population. With ZPG the death rate would increase by over 50 percent to more than fourteen per 1000 population, which is the equivalent of our current life expectancy of seventy.

Continued population growth will help to improve medical treatment of the elderly by keeping the death rate at a low level and thus holding down the per capita cost to society of treating health problems related to death. Conversely, lack of population growth would make it more difficult to improve elderly health care because it would have the effect of increasing the death rate and the per capita costs of attending to death-related medical problems.

Education

As the country has grown in population from 4 million to more than 200 million, the educational level of the people has risen accordingly. In 1870, for example, only 2 percent of seventeen-year-olds were high school graduates.[23] Today, more 75 percent of persons twenty-five to thirty-four years old have completed four years of high school.[24]

The median number of years of school completed by persons twenty-five years old and over has been gradually rising throughout the history of the country. By 1940, median years of school completed had reached 8.6. In 1974, this figure had risen to 12.3.[25] In addition, the proportion of high school graduates who completed one year of college or more rose from about 27 percent in 1940 to 47 percent in 1974.[26]

These educational advances have been achieved primarily as a result of the rising real income produced by population growth. A remarkable illustration of this process occurred during the period 1952–72, when, as a result of the rapid rise in the rate of population growth through 1957, the number of students in public schools more than doubled, from 28 to 52 million. A great cry went up at the time concerning how society was going to be able to pay for all the new schools and teachers required to handle this tremendous influx of additional students. Yet, as pointed out by Roger A. Freeman, senior fellow at the Hoover Institution, expenditures on public education during this period increased not merely twice but eight times, from $8.4 billion to $67.5 billion. Simultaneously, expenditures per student leapt four times, from $301 to $1294.[27]

Today, the shoe is on the other foot. The number of students in schools is shrinking due to the reduction in the rate of population growth that began in 1957. Supposedly, this decline in student population was to result in better education because it would free up school space for more types of "enrich-ment" activities and make it possible to reduce class sizes. But the opposite has turned out to be the case. Typical of conditions in school systems through-out the country is the situation in Illinois' suburban Cook County, where "the decline in public school enrollment is reaching landslide proportions. The dramatic drop in the number of children attending school has touched every corner of the country and is sending a shudder through those who must administer education programs in elementary school districts. Having lived through fat times—thanks to the post–World War II baby boom—they now face lean ones. The boom is over. During the last eight years, enrollment declined in 53 percent of the country's suburban elementary school districts. The results touch everyone with children in school or a tax collector at the door. Schools are closing, the buildings being leased out or put up for auction. Teachers are being laid off. And most important in the long run, there is a threat in many districts that the scope and quality of the curriculum will eventually be curtailed."[28]

Housing

In the area of housing, the American people have obviously come a long way from the one-room log cabin of two centuries ago. What is not so obvious is that this improvement has continued in recent years. For example, population grew by 13.3 percent between 1960 and 1970. At the same time, the number of housing units increased by 17.7 percent. During this same period, the

110

proportion of housing units with one or more rooms per person—an indication of the absence of overcrowding—increased from 88.5 percent to 91.8 percent. At the same time, the proportion of housing units with complete plumbing facilities increased from 83.2 percent to 93.1 percent. There was also a slight increase in the category of owner-occupied homes, from 62 to 63 percent.[29]

The housing industry, of course, is particularly sensitive to positive population growth trends. Consequently, further housing improvements can be expected to occur faster under conditions of population growth than under ZPG.

Consumption

Along with the rising real income that has accompanied population growth has come increasing consumption of an ever-broadening variety of goods and services. The reason why these goods and services have become more available is shown in the following table, which compares how long a typical factory worker had to work to buy various items in 1925 and 1975.[30]

To Buy This	A Worker Would Have to Put in	
	1925	**1975**
New car	41.5 wks.	26.5 wks.
Year at state university	31 wks.	15 wks.
Rail fare, Washington, D.C., to Atlanta	1 wk.	1.5 days
Gas range	138 hrs.	61.5 hrs.
Electric clothes washer	120.5 hrs.	54 hrs.
Electric sewing machine	101.5 hrs.	22 hrs.
Vacuum cleaner	59.5 hrs.	13.5 hrs.
Man's shoes	7.5 hrs.	7 hrs.
Lady's wool skirt	6.5 hrs.	3 hrs.
Man's dress shirt	3 hrs.	2.5 hrs.
Oranges, doz.	49 min.	19 min.
Potatoes, 10 lbs.	30 min.	19 min.
Coffee, lb.	48 min.	20 min.
Milk, half-gal.	31 min.	12 min.
Butter, lb.	57 min.	15 min.
Margarine, lb.	33 min.	11 min.
Eggs, doz.	53 min.	13 min.
Bread, lb.	10 min.	6 min.
Round steak, lb.	38 min.	27 min.
Chicken, whole, lb.	39 min.	9 min.

The leisure to enjoy these goods and services increased as the number of hours worked each week decreased from about fifty-five in 1870 to less than forty in 1970.[31] In addition, the physical mobility required to enjoy "goods" such as national and state parks and national forests simultaneously increased, as is shown by the fact that the rate of growth in attendance at these and other outdoor recreational facilities has averaged 8 to 10 percent annually for the past several decades, while population was increasing at a rate of only one to 2 percent a year.[32]

Social Atmosphere

Underlying all of these improvements in human welfare brought on by population growth is a relatively open and progressive social atmosphere, consisting of a willingness to improve and an eagerness to find a "better way," which has not only helped to create these social advancements but caused their benefits to be shared with an ever-broadening circle of Americans. For, as Walter Heller observes in commenting on the results of economic growth, apart from the "tangible bounties that growth can bestow, we should keep in mind some of its intangible dividends. Change, innovation, and risk thrive in an atmosphere of growth. It fosters a social mobility and opens up options that no stationary state can provide."[33]

Conversely, as Ansley Coale notes, there is a "non-negligible cost associated with attaining a stationary population. . . . A stationary population with the mortality levels that we have already attained has a much older age distribution than any the United States has ever experienced. It has more people over 60 than under 15, and half the population would be over 37 rather than over 27, as is the case today. It would be an age distribution much like that of a health resort. . . ."[34]

Urbanization and Social Welfare

Advances in social welfare have been achieved in the United States not only directly as a result of population growth but indirectly as a consequence of the vast population redistribution process called urbanization. Basically consisting of the redistribution of population from rural to urban areas, urbanization has played a major role in enabling the American people to significantly improve their social welfare.

The reason for this is that, by definition, urbanization concentrates large numbers of people in relatively small areas, resulting in high population density. And this combination of large numbers of people living and working under high population density maximizes beneficial socioeconomic interac-

112

tions, while minimizing the costs, time, and effort involved in achieving these interactions.

Thus, population growth provides the impetus for improving social welfare. And this social improvement is maximized through urbanization. But, although population growth helps to spur the urbanization process, it is not directly related to either the rate of urbanization or the population density of metropolitan areas. This is because urbanization is entirely a consequence of population *redistribution* from rural to urban areas. Population growth affects the ultimate size of urban or metropolitan areas. But, if population growth in rural areas is the same as population growth in metropolitan areas, no urbanization occurs. It is only where immigration from rural to urban areas occurs that there is urbanization.

Likewise, average U.S. population density in 1790 was about 4.5 persons per square mile. Today, as a result of population growth (along with expansion in land area), average population density is close to sixty persons per square mile. Yet people today live in metropolitan areas with population densities up to 70,000 persons per square mile or more, as is the case in certain sections of Manhattan. However, this high population density is not a direct function of population growth because the density at which people live and work together is socially determined independently of the rate of population growth.

For example, at our current average population density, there are about ten acres of land, the equivalent of nine football fields, for every man, woman, and child in the United States. But, far from spreading out to occupy this maximum amount of land per person, the American people have instead concentrated in metropolitan areas at population densities up to 1000 times the average population density of the country. This has occurred for no other reason than that it is economically and socially beneficial to do so. Jane Jacobs, author of *The Death and Life of Great American Cities,* for instance, cites the remark of Samuel Johnson to Boswell in 1785 that "men, thinly scattered, make a shift, but a bad shift, without many things. . . . It is being concentrated which produces convenience."[35]

Dr. Philip M. Hauser, director of the University of Chicago's population research center, observes that "agglomerations of population represent the most efficient producer and consumer units that our society has yet devised. The very size, density and congestion of our Standard Metropolitan Areas, to which some city planners object, are among our most precious economic assets."[36]

Says Edwin S. Mills of the Department of Economics at Princeton University: "Large cities economize on the use of resources in transportation and communication by the proximate locations of many related economic activities. Large buildings crowded together in downtown areas are the most prominent physical manifestation of this attempt to economize. Less dramatic but equally important is the rapid growth of an enormous range of business and consumer services in metropolitan areas where they can be close to customers and to related enterprises."[37]

Consequently, as Peter A. Morrison of the RAND Corporation states, the "transition to a metropolitan society has been broadly beneficial, measured by improvements in living standards and employment opportunities. Increasingly, an individual's social status depends more on his achievements and less on inherited advantage or disadvantage. He also has a greater range of ways to realize his potentialities. On the average, residents of large metropolitan centers have access to better health and education; higher income; a wider range of employment options, broader avenues of advancement for disadvantaged members of the population, especially blacks; and a greater diversity of residential environments."[38]

For example, the 1973 median annual income of American families was $14,007 in the suburbs of metropolitan areas, $11,343 in metropolitan central cities, and $10,327 in nonmetropolitan areas.[39] The mean earnings of men were $13,179 in metropolitan suburbs, $11,488 in metropolitan cities, and $9888 in nonmetropolitan areas, while the mean earnings of women were $6369, $6258, and $5062, respectively, in metropolitan suburbs, metropolitan cities, and nonmetropolitan areas.[40]

From the standpoint of education, 84.5 percent of all people twenty-five to thirty-four years old residing in metropolitan area suburbs and 79 percent of this same age bracket in metropolitan cities were at least high school graduates in 1974, compared to 75.1 percent of the 25-to-34-year-old population in nonmetropolitan areas.[41]

As for health care, the availability of physicians shows a relatively steady progression from 205 per 100,000 population in greater metropolitan areas of more than one million people to 153 in smaller metropolitan areas of less than one million, to 100 or less in rural areas.[42]

In terms of housing, the proportion of housing units with complete plumbing facilities in 1970 was 93.1 percent in metropolitan areas and 85.7 percent in nonmetropolitan areas. In addition, metropolitan housing was slightly more spacious, with 91.8 percent of the housing units having one or more rooms per person compared to 90.7 percent in nonmetropolitan areas.[43]

Moreover, social conditions are not only generally better for people living in metropolitan areas. They are particularly better for minorities. For, as Princeton's Edwin Mills points out, few people

resist the notion that whites have migrated to cities because income, employment, shopping, cultural, educational and social opportunities are better there than in the small towns and rural areas from which they have come. Yet people who see how badly blacks live in the ghettos of large central cities find it hard to believe that blacks have urbanized for much the same reasons. Nevertheless, the evidence is overwhelming that discrepancies between urban and rural life are greater for blacks

114

than for whites and that blacks have greatly improved their economic and political life by urbanization.

Throughout the postwar period, family incomes of blacks in metropolitan areas have been about twice as high as those of blacks living elsewhere. The corresponding discrepancy for whites has been between 25 and 50 percent. In 1968, after a quarter century of rapid migration to metropolitan areas, urban black family incomes were still 70 percent higher there than those of blacks elsewhere. Poverty statistics tell an even more dramatic story. In 1959, 78 percent of blacks living outside metropolitan areas, and 43 percent of those in metropolitan areas, were below the official poverty line. By 1968, the figures were 55 percent and 27 percent. Not only is the incidence of poverty among blacks much lower in metropolitan areas than elsewhere, but also poverty among blacks has decreased much more rapidly in metropolitan areas.

Housing statistics tell a similar story. In 1960, 77 percent of blacks living outside metropolitan areas, and 43 percent of those in metropolitan areas, lived in substandard housing. By 1968, the figures were 55 percent and 16 percent. Again, conditions are better and progress has been faster in metropolitan areas than elsewhere.

The story can be repeated with data on health, mortality, and education. By almost any measure, life is better for blacks in the cities than in small towns and rural areas from which they came, and the differences have persisted throughout the period of rapid migration since World War II.[44]

These metropolitan socioeconomic benefits have occurred because, in Mills' words, large cities "economize on the use of resources in transportation and communications by the proximate locations of many related economic activities." What this means in terms of the increasing potential for social interactions or human contacts resulting from urbanization has been amply delineated by Philip Hauser. He points out that "in aboriginal America a person moving within a ten-mile circle could potentially make only 313 different contacts with other human beings. In contrast, the density of the United States as a whole today would make possible 15,699 contacts in the same land area. The density of the average central city in the United States would permit over 2.5 million contacts, the density of Chicago over 5.3 million contacts, the density of New York City over 7.8 million contacts, and the density of Manhattan over 23.5 million contacts in the same land area. The potential number of contacts, when considered as a measure of potential human interaction, provides, in a simplistic way to be sure, a basis for understanding the difference that city living makes."[45]

Of course, urbanization began in the United States in the mid-1800s when the fastest means of intraurban transportation was the horse-drawn conveyance and the fastest method of communications was a messenger boy. To achieve the socioeconomic benefits of urbanization, it was therefore necessary to have a very high population density to make up in close physical proximity what was lacking in the speed and flexibility of transportation and communications facilities. As transportation and communications capabilities improved over time, it might be expected that this socioeconomic need for high population density or close physical proximity would decline. And this is exactly what happened.

The development of the electrified elevated, or street, car, the "horseless carriage," and the telephone around the turn of the century made it possible for people to begin to spread out from high-density urban cores while still maintaining a high degree of human interaction. As Charles L. Leven of Washington University's Institute for Urban and Regional Studies comments, probably

the most important single determinant of the urban process is the intrametropolitan transportation system. That transportation should have such a central role stems from the central purpose of the urban process: the gathering together of people and firms so that they can achieve economies of scale in production, consumption, and social interaction. If these scale economies are to be realized, interaction must be possible and the major barrier to interaction is the friction of distance. In the absence of a change in the transportation system, the only way to accommodate more people is with very considerable increases in settlement density. This produces very high construction costs and an ability of people to consume only very small amounts of land. Expansion of the system or moving to a new technology (from street railways to automobiles) opens up new territory so that more people can have the same access without incurring the crowding and construction costs of higher density. Historically, urbanites have used expanding transport to obtain both a larger collection of population within some time distance from each other and more space per person. . . . The communication system on the other hand affects the urban process in a somewhat different way; in large measure, it is a substitute for transportation. In viewing past developments, the role of communication in shaping urban form has largely been neglected. It seems clear, however, that the telephone has contributed to megalopolitan sprawl. By reducing the aggregate need for personal travel, it allows more people in a single community at any given cost.[46]

As a result of transportation and communications improvements, the early 1900s marked the high point of urban population density. Since then, although urbanization has continued to increase, the average population density of major urbanized areas has declined due to the fact that urban boundaries have expanded faster than populations. As Peter Morrison puts it, in "major urbanized areas (upwards of 100,000 people), average population density per square mile has dropped consistently since 1920, and is expected to decline further in the future. The paradox of numerical increase accompanied by declining density is explained by more rapid expansion of urbanized territory than of population."[47]

In 1920, the average population density of major urban areas was 6580 persons per square mile. By 1940, this density figure had dropped to 5870. In

116

1960, there was a further decline to 4230. Nor is this trend expected to be reversed in the future. By 1980, a population density of 3840 persons per square mile is anticipated in major urban areas, with a further decrease to 3732 persons per square mile to come in 2000.[48]

This decrease in metropolitan population density is primarily resulting from the continuing exodus of people from central cities of metropolitan areas to the suburbs. Due to this migration, population growth of central cities in major metropolitan areas has not only slowed down but gone into reverse. Between 1960 and 1970, for example, the population of metropolitan areas increased 16.6 percent, but the population of their central cities increased only 5.3 percent, while the population of central cities in metropolitan areas with more than 2 million people actually declined 1.8 percent.[49] This decline was led by cities such as Chicago, with a population loss of 5.2 percent, Philadelphia, which experienced a loss of 2.7 percent, Detroit, with a decline of 9.5 percent, Pittsburgh, where there was a drop of 14 percent, and Saint Louis, which decreased a startling 17.1 percent.[50]

Since 1970, this decline in population of metropolitan central cities has accelerated. Between 1970 and 1974, for example, the total population of *all* metropolitan central cities decreased by 1.9 percent. This was a result of a drop of 3.8 percent in central cities of metropolitan areas with more than one million people, which more than cancelled out a slight increase of 0.3 percent in central cities of metropolitan areas with less than one million people.[51] New York City, for example, was down 4.2 percent,[52] Chicago declined 5.8 percent,[53] and even Los Angeles County went into reverse, with a decrease of 1.7 percent.[54]

For the last several decades, while the population growth of metropolitan central cities has been slowing down, population in metropolitan suburbs has been growing at a very rapid rate. Between 1960 and 1970, for example, while central city populations were growing only 5.3 percent, suburban populations increased by 28.2 percent.[55] However, the rate of population growth in metropolitan suburbs has also declined in more recent years. For the near half-decade from 1970 to 1974, for example, suburban population grew only 8.4 percent,[56] in comparison to the 28.2 percent growth figure for the previous decade.

At the same time, the rate of population growth in nonmetropolitan areas has increased as people have moved to these areas from not only metropolitan central cities but suburbs, too. Between 1960 and 1970, for example, the U.S. nonmetropolitan population increased by 6.5 percent.[57] Then, from 1970 to 1974, nonmetropolitan population grew another 5 percent[58]—almost the same percentage in less than half a decade.

As a result of this continuing outward spread of population from metropolitan central cities to metropolitan suburbs to nonmetropolitan areas, the 1970–74 population growth rate of 5 percent in nonmetropolitan areas was greater than the growth rate of 3.6 percent in metropolitan areas. Thus, for the first time since the founding of the United States, urbanization as it is currently defined is declining instead of rising, even as the population of the country continues to grow. And there is a good possibility that this trend will continue in the future as an increasing proportion of people, jobs, and industries locate outside metropolitan areas. For, as Calvin L. Beale of the Department of Agriculture's Economic Research Service notes, the "new trend, a turn-around unexpected by most demographers, will have a continuing impact on U.S. population distribution at least to the end of the century."[59]

What this trend is leading towards, of course, is the formation of so-called megalopolises, which will merge a number of current metropolitan areas into a single larger area within which average population density will decline even further and the distinction between metropolitan and nonmetropolitan will become increasingly blurred. Sociologist Ben Wattenberg and former U.S. Census Bureau Director Richard Scammon describe the current development of one megalopolis in the Northeast, which "runs from Boston to Washington —along the coast here, inland there—and is highly industrial. This huge belt is about five hundred miles long, takes in parts of thirty-two different SMSA's (Standard Metropolitan Statistical Areas), and for much of its route is serviced by super-cities: Boston, New York, Philadelphia, Baltimore, and Washington." Wattenberg and Scammon see other megalopolises forming in the areas occupied by Gary-Chicago-Milwaukee, Detroit-Toledo-Cleveland, Cleveland-Youngstown, Pittsburgh, Los Angeles-Fresno-San Francisco-Oakland, and Miami–Fort Lauderdale.[60]

That the American people are ready and willing to effect this population redistribution to the megalopolis of the future is readily apparent. For, as the Stanford Research Institute reports, there "exists a strong and pervasive preference for smaller scale living environments—typically, in national polls regarding preferred residence, an absolute majority of Americans indicated they would prefer to live in a small town or rural environment."[61] The findings in one survey, in fact, suggest that "if the American people could follow their inclinations, the population of our cities would be cut in half. The proportion of suburbanites would remain the same. The percentage of people living in towns and villages would increase significantly. And the proportion enjoying country life would more than double, from less than two to almost four in ten."[62]

The megalopolitan trend of the future thus provides an opportunity for Americans to further improve their social welfare. And continuing population growth will play a vital role in helping to achieve this goal. The feasibility of the megalopolis depends on continuing economic growth and the technological development and implementation of a host of more efficient and effective forms of transportation and communications, including expanded expressway and highway systems, improved public transport facilities, and more available and

118

economical computer technology, data communications, microwave transmission, "phonevision," cable television, facsimile transmission, and the like. This economic and technological advancement can best be achieved under the impetus of population growth.

Also, the urbanization process has apparently run its course, with the result that social benefits in the future must be derived wholly and directly from population growth rather than partially and indirectly from population concentration. And, due to the fact that more people are emigrating from than immigrating to major cities, these cities must depend on population growth simply to maintain their present populations. Continuing population growth is thus vital in helping the cities to conserve their economic and social viability. Conversely, zero population growth combined with continuing population outflow will result in a multitude of urban depopulation disasters.

There are, of course, a number of factors involved in the financial collapse of New York City. But the fact that the city is not only not gaining but actually losing population is at the heart of many of them. In the Detroit area, depopulation is advanced to the point where even older suburbs such as Dearborn, Royal Oak, Birmingham, and Warren are "beginning to experience a decline in population, just as Detroit did two decades ago. Shrinking population was a first indication of urban decay for Detroit. For the suburbs, at the very least, it means an increased tax burden on remaining residents. It could also be the first step toward decline. In some of the older suburbs, first stages of decay like Detroit's can already be easily seen."[63]

In Chicago, Richard L. Thomas, president of First Chicago Corporation and its subsidiary, the First National Bank of Chicago, comments that the "loss of population in Chicago should also be a matter of concern. Between 1960 and 1970, Chicago's population fell by more than 5 per cent. Even more alarming are the latest census bureau estimates which indicate a further decline of nearly 6 per cent in the 1970–73 period."[64]

As was pointed out by Donald Haider, associate professor of the Chicago area's Northwestern University Graduate School, if we "talk about a turn-around situation, one of conservation and stabilization, we're really talking about the mix of policies—state, county and local, both public and private—that combine zero or slow population growth with economic wellbeing. These are uncharted waters as metropolitan areas in our country's history have not been able to attain this balance."[65]

Uncharted waters, indeed, for, although a majority of people say they would opt to live in a small town or rural environment if they could, most of them still want to live "within commuting distance of a large city."[66] However, lacking population growth, there will not be many big cities left that will be worth commuting to.

The Arguments against Population Growth

Population growth is blamed for a host of social ills. The major ones are probably what might be called the "three Cs": congestion, crowding, and crime. But critics also state that population growth is causing us to "run out of space," that it results in larger, socially undesirable family sizes, and that changes wrought by population growth are resulting in a breakdown in social structure.

Congestion. Congestion is one of the prices paid in obtaining the socioeconomic benefits of high population density created by urbanization. On the one hand, high population density maximizes social welfare by minimizing the costs of socioeconomic interactions. But, on the other hand, it concentrates large numbers of people in small areas, making it difficult for them to simultaneously move by car or public transportation from one place to another.

Traffic congestion within cities is perhaps particularly galling because of the invidious comparisons that can be made with the obviously great advancements achieved in intercity travel. Traveling on expressways or in the air, people today go between cities in a small fraction of the time it used to take. It is thus somewhat ludicrous that, due to intracity congestion, it is often necessary to spend more time traveling to and from a local city airport than is spent traveling intercity.

However, although everybody is aware of and complains about the problem of urban traffic congestion, very few actually attempt to accurately define or measure the problem. This is unfortunate because, as Peter G. Koltnow of the Highway Users Federation points out, current "lamentations about the 'urban transportation crisis' hinge on the generally accepted belief that our cities, and particularly our city centers, are suffering from increased vehicular congestion." But, he goes on to say, the "generalization that urban mobility is experiencing a congestion crisis obscures reality. Some mobility changes are for the better, some for the worse, some neither good nor bad but indicative of new needs, calling for new programs."[67]

The Highway Users Federation for a number of years has collected data on travel times in urban areas. The most important conclusion to emerge from this research is that "the cliche about imminent strangulation of American cities is essentially inaccurate; most cities have enjoyed improved mobility in recent years." A corollary to this is that "mobility, like J. P. Morgan's stock market, 'fluctuates.' Travel conditions get better, they get worse, and they get better again. There are no apparent irreversible trends." Furthermore, the idea that "rapid urban growth is the stimulus to a decay in urban transportation is not supported by our survey. In fact, we found that our most mobile and rapidly improving cities are those experiencing the greatest growth. Apparently an energetic program of transportation improvement can keep pace with the rapid growth experienced by our large and middle-size cities."[68]

120

The federation points out that New York, and particularly Manhattan, is commonly used as the example of the area with the worst automotive congestion in the United States. As long ago as the mid-1920s, observers pointed out that half the time spent by vehicles in transit was consumed by street delays. Yet, in general, surveys show that travel speeds on Manhattan have changed little between the twenties and the sixties, in spite of substantial—even spectacular—growth. The following table, based on a 1967 report for the Triborough Bridge and Tunnel Authority, shows changes in Manhattan uptown-downtown and crosstown traffic speeds between 1929 and 1966.[69]

Manhattan Average Speeds (mph)

Year	Uptown-Downtown	Crosstown
1929	10	7
1935	13	6
1949	12	9
1966	12	7

N.Y.

Meanwhile, travel times in off-peak hours between locations throughout the area for the most part show significant improvements, as the table below shows.

Off-Peak Trips	Travel Times by Year	
Times Square/JFK Airport	1946: 40 min.	1966: 30 min.
Times Square/Elizabeth, N.J.	1949: 40 min.	1966: 25 min.
Elizabeth/JFK Airport	1949: 80 min.	1966: 40 min.
New Dorp, S.I./City Hall	1949: 70 min.	1966: 25 min.
Geo. Washington Bridge/Nassau Co. line	1959: 45 min.	1966: 25 min.
Queens Plaza/Southern Queens	1938: 30 min.	1966: 30 min.

In January, 1970, the Federal Highway Administration of the Department of Transportation produced a travel-time report for nine other cities in addition to New York. The results of this report are as follows:[70]

Los Angeles. Despite the fact that vehicle registration has more than tripled from 1936 to 1960, travel times to all parts of the area have decreased.

Detroit. Between 1953 and 1965, the average speed of a work trip increased 19 percent despite the fact that the number of work trips made increased by 26 percent.

121

San Francisco. Between 1937 and 1959, average travel speed has increased in all corridors in spite of the fact that traffic volumes have increased from 50 to 146 percent.

Milwaukee. Between 1963 and 1967, the number of miles of regional system operating over design capacity was reduced from 191.8 miles to 144.5 miles. In the same period, total vehicle-miles of travel increased 20 percent. A motorist traveling to Milwaukee's central business district arrived ten minutes sooner than he would have in 1963.

Kansas City. On the average in 1965, an auto driver could travel twice as far in a twenty-minute period as he could in 1957.

Phoenix. Although average traffic speeds have declined slightly in recent years, the 1966 peak-hour speeds showed an increase over the 1947 level. This occurred despite a 250 percent increase in traffic.

San Diego. The average peak-hour speed has more than doubled from 1955 to 1964.

Columbus, Ohio. In three corridors, travel has tripled since 1936; however, the trips are being made in up to 43 percent less time.

Albuquerque. The addition of an Interstate link has held the overall average freeway speeds high, with a slight increase from 53 mph to 56 mph (1967–69). However, increased traffic volumes with little change in the arterial system have caused speeds to decrease slightly on the arterials.

The overall picture during the past half century is thus one of population growth resulting not in increasing urban congestion but generally faster travel times except in central business districts, where vehicle speeds have remained approximately the same. The reason for this improvement is that population growth has made it possible to expand urban metropolitan expressway and arterial road systems faster than the increase in population, vehicles, and vehicle-miles traveled.

This, of course, is not to say that there are not some metropolitan routes on which travel times are longer than they used to be. Nor is it to say that current vehicle mobility, even though it is better than before, is acceptably better. As the Highway Users Federation points out, the "public's perception of mobility, or the standards of mobility it considers acceptable, may change more drastically than mobility itself, confusing the question of whether or not matters are improving—or improving enough."[71] But it is to say that population growth has generally been a positive force increasing metropolitan mobility rather than a negative force causing increased congestion, and it can be expected to continue to have this positive impact in the future.

Improvements in metropolitan mobility have generally taken place during a period of increasing population but decreasing population density. This decrease in population density, of course, has been in large part a result of the vast increase in automotive usage, which has enabled people to spread throughout metropolitan areas over the years. But, at the same time, the density decrease has been primarily responsible for the decline of urban mass transportation systems. This is because the success of urban transit is primarily dependent on high population density—the concentration of people along transit routes. However, since the twenties and even before, urban population density has been decreasing. Consequently, it is no coincidence that "since 1920, excepting two short periods (the Depression in the 1930's and World War II), transit ridership has continuously fallen. . . . From 288 rides per capita in 1920, the average reached 49 rides per capita in 1970, and 44 in 1972. . . . The decline of the industry is evidenced by reduced ridership, curtailment of services, increased costs, growing deficits, failures of firms, and increased public acquisition of firms to prevent abandonment of service."[72]

In response to declining population density, urban areas today are developing more flexible mass transit systems, such as "park-and-ride" facilities and "dial-a-bus" services. However, lacking population growth, urban population density will decline even more in the future, resulting in a need for even greater public subsidies, further cutbacks in service, or both. Conversely, population growth will make it possible to at least maintain and perhaps even increase urban population densities required for the economical operation and technological improvement of mass transit systems.

Crowding and Crime. Crowding is thought to have all kinds of bad effects on people. As Columbia University psychology professor Jonathan Freedman says, "everyone knows that crowding is bad. Politicians, environmentalists, ethologists, and biologists constantly warn of the evils of high density living. They assert that crowding causes tension, anxiety, family troubles, divorce, aggressiveness, neurosis, schizophrenia, rape, murder, and even war."

So, as Freedman adds, it is "a wonder that the world survives at all given that so many people live under conditions of severe crowding. Yet live they do, and there are few reports of people in New York subway cars turning on each other in a violent frenzy or of shoppers in Macy's going berserk and tearing the merchandise and each other to shreds. How can this be if crowding is so bad?"

The answer, responds Freedman, according to research accumulated over the past few years, is that "high population density has been much maligned, at least as it affects humans. Intuitions, speculations, political and philosophical theory appear to be wrong in this respect. Under some circumstances, crowding may have disastrous effects on rats, mice, rabbits, and other animals, but crowding does not have generally negative effects on humans. People who live under crowded conditions do not suffer from being crowded. Other things being equal, they are no worse off than other people."[73]

123

Crowding, of course, can be a very subjective concept. One hundred thousand people may jam into a football stadium to cheer their team on to victory and not feel crowded at all. But two lovers who want to be alone can sit in the same stadium after the game and feel "crowded" if there is one other person there.

However, crowding can also be defined objectively, or physically, in terms of, say, the number of persons per room or the number of persons per square mile. The former is the technical measurement in which crowding is usually expressed, while the latter is normally called population density. It should be pointed out, too, that crowding and population density, as defined above, do not necessarily go together. A rural family living in a one-room house may be crowded, for example, even though the population density of the area is very low. Conversely, a family may live in a spacious uncrowded apartment in an urban high-rise area with high population density.

Most theories concerning the effects of crowding on human behavior are based on experiments with rats and observations of other animals. John B. Calhoun, for example, did numerous studies of the effects of crowding on Norway rats, concluding that "the behavioral repertory with which the Norway rat has emerged from the trials of evolution and domestication must break down under the social pressures generated by population density. In time, refinement of experimental procedures and of the interpretation of these studies may advance our understanding to the point where they may contribute to the making of value judgments about analogous problems confronting the human species."[74] Following in a similar path, others such as Desmond Morris *(The Naked Ape),* Lionel Tiger *(Men in Groups),* and Robert Ardrey *(The Territorial Imperative)* have written books attempting to interpret human actions in terms of animal behavior. But, as Freedman points out, this is "a grave mistake. It is always misleading, often foolish. Even Konrad Lorenz, the Nobel Prize–winning ethologist, has had a tendency in recent years to make broad statements about human behavior based on his studies of tropical fish. And when men such as Desmond Morris, Lionel Tiger, and Robert Ardrey write whole books in which they make profound statements about humans based on other animals, it is truly disheartening."[75]

Encouraged by *Population Bomb* author Paul Ehrlich, who convinced him that "over-population was one of the most important problems facing the world," Freedman decided to do research on the subject of population density because it was obvious that high density was to be a fact of life for the foreseeable future and it was important to know "what effect it had."[76]

He and his research collaborators "started with the familiar naive assumption that crowding was 'a bad thing' and would have negative effects on people's behavior. In particular, we thought that crowding probably was very stressful, would produce tension, and would then produce all the effects that psychologists have found to be associated with high drive."[77]

124

The question was examined using two different measures of density: number of people living per square mile in an area and number of people per room in housing units. The relationship between these measures and the juvenile delinquency crime rate was then explored. The results, according to Freedman, indicated that

income level is strongly related to juvenile delinquency. The poorer the neighborhood, the higher the crime rate. But with income level and ethnicity equated, there is no relationship between either measure of population density and juvenile delinquency. There are about as many high-density areas that have low crime rates as there are that have high crime rates; and about as many low density areas have high crime rates as have low crime rates. This holds for population per acre and perhaps even more surprisingly for density in the houses themselves. Living in a crowded neighborhood or crowded apartment is not associated with committing more crimes.[78]

Freedman next looked at just lower-income areas to see what relationship would hold in these areas between density and juvenile delinquency. "Quite startlingly," he reports, "there is actually a reverse relationship between density and juvenile delinquency in low-income areas—people who live under higher density have a *lower* rate of juvenile delinquency than those who live in low-density areas. Even in low-income areas, density is not associated with crime rates."[79]

Freedman also reports results of analyses of relationships between density and other human problems, summing up that

evidence indicates no effect of density on other types of mental, physical and social pathology. . . . studies of Chicago and New York . . . found that when economic and ethnic factors are controlled, there is little or no relationship between density and such pathologies as mental illness, infant mortality, venereal disease, and adult mortality. People living in high-density areas do not have higher death rates, they do not suffer more from venereal disease or other diseases, they do not enter mental hospitals more often. There is a slight hint that high density might be associated with minor mental disturbances, but the evidence is inconsistent. In general, this research provides no evidence to support the notion that high density is bad for people. There is no consistent or even substantial relationship between the density of a neighborhood, measured either by people per acre or the amount of space in the living quarters, and any pathology.[80]

Apparently not completely satisfied with these results, Freedman proceeded to perform a series of experiments with various groups of people in which room sizes were varied to find out what effect this would have on their performance and behavior. But these tests also resulted in the primary conclusion that crowding per se had no general negative or positive effect on human behavior, leading Freedman to the principle that crowding by itself has neither good effects nor bad effects on people but rather *serves to intensify the individual's typical reactions to the situation.* If he ordinarily would find the circumstances pleasant, would enjoy having people around him, would think of the other people as friends, would in a word have a positive reaction to the other people, he will have a more positive reaction under conditions of high density. On the other hand, if ordinarily he would dislike the other people, find it unpleasant having them around, feel aggressive toward them, and in general have a negative reaction to the presence of the other people, he will have a more negative reaction under conditions of high density. . . . Thus, people do not respond to density in a uniform way, they do not find it either always pleasant or always unpleasant. Rather, their response to density depends almost entirely on their response to the situation itself. Density acts primarily to make this response, whatever it is, stronger.[81]

Thus, 100,000 people crowded into a football stadium respond more lustily and enthusiastically than if the stadium is only half-filled. Conversely, a ride on a subway car is much less pleasant if the car is crowded instead of only half filled. Or, to look at it from an opposite point of view, people at a house party oftentimes all crowd into the kitchen to increase their enjoyment, but people sitting in a courtroom waiting for the judge to hear their traffic violations all spread out to reduce the unpleasantness of the situation. The unifying principle in all of these situations is that, as Freedman sums it up, crowding "intensifies the normal reaction—making a bad experience worse and a good experience better."[82]

Consequently, Freedman concludes, the "cities of the world are not doomed. They are not necessarily condemned to high crime rates, riots, and violence. As the population of the world increases, there will not necessarily be an increase in aggressiveness and antisocial behavior and a general breakdown in society. Homo sapiens is not doomed to extinction because of population density; the race will not destroy itself simply because it will be crowded."[83]

However, although Freedman establishes that population density in itself does not *cause* crime and other deviant behavior, this does not necessarily mean that density may not provide an increased *occasion* for crime. For example, it is well known that the crime rate in rural areas of relatively low population density is less than that in urban areas with higher population density. As Freedman notes, the "crime rate per 100,000 people is approximately 1,000 crimes per year in rural areas, 2,300 in the suburbs, 3,400 in small cities, and 5,300 in larger cities."[84]

Freedman suggests that this variation in crime rates is due to population size rather than population density. But his analysis in this case concerns itself only with comparisons between various metropolitan areas rather than between metropolitan and rural areas.

Density clearly is not the cause of this variation in terms of creating pathological behavior, as Freedman so ably demonstrates. But, since population density increases social interactions between people, there is no reason to think that density may not provide an increased occasion for crime, just as it provides greater opportunities for beneficial transactions. Merchants, for example, love crowds, but so do pickpockets—and crowds are more prevalent in big cities than in rural areas. Crime would thus appear to be a possible function of density insofar as density increases opportunities for antisocial as well as socially beneficial interactions.

Population density in major metropolitan areas—where most crimes are committed—has been decreasing in recent years. Yet, between 1960 and 1971, the national crime rate per 100,000 population increased about 190 percent—hardly an indictment of density as the controlling factor.

Still, we are often told that population growth is a main "cause" of this escalating crime wave. A classic example of this view is a full-page advertisement that appeared in the *New York Times* sponsored by an organization called the Campaign to Check the Population Explosion. Under the headline, "Have you ever been mugged? Well, you may be," was a picture of a man grappling with a mugger. "Is there an answer?" the ad copy asked. "Yes, birth control is one," it responded. But, during the period when population growth was supposedly causing a crime explosion, the rate of population growth was being rapidly shaved in half, from almost 2 percent to one percent, and population grew only about 14 percent.

The ad went on to state that "city slums—jampacked with juveniles, thousands of them idle—breed discontent, drug addiction and chaos." There is a grain of a half-truth here insofar as juvenile delinquency goes up disproportionately during a period of population growth because there are more young people around in relation to the rest of the population and it is young people who, by definition, are juvenile delinquents.

Because of the "baby boom" of the late forties and early fifties, there was an increase of more than 50 percent in the number of young people in their teens and early twenties during the 1960–71 period. Since this age group in 1972 accounted for about 50 percent of all arrests, it is apparent that this change in age distribution had an impact on the total crime rate. But, all other things being equal, this impact would have been no more than 25 percent, not 191 percent. So the change in the age distribution can in no way be used to explain the explosion in the crime rate during the sixties. Nor does it make any sense to propose population control as a solution to crime or youth problems, since not only would the results of such an approach be relatively insignificant but they would amount to nothing more than throwing out the baby with the bath water.

Thus, reasons for the rapid increase in crime during the sixties and solutions to the problem must be found elsewhere—most probably in society's attitude towards crime and the ability of government to mete out swift, assured

127

justice to criminal offenders. Meanwhile, population growth can help to alleviate crime in the future by providing continuing economic advancement for lower-income groups among whom the incidence of crime tends to be the highest.

Space. Population density in metropolitan areas is currently declining rather than increasing, resulting in more land area per person. For example, as is pointed out by Kingsley Davis, Ford Professor of Sociology and director of international population and urban research at the University of California, the "density of the New York urbanized region is dropping, not increasing, as the population grows. The reason is that the territory covered by the urban agglomeration is growing faster than the population: it grew by 51 per cent from 1950 to 1960, whereas the population rose by 15 per cent."

However, Davis goes on to say, New York is not the only city in the region that is expanding. So are Philadelphia, Trenton, New Haven, and so on. Consequently, since the whole area is becoming one big polynucleated city, its population cannot long expand without a rise in density. "One can of course imagine," comments Davis, "that cities may cease to grow and may even shrink in size while the population in general continues to multiply. Even this dream, however, would not permanently solve the problem of space." Thus, he sums up, it "seems plain that the only way to stop urban crowding . . . is to reduce the overall rate of population growth."[85]

The first thing that can be said about Davis' observations is that they reflect a bias against high population density that is not borne out by the facts. Some people may prefer high-density living; others may not. And the same people may prefer it at one stage of their lives and not prefer it at another.

The second thing that can be said is that those people who prefer a low level of density that is not available in their region can always move to another less populated region. It is a big country. But this, of course, brings up the inevitable question: Are we not eventually going to run out of space?

From the standpoint of the whole country, the fact is that the United States is one of the most sparsely populated nations in the world, with less than a tenth of the population density of a country such as the Netherlands and also much less density than many other advanced as well as developing nations of the world. Currently, there are more than ten acres of land, the equivalent of nine football fields, for every man, woman, and child in the United States. If our population should double, the amount of land area per person will be reduced to five acres. Will this mean that the amount of space will also be cut in half? Answer: No, the exact opposite is the case, since space is three-dimensional rather than two-dimensional, and population growth increases man's ability to utilize this three-dimensional space more fully and effectively.

For example, up until the latter part of the nineteenth century, we had the capability of constructing buildings with maximum heights of perhaps fifty feet, or three or four stories. Since then, our population has approximately quadrupled, but our building ability has increased more than twenty or twenty-five times, to 100 stories and 1000 feet and more. In addition, we now have the capability of using space up to 100,000 feet above ground level for travel. Furthermore, technological advances in underground excavation, such as new tunneling techniques, now provide the opportunity to utilize space down to several hundred feet below ground for transportation facilities, power plants, industrial operations, and other economic activities, freeing ground-level space for residences, parks, and other uses more directly associated with increased social welfare. Thus, far from causing us to "run out of space," population growth is resulting in an increase per person in the amount of usable space effectively available for human betterment.

Family Size. In recent years, a number of studies and articles have appeared claiming that children from small families do better than children from large families. In "Dumber by the Dozen," for example, University of Michigan psychology professor Robert B. Zajonc states that research has found a "clear effect of family size on IQ, and an effect of birth order within a given family size. The brightest children came from the smallest families, and within a given family size, the brightest children were those who came along early. The first child in a family of two, for example, got the highest scores, while the last child in a family of nine produced the lowest scores."[86] In "The Case for Small Families," E. James Lieberman, psychiatrist and consultant at the National Institute of Mental Health, states that the child from the small family is not only brighter but more creative, bigger and taller, and more vigorous and independent than his large-family counterpart.[87]

Claims such as these are based on studies derived from analyses of large groups of children and young adults. But the results of such studies are only as good as the data fed into them. How good is the data? Not very.

Kenneth W. Terhune, principal psychologist at the environmental systems department of the National Institutes of Health, reviewed more than 400 books and articles analyzing the consequences of family size. According to Terhune, one of the major pitfalls in such studies is "to interpret as family size consequences those effects that are due to other variables."[88]

For example, it is well known that people in higher socioeconomic classes tend to have small families, while people in lower socioeconomic brackets tend to have large families. Consequently, any study that purports to show the effects of family size must control for these socioeconomic variables. Otherwise, what the study will measure is not the effects of family size but the effects of socioeconomic class.

But, as Terhune notes, this is very difficult to do since family size has been found to correlate with so many different kinds of socioeconomic or demographic variables as to defy their complete control in studying family-size effects. Among these variables are religion, race, income of parents, occupational status of parents, educational level of parents, rural/urban residence, country of birth of parents, and an individual's year of birth.

Terhune points out that "frequently studies of family size effects will have intentionally or unintentionally controlled for one or more of these variables by restricting the samples to certain groups, such as urban dwellers, whites, or eleven-year-olds. Seldom, however, will studies control for more than one or two variables so that family size effects may be compared across categories, such as between middle class and working class groups. In nearly all studies, consequently, questions will remain of whether the results would be the same in other groups and/or whether the apparent effects of family size may be explained by demographic variables."[89]

Based on these qualifications, Terhune concludes, in the case of the relationship between family size and intelligence, that "only about one to three percent of variance in intelligence is associated with family size differentials. And of that limited variance, part is due to heredity (duller people having larger families) and part is due to environment. Only in the latter effects can intelligence be said to be a *consequence* of family size."[90]

What this means is that, if the first child in a large family has an IQ of 110, succeeding children will have progressively lower IQs ranging from 109 to 107. But even this conclusion is not firm because, as Terhune notes, it "still is not clear what proportion of the intelligence–family size relationship is due to 'nurture' as opposed to 'nature.' " In other words, if the one to three percent variance suggested by Terhune is due to "nature," or heredity, rather than "nurture," or environment, then the effect of family size on intelligence is nil.

At the same time, it should be noted that studies have also found that only-children and first-borns have lower intelligence levels than second- and third-born children. In addition, the small family has been found to have some problems of its own, for, as Terhune reports, the "only evidence that family size is related to severe mental illness (psychosis) is the tendency for only children and perhaps small family children generally to develop schizophrenia. This could be explainable as the combined result of inheritance and low fertility of schizophrenics. The relation of family size to neurosis is unclear, but . . . there are indications that identified neurotics come disproportionately from one- and possibly two-child families. Tentatively, evidence suggests that the only child may be more prone to alcoholism."[91]

The effect of family size has also been analyzed in relation to a variety of other social, psychological, and health factors. But all of these analyses are subject to the same qualifications as the analyses of family size and intelligence discussed above. The data are at best inconclusive and, as Terhune sums up, the "caveat that must be made . . . is that in nearly all cases the data have established relationships but not causal effects of family size."[92]

Because of past population growth, the United States is a nation of large families, and the results have hardly been bad. Conversely, we have no experience with what it would be like to be a nation of small families under zero population growth, but the current state of such countries as Sweden where such families prevail is not all that inviting.

Perhaps the most sensible thing that can be said about the effects of family size is the observation of Jane Jacobs, who asks "who knows whether it isn't extremely important for some human beings to come from large families and some from small ones? We ought to be wary of anything that tends to destroy human diversity. We surely need diversity in sizes and kinds of families just as much as we need diversity of talents, occupational preferences, and personalities."[93]

Social Structure. Perhaps the most basic argument against population growth from the viewpoint of social welfare is that it causes change that can result in a breakdown of social structure. There is no doubt that population growth causes change, and change, according to Alvin Toffler, author of *Future Shock,* is a "current so powerful today that it overturns institutions, shifts our values and shrivels our roots."[94] Moreover, Toffler goes on to say, "future shock" caused by change "is no longer a distantly potential danger, but a real sickness from which increasingly large numbers already suffer. This psycho-biological condition can be described in medical and psychiatric terms. It is the disease of change."[95]

However, the most basic change that might affect social structure is probably physical mobility. The United States is indeed a mobile country, but as Ben Wattenberg and Richard Scammon comment, this has been exaggerated well out of proportion. We have all heard the Census Bureau estimate that one out of five (actually 19 percent) of all Americans move every year, a huge figure that conjures up the image of a population rootlessly flitting about the country in search of who knows what. But, the fact is that, each year, of every 100 Americans, 80 do not move at all, 13 move only to a different residence within the same county, 3 move to another county within the same state, and 3 move to another state (0.5 came to the U.S. from another country). As Wattenberg and Scammon point out, the key figure from the standpoint of mobility is the 3 percent of people who move to another state, since the others generally remain in close physical and cultural proximity to their former homes. But even this 3 percent figure is somewhat inflated, since it includes out-of-state college students and young persons joining the military, many of whom will eventually return home, and "local movers," who move across state lines but remain in the same metropolitan area or urban community.

Consequently, the total percentage of Americans who made a major move from their state of birth in the decade from 1950 to 1960 was not 200, as would be implied by the one-in-five mobility figure, but 9. And this interstate mobility is not a current phenomenon, but has been common for the past century at least, ranging from a low of 4 percent in the Depression to a high of 11 percent in the period 1850–60, and probably even higher in the preceding years. But, even with this significant degree of mobility, the 1960 census revealed that 70 percent of native Americans were living in the same state in which they were born. "Rootless people?" ask Wattenberg and Scammon. "If anything, we seem to be developing a strong system of national roots, American roots. . . . Non-statistically, it was all summed up neatly by John Steinbeck in his recent *Travels with Charley,* an account of a trip around the entire continental United States. Said Steinbeck: 'From start to finish I found no strangers. . . . These are my people and this is my country.' "[96]

But what about the sense of community in American life today? It is sometimes said, for example, that the neighborhood spirit that binds people together is declining. But, insofar as this may be the case, it is due not to social apathy but the fact that improved transportation and communications and increased leisure make it possible today to be a member of a diverse number of area-wide, city-wide, country-wide, and even worldwide communities of a social, economic, and political nature. Thus, if the neighborhood community is being neglected today, it is a result of oversight rather than anomie, and, if the number of local community groups now operating throughout the country is any indication, it is a situation that apparently quickly corrects itself when a neighborhood problem arises.

What about the effects of change on the family? Certainly, here the effects are deleterious. We have all read about how changing social conditions are buffeting the family unmercifully and that it may be only a few more years before it entirely disappears. Undoubtedly, the family is under considerable strain today, but much of this is due not to social changes per se, but the attack of antifamily critics who would do away with it if they could. Still, funeral notices for the family are premature, for as Kingsley Davis of the University of California observes, the "preoccupation with change in most studies of the modern family is ironic. Of all social institutions, the family shows least evidence of change. The family in industrial society is amazingly similar to that in primitive society. In fact, in many ways, the modern family is more 'primitive,' in the sense of being elementary, than the family in primitive societies."[97]

Finally, what about technological changes that might overturn other types of social institutions? All that can be said here is: The sooner, the better. One of the problems of any society is that social institutions tend to resist change, while one of the beneficial results of population growth is that it forces continual change on these institutions. It forces them either to improve or get out of the way for new social arrangements to be made. This is what is happening, for example, in some of our older cities, where people are "fleeing" not because of high density, but because these urban areas are no longer functioning well due to government mismanagement or outmoded methods or both.

This is what social commentator Caroline Bird, author of *The Crowding Syndrome,* has in mind when she comments that

most of the systems on which our society rests—both private and public—are near collapse because of sheer weight of numbers, and just adding on to them or simply building bigger systems of the same type won't solve the problem. We need to allow some of the most antiquated to actually break down completely. And then we need to come up with entirely new systems designed to handle the greater numbers. . . . We're so used to simply slapping on another patch that I think it will take real breakdowns to jog people into coming up with new ways of doing things. I'm an optimist in that I think that once jogged, the people of this country are very resourceful, responsible and constructive. . . . One of the virtues of having a complex society is that breakdowns can be sustained without the whole system going out. . . . Basically, we've been trying to preserve the status quo, with a moderate allowance for orderly expansion. But even if our systems continued to be productive at the rates we assumed—and once they're overloaded they can't—we would be losing ground. We have to come up with ways of increasing productivity—thru technological and social reform and by ditching the obsolete facilities we can no longer afford to carry.[98]

Conclusion

Population growth plays a major role in helping to improve the social welfare of all Americans. It provides not only the economic advancement and technological development necessary for human betterment, but also results in a society that is more open and responsive to opportunities for improvement and more progressive in achieving social advancement for all people, in particular, minorities.

By contrast, a stationary population will make improvements in social welfare more difficult to achieve because it will result in a slowdown in material progress, aging of the population, and increasing social rigidity. In addition, lack of population growth will seriously endanger the economic and health status of the elderly and the viability and livability of cities.

Continuing improvements in social welfare are thus greatly dependent on population growth. For with growth will come a change from our current metropolitan to the megalopolitan community of the future. And, as Wattenberg and Scammon sum up, there is "one thing that can be stated—and restated—with certainty: there are no apparent urban-growth problems in the United States generally, or in the megalopolis specifically, that are unsolvable. More important, there is every indication that the solutions to the solvable problems will provide an even better—if somewhat different—way of life."[99]

6

U.S. POPULATION GROWTH AND POLITICAL FREEDOM

The United States was born in an atmosphere of population growth and political freedom. The fact that these two conditions existed at the time of the country's founding is no coincidence.

Population growth was one of the major factors prompting the colonies to throw off the yoke of England and declare their independence. When the colonies were small and relatively isolated, they had no choice but to accommodate themselves to economic restrictions placed on them by England. But with population growth came both economic development and increasing colonial power. The restrictions on economic activity thus became increasingly more onerous at the same time that the power of the colonies to resist them became greater. Population growth in the colonies consequently set in motion a chain of events that eventually issued in the Declaration of Independence, wherein one of the specific charges made against King George III is that he "endeavoured to prevent the population of these states."

Nor is this relationship between population growth and political freedom peculiar to the United States. In practically all the countries of Western Europe, the flowering of democracy and political freedom also coincided with a rise in the rate of population growth.

Furthermore, in more recent times, the same symbiosis between population growth and political freedom can be observed. For example, whereas major population growth in developed countries occurred a century or two ago, population growth in developing nations did not begin in earnest until after World War II. And there, too, population growth has been accompanied by growing political independence, as country after country in the Third World has rejected colonialism.

135

By contrast, one can look back into history over thousands of years—a time when population growth was infinitesimally slow—and find no examples of the broad political freedoms we take for granted today. Perhaps it could be said that these freedoms were first conceived and developed in ancient Greece and Rome. But there, too, population growth played an important role in the development of the concept of freedom, a concept which vanished with depopulation. Then as today, it is only under the impetus of population growth that political freedom becomes an idea whose time has come.

As Colin Clark puts it, the problem is that

progress—toward a more productive economy, toward better and freer political forms, toward better education, science, and culture—does not come easily or automatically. The forces opposing progress toward these desirable ends are always formidable. There are many examples to show that population growth provides a beneficial stimulus, often indeed is the only stimulus powerful enough to shake men out of their established ways and customs, and make them seek something better. Americans, who have had a history of steady and rapid population growth for three centuries, tend to take it for granted, and so underestimate the important part it has played in developing their institutions. This proposition becomes clear enough once we state its converse—had population been stationary, or only slowly growing, over this period, the American economy, political institutions, and culture would all be quite unrecognizably different from what they are now. This relationship between population growth and progress holds true not only in the realm of fact, but also in the realm of ideas. It is when populations are (or are expected to be) comparatively stationary that statist ideas are likely to flourish. . . . It is as communities become larger and move into a stream of progress that governmental control of economic life is found to be both impracticable and undesirable.[1]

How Population Growth Promotes Political Freedom

Federalist Paper No. 10 is justly famous for its brilliant exposition of the basic problem facing popular or representative government. In the words of James Madison, the paper's author, this problem, which is at the heart of individual liberty, is how to "break and control the violence of faction" which otherwise results in measures being "decided, not according to the rule of justice and the rights of the minor party, but by the superior force of an interested and overbearing majority."[2]

By faction, Madison meant a "number of citizens, whether amounting to a majority or minority of the whole, who are united and actuated by some common impulse of passion, or of interest, adverse to the rights of other citizens, or to the permanent and aggregate interests of the community."[3]

Madison was primarily concerned with showing that a republic is far superior to a pure democracy in terms of its ability to control the mischief caused by faction. The major reason for this, he pointed out, is that a republic is a representative government in which responsibility is delegated to a small number of citizens elected by the rest, thus effectively short-circuiting factional passions. But the question then arose as to "whether small or extensive republics are most favorable to the election of proper guardians of the public weal."

An extensive republic is more favorable in this regard for two reasons, Madison responded. In the first place, it

is to be remarked that however small the republic may be the representatives must be raised to a certain number in order to guard against the cabals of a few; and that however large it may be they must be limited to a certain number in order to guard against the confusion of a multitude. Hence, the number of representatives in the two cases not being in proportion to that of the constituents, and being proportionally greatest in the small republic, it follows that if the proportion of fit characters be not less in the large than in the small republic, the former will present a greater option, and consequently a greater probability of a fit choice. In the next place, as each representative will be chosen by a greater number of citizens in the large than in the small republic, it will be more difficult for unworthy candidates to practice with success the vicious arts by which elections are too often carried; and the suffrages of the people being more free, will be more likely to center on men who possess the most attractive merit and the most diffusive and established characters.

Furthermore, Madison stated, factious combinations are to be dreaded less in large republics because the

smaller the society, the fewer probably will be the distinct parties and interests composing it; the fewer the distinct parties and interests, the more frequently will a majority be found of the same party; and the smaller the number of individuals composing a majority, and the smaller the compass within which they are placed, the more easily will they concert and execute their plans of oppression. Extend the sphere and you take in a greater variety of parties and interests; you make it less probable that a majority of the whole will have a common motive to invade the rights of other citizens; or if such a common motive exists, it will be more difficult for all who feel it to discover their own strength and to act in unison with each other. Besides other impediments, it may be remarked that, where there is a consciousness of unjust or dishonorable purposes, communication is always checked by distrust in proportion to the number whose concurrence is necessary. Hence, it clearly appears that the same advantage which a republic has over a democracy in controlling the effects of faction is enjoyed by a large over a small republic.[4]

But it is not only population size that provides protection against the power-hungry manipulations of contesting factions. It is also the existence of population growth, for with population growth comes a general improvement in the lot of people, minimizing the desire of citizens to form factions and blunting the thrust of those that are formed. Conversely, decline in population

137

growth, with its accompanying slowdown in economic and social advancement, increases pressures to use factional politics to secure by governmental decree those benefits that are not being attained because of a lack of normal growth. However, as Madison clearly foresaw, the consequence of such factionalism is an inevitable increase in governmental power and special privilege at the expense of individual liberty and political freedom.

This inverse relationship between population and governmental growth can be traced from the founding of the country. During the nineteenth century and into the first decade of this century, population grew rapidly, although at gradually declining rates varying from a high of more than 35 percent per decade at the start of the period to a low of 21 percent per decade at the period's end. Yet, after this century and more of very rapid population growth, total governmental expenditures in 1913 accounted for only 8.8 percent of gross national product.[5]

For the next thirty years, population growth slowed down further and then went into a precipitous decline in the thirties, decreasing from 21 percent per decade in 1900–10 to only 7.2 percent per decade in 1930–40. During approximately the same period, total government expenditures as a percentage of gross national product did not decline, but increased nearly four times, from 8.8 percent in 1913 to 19.6 percent in 1932 and 32.7 percent in 1942,[6] although it should of course be noted that 1942 was a war year with heavy expenditures for national defense.

The next two decades saw an upsurge in population growth, from the 7.1 percent per decade in 1940 to 18.4 percent per decade in 1960. But, the percentage of total governmental expenditures to GNP actually decreased slightly during this time, from 32.7 percent in 1942 to 32.5 percent in 1962.[7]

Beginning in the late fifties and early sixties, population growth once again went into a sharp decline, decreasing from 18.5 percent per decade in the fifties to 13.3 percent per decade during the seventies, and down to a current decadal rate well below 10 percent. Meanwhile, total government expenditures as a percentage of GNP once again began to rise, from 32.5 percent in 1962 to 36.1 percent in 1972.[8]

The pattern shown over the past two centuries of American history is thus one of governmental power and control increasing as the rate of population growth decreases. This inverse relationship first came to light in public discussion in the thirties, when it appeared to many that zero population growth was to be the wave of the future. It was Keynes who first pointed out that population growth in the past had evoked a good volume of free-market investment that had on the whole been well directed and had maintained the economy in a state of reasonably full employment. However, with population stagnation, Keynes observed, much of this would inevitably be replaced by government direction of investment.[9]

In America, Alvin H. Hansen, a leading economist of the thirties, applied

Keynes' observations to the United States, pointing out that the economy formerly had been stimulated by rapid population growth and the discovery and settlement of new territory. But, with population becoming static and the frontier closed, the only dynamic element that remained, he thought, was technological innovation. But innovation, he feared, would not absorb as much investment for economic expansion as the other two factors had in the past. Hansen thus concluded that more federal regulation of economic life was inevitable in a "mature economy."[10]

But Hansen's belief in the dynamism of technological innovation as a positive counterbalance to the negative economic forces brought on by a stationary population was misplaced, not only because declining population growth sucks the vitality from technological as well as economic advancement but because zero population growth positively requires that technological innovations be suppressed by governmental regulation.

Colin Clark relates how this connection between zero population growth and zero technological development was stated clearly and directly by England's Lord Stamp in a presidential address to the British Association for the Advancement of Science in 1936.

"Perhaps birth control for people," stated Stamp, "demands ultimately birth control for their impedimenta." For, so long as population is rising, he explained, the product of new inventions and new investments can be readily absorbed. But when populations become stationary or decline (which Stamp expected soon to be the case in all Western industrial countries), then the effects of new plans and processes in displacing the old will be much more keenly felt.

According to Clark, Stamp then went on to make, in all seriousness, the "astonishing" proposal that the introduction of all new processes should be deliberately slowed down so as to insure that all the men working on the older process had retired, and all the plant was physically worn out, before the new process was allowed. This state of affairs, he added, would be much easier to bring about if industry were cartelized, and not subject to competition. "It might," he added, "be deemed proper to put a special levy on those new industries that turn out to be profitable and to use it to relieve the social charges of the dislocation of labor and the obsolescence of capital."[11]

Currently, we are in a period comparable to the thirties from the standpoint of a rapid decline in the rate of population growth. And proposals similar to those made in the thirties for a "planned economy" and "technology assessment" are once again surfacing.

Increasing government control is dramatically reflected in the growth of the federal budget. It took 186 years for the federal budget to reach $100 billion in 1962. It took only nine more years for the budget to hit $200 billion. Only four more years were required for the budget to break $300 billion in 1975.

This tripling of the federal budget from $100 billion in 1962 to $300 billion in 1975 occurred at a time when the population growth rate was being cut by more than half, from close to 2 percent to 0.7 percent. This was a time when government was telling us that we were being threatened by a "population explosion"!

There was, of course, an explosion during this period. However, it was an explosion not in population but in government, an explosion stimulated by declining population growth and now resulting in ever-increasing restrictions on individual liberty and political freedom. As Caspar W. Weinberger, former secretary of Health, Education and Welfare, states, after "5½ years in Washington, my single over-riding observation is that an all-pervasive federal government, unless checked, may take away our most precious personal freedoms while shattering the very foundations of our economic system. Consider this: In 1970, the federal-budget outlay stood at $196.6 billion; it is now $358.9 billion—an increase of 83 percent! Apart from its sheer magnitude, federal spending has shifted toward programs that reduce the remaining freedom of individuals. We are creating an edifice of law and regulation that has intruded into the lives of all of us—both those it seeks to help and those who do the helping."[12]

Nor are the prospects any brighter for the future, for 75 percent, or $261 billion, of the U.S. federal budget for 1976 was for so-called uncontrollable expenditures.[13] These are budget outlays over which neither the president nor Congress can exercise effective control during the year ahead because the expenditures have been mandated by law in previous years. To put this another way, 75 percent of 1976 federal expenditures consisted of outlays that had to be made regardless of whether population increased, decreased, or remained the same. And, between 1967 and 1976, these "uncontrollable" expenditures dramatically increased, from about 50 percent to the 1976 proportion of 75 percent of the total federal budget.

The rate at which the per capita cost of these uncontrollable expenditures increases in the future would be slowed as a result of population growth. But, lacking population growth, these expenditures will create an increasingly intolerable per capita burden on taxpayers.

This is not to say that these "uncontrollable" expenditures cannot ever be controlled. But this would require that government oppose the desires of various pressure groups—factions—whose income is dependent on the expenditures, two-thirds of which are payments to individuals. By spurring economic and social progress, population growth would make such government decisions at least politically feasible. But, without the economic and social advancement provided by population growth to alleviate factional pressures for increasing shares of a static economic pie, it is difficult to imagine such governmental decisions being made.

Instead, in the face of the slowdown in economic and social progress resulting from declining population growth, government is more likely to use fiscal and monetary policy to devalue the currency and pay off the demands of factional pressure groups with inflated dollars. But this can only result in a further erosion of freedom and an increased dependence of the citizen on the state. For, as Colin Clark points out, in a

> well-governed country, where the currency maintains its value, a prudent citizen does and should try to make provision for old age and similar needs through his own savings and insurance. Once confidence in the currency has been lost, however, people are naturally much less willing to make the sacrifice entailed in such savings: they set up political demands for the state to carry these responsibilities for them. "Devaluation" or "inflation," as it is commonly though mistakenly called, is welcomed by shortsighted businessmen who see immediate profits for themselves, but who do not see the ultimate consequences; and it is also welcomed by longsighted statists who look forward to the increasing subordination of the individual's decisions to the state's decisions.[14]

The fantastic explosion in recent years of "state decisions" in the form of the federal welfare state is well documented by Roger A. Freeman, senior fellow at the Hoover Institution. Freeman points out that, between 1952 and 1972, when the rate of population growth was for the most part declining, spending for domestic public services (health, education, welfare, et cetera) multiplied more than ten times, from $12.3 billion to $131 billion.[15] During the same period, GNP increased 3.5 times, or only about one-third as fast.

But there is an interesting paradox here, which Freeman notes. This is that, although federal expenditures on *domestic* programs increased three times faster than GNP, *total* federal expenditures increased at about the same rate as GNP, or about 3.5 times.[16] Consequently, total federal expenditures in 1952 amounted to 21.2 percent of GNP, while in 1972 they accounted for 22 percent of GNP, an increase of only 0.8 percent.

How do we account for this paradox? Simple. While spending on health, education, welfare, and other domestic programs was increasing more than ten times, or plus 962 percent, between 1952 and 1972, expenditures on national defense increased only 68 percent, paralleling the simultaneous rise in prices. As Freeman observes, expressed in *constant* dollars, military outlays in 1972 were no higher than they were in 1952; they were substantially lower than they were in 1967. In relative terms, defense spending fell during this period, from 66 to 32 percent of the total budget and from 13.5 to 6.8 percent of the GNP. Spending for domestic public services meanwhile multiplied more than ten times (plus 962 percent), and its share of the budget jumped from 17 to 54 percent (the remaining 14 percent of the budget went for interest, veterans, international affairs, and space). Outlays for education, health, and welfare multiplied more than fifteen times—an increase of 1416 percent; outlays for all other domestic purposes combined multiplied more than six times. Over

141

two-thirds of the $174 billion increase in federal revenues and expenditures between 1952 and 1972 was allocated to domestic programs. Approximately one-half of the total budget growth went just to education, health, and welfare, approximately one-seventh to interest, veterans, international affairs, and space, and approximately one-fifth to national defense.

"It is becoming apparent," Freeman sums up, "that the shift in national priorities, which some political and academic groups have been demanding for years, that is, 'from the warfare state to the welfare state,' has taken place. It probably would have been impossible to expand social welfare programs at the rapid rate we experienced since the mid-fifties without cutting into national defense. Congress could not have provided sufficient revenues by boosting taxes."[17]

For, as Freeman notes, even with the massive reduction in spending on national defense, all governmental revenues (federal, state, and local) went up 310 percent between 1952 and 1972, while GNP and national income increased only 234 and 224 percent, respectively. As a result, total receipts of all governments went up from 26 percent of GNP and 30.8 percent of national income in 1952 to 31.9 percent of GNP and 39.1 percent of national income in 1972.[18] One can imagine what the increase in taxes would have been like if the percentage of national defense expenditures had remained the same instead of decreasing 50 percent in relation to GNP during this twenty-year period.

Furthermore, although the vast infusion of money into domestic programs that occurred from 1952 to 1972 undoubtedly helped some people (although not necessarily in all cases the people it was supposed to help), there is no denying that whatever improvements resulted were in no way proportional to the expenditures. Freeman points out, for example, that "the status and products of our educational system do not reflect the fact that eight times as much public money is now being allocated to it each year as two decades ago, while enrollment meanwhile only doubled. . . . Attempts to correlate tangible achievements with the resources applied to a program have cast great doubt on the idea that improvements are necessarily proportionate to the amounts spent or even tend to be favorably affected. In case after case we must question whether there is a positive cost-quality relationship or whether expenditures have been counterproductive. Huge federal spending has not brought forth social miracles, but has instead created resentment among those who felt cheated when the promised results failed to materialize as the money was dissipated."[19]

Expenditures on national defense, of course, have also been cited for excessive waste in the past. But a reduction of 50 percent in the percentage of these expenditures in relation to gross national product has left even less room for Pentagon snafus, while seriously endangering the security of the country and, ultimately, the political freedom of all of its people.

One would have to be a confirmed recluse not to be aware of the potentially disastrous shift in the balance of power that has occurred in recent years between the United States and the Soviet Union as a result of the shriveling up of American national defense expenditures. For example, according to an extensive 1976 study made by John Collins, senior defense specialist for the Library of Congress, the balance of military power is beginning to tip so definitely toward the Soviet Union that the United States may have to reassess its position as a global power. If the United States is to remedy its eroding military position, the study stated, it must significantly increase its military spending, redirect its military budget, and concentrate on fewer areas. Otherwise, the U.S. must accept reduced status as a world power because the Soviet Union continues to increase its numerical superiority over U.S. military forces in almost all important categories, and the country's former qualitative advantage in certain high-technology areas is "slowly slipping away."[20]

A similar warning was sounded by former Secretary of Defense James Schlesinger in an article published in the February, 1976, issue of *Fortune* magazine. Schlesinger cited the expansion of Soviet military power, coupled with the retrenchment of American power and policy, as posing the most formidable threat to the survival of the western world since the 1930s. He said the "specter of Soviet hegemony" is haunting not only Europe but Japan, Korea, and the Middle East. "That specter arises from the steady expansion of the military power of the Soviet state, but it remains contingent upon the faltering of American purpose, as America . . . becomes preoccupied with its internal problems and internal divisions," he stated. "The growing reach of Soviet military power and the psychological aura it increasingly conveys . . . may be employed directly for intervention or seizure, but is more likely to be exploited indirectly to extract political, economic, or military concessions. To avoid such concessions, deterrence through countervailing military power remains an indispensable requirement."[21]

In the January, 1976, issue of *Foreign Affairs,* Paul H. Nitze, a former deputy secretary of defense in a Democratic administration and later a member of the strategic arms limitation delegation in the Republican White House, had this to say about the balance of nuclear power: "In sum, the ability of U.S. nuclear power to destroy without question the bulk of Soviet industry and a large proportion of the Soviet population is by no means as clear as it once was, even if one assumes most of the U.S. striking power to be available and directed to this end."[22]

Meanwhile, Malcolm R. Currie, the Defense Department's research director, told Congress in February, 1976, that "the Soviet Union can achieve dominance in deployed military technology in the 1980's." He said he based this judgment on "a very large and determined effort" by Russia as United States investment in military research, development, and procurement declines.[23]

Also testifying before Congress at the same time, General Fred C. Weyand,

Army chief of staff, said the U.S. continues to hold a technological lead over the Soviet Union in most areas critical to national security. "But that lead has been diminishing," he said. "In some important areas it is gone; the Soviets are ahead." According to Weyand, Russia is now able to "project power at great distances"; is improving its ability to operate naval units, aircraft, and resupply forces far from its shores; and has global command, control, and communications ability. "This is a striking transformation for a nation historically preoccupied with defense of the homeland," he said. "From all indications, the future Soviet strategy will be world dominance, with technology as one of the key drivers. It is by no means clear that the Soviet Union regards nuclear war as unthinkable. There is strong evidence to the contrary, that the Soviets do not accept the premise of mutual suicide. . . . Their growing countermilitary offensive capability and damage-limiting defensive capabilities at least open the door some day for potential blackmail or offensive probes."[24]

However, whereas decreasing population growth has hastened the decline of American defense capabilities, increasing population growth can greatly expand the nation's ability to improve its military preparedness in the future. This is because expenditures on national defense, in contrast to domestic expenditures, are not population-intensive, that is, it does not require proportionally greater expenditures to defend a country of 300 million people than it does a country of 200 million people. In fact, the exact opposite is more likely the case; it probably requires little if anything more. Consequently, a country growing towards a population of 300 million is much better able than a country stagnating at 200 million to afford a strong national defense because the former will not only have more funds to spend but the per capita costs will be lower.

In addition, population size itself is a critical factor in the determination of national power. For as A.F.K. Organski and Alan Lamborn of the University of Michigan and Bruce Bueno de Mesquita of Michigan State University point out, the "three variables generally considered the most important of the many determinants of national power are population size, level of economic productivity, and level of political mobilization. . . . The rationale for considering population size a major determinant of national power is fairly clear. After all, it is people who fight and work and consume and carry within themselves the national culture and ideology; and it is these activities that are the sources of the capacity of one nation to influence the behavior of other nations."[25]

According to these authors, the

major world powers all have populations of at least 50 million. A population of this size appears to be at least a prerequisite of great power status, though not a guarantee. The two great super-powers (and their most troublesome rivals: China and Japan) have populations of over 100 million. Total population size alone provides at least a partial explanation of the diminishing importance of the West European powers that dominated the world in the 19th Century. They simply do not possess

144

the demographic resources to compete with nations four times their size once these nations become economically developed and politically mobilized. On the basis of their size, the United States and the Soviet Union appear assured of continued leadership for some time to come, but face clear future threats from China (increasingly recognized), India (generally overlooked), and a United Europe if true political unity is ever achieved.[26]

Organski et al. go on to note that it is not population size alone that helps to determine national power but *effective* population, which they define as the number of employed nonagricultural workers.[27] In 1970, for example, the Soviet Union had 241 million people, while the United States had 203 million. But the U.S. had an effective population of 33 percent of total population, or 60.5 million, in comparison to 27 percent, or 58 million, for the USSR. By contrast, China and India had populations of 740 and 537 million, but their effective populations were only 10 and 9 percent of total population, or 62.1 and 38 million people, respectively.[28] China and India also had gross national products of only $90 billion and $43 billion, respectively, in comparison to $866 billion and $413 billion, respectively, for the United States and the Soviet Union.[29] So, as Organski *et al.* note, China and India owe their present power status not to economic productivity but simply to sheer population size.[30] But, as they add, because these nations have a low percentage of effective to total population, they have an "immense reservoir of untapped power compared to a nation like the United States that is already using its population relatively effectively."[31] Thus, for the United States, population growth will continue to be a critical factor for many years in maintaining and enhancing national power and independence.

The Arguments against Population Growth

One of the major arguments against population growth is that as a society gets larger it becomes more complex and requires increasing government regulation, thus reducing individual freedom. The example is oftentimes given of the need for increased regulation represented by traffic lights as the number of cars grows. But, by concentrating only on the regulatory aspect of growing complexity, this argument fails to take into account the diverse new opportunities and capabilities that are created by this same complex growth. Of course, growth requires an increasing number of traffic lights. But this same growth also makes it possible to drive the length and breadth of the country on expressways that do not have stop signs, much less traffic lights. From this point of view, traffic lights are a small regulatory price to pay for the immensely expanded physical mobility provided by growth.

Consequently, as long as regulation is in proportion to real human need,

145

it is a necessary and not particularly invidious accompaniment of growth. What is not tolerable from the standpoint of personal freedom, however, is unnecessary or ill-conceived or positively counterproductive regulation that is related not to real needs but the passion for power and influence of those at the regulatory controls.

From 1960 to 1972, for example, while the growth of complexity was supposedly slowing down due to a decrease of 60 percent in the population growth rate, new control legislation related to consumer interests rapidly accelerated. As reported by Murray L. Weidenbaum, director of the Center for the Study of American Business at Washington University, the number of "control" laws more than doubled, from twenty to fifty, and not only were more laws passed, but the laws were broader and more far-reaching than previous legislation.[32] Meanwhile, according to the U.S. Office of Management and Budget, the reporting burden imposed on American business by the federal government increased by 50 percent between December, 1967, and June, 1974. Major new programs—occupational safety and health activities, medicare and medicaid, environmental protection legislation, and equal employment opportunity compliance—were the principal sources of the increase.[33]

The only way to justify regulatory controls is on the basis that their benefits outweigh their costs. Or, as Weidenbaum puts it, a "regulatory activity generates costs as well as benefits. Hence, consideration of proposals—and they are numerous—to extend the scope of federal regulation should not be limited, as is usually the case, to a recital of the advantages of regulation. Rather, the costs need to be considered also, both those which are tangible and those which may be intangible."[34]

Yet, in the recent rush to regulation this basic point has apparently been largely ignored. Weidenbaum, for example, cites an assistant administrator of the Environmental Protection Agency who cavalierly states that the "whole thrust of the new legislation is to push technology and not get bogged down in deciding whether costs justify water-quality needs in a particular area."[35] Or consider the comment of R. David Pittle, a commissioner on the Consumer Product Safety Commission (CPSC), who vows that "when it involves a product that is unsafe, I don't care how much it costs the company to correct the problem,"[36] ignoring the fact that consumers "have unequal tastes for safety as well as for other characteristics of product performance" and thus there is, in the words of Professor J. Fred Weston of UCLA, a "need to recognize trade-offs between safety and other criteria important to consumers."[37]

Such high-handed regulatory policies not only vastly and unnecessarily increase costs to the American consumer, but work against consumers' ultimate best interests. For, as Professor Max Brunk of Cornell University explains, consumerism is intended to protect the consumer, but look what the regulations do to the consumer "who pays the cost and loses the benefits that

146

a prohibited product or service could have provided." Furthermore, adds Brunk, consumerists "sometimes have as much difficulty in convincing the consumer of his or her need for protection as they do in convincing a regulatory body to provide the protection."[38]

Clearly, the increase in regulatory controls in many areas today is not designed so much to achieve societal benefits, although that is the stated intent, as it is to massage what Weidenbaum calls the "Big Motherism" mentality of those who think up and enforce the regulations, regardless of costs or incursions on personal freedoms. One CPSC commissioner, for example, has reportedly argued that a house is "a hazardous consumer product" and thus qualifies for CPSC regulation.[39] Presumably, this might mean that every homeowner and apartment dweller in the country would have to fill out a form indicating satisfactory compliance with the commission's safety requirements or otherwise face the possibility of a fine or perhaps even a jail sentence for failing to take the prescribed precautions. Has growth really resulted in such complexity that a regulation such as this should even be imagined, much less seriously proposed?

The answer, of course, is no. Growth, in fact, provides the impetus for society to improve living conditions, while revising and removing outdated and anachronistic regulations because it so strikingly indicts those that clearly have outlived their usefulness. By contrast, it is the static society that, once encumbered by regulations and restrictions that increasingly serve no useful purpose and in many cases even an antisocial function, finds it increasingly difficult if not impossible to resist succumbing to their deadening effect.

Another argument is, as the report of the Commission on Population Growth and the American Future states, that "representation at the national level is diluted by population growth. The constituency of an individual congressman has grown enormously since the size of the House of Representatives was fixed at 435 members in 1910. Then, each congressman represented 211,000 citizens, on the average. In 1970, a congressional constituency averaged 470,000 citizens. By the year 2000, each congressman in a 435-seat House will represent 623,000 persons under the 2-child growth rate, or 741,000 persons in the 3-child case."[40]

But, as the commission itself states, the "size of the constituency is clearly not the sole factor determining excellence in government. Perhaps it may not even be very important, compared with the quality of the representatives, the size and professionalism of their staffs, the size of the governing body itself, and other factors."[41] Furthermore, the argument ignores Madison's insight that, once an effective number of representatives is attained, the overall quality of representation increases with larger districts because of a greater number of potential legislators from which to choose and the greater difficulty faced by unworthy candidates in getting elected to office. Nor is it accurate to say, as the commission does, that the individual constituent's voice will be diminished with population growth.[42] Contrary to this commission view, which is derived from simplistic arithmetic, the vast improvement in communications and transportation resulting from population growth amplifies each individual's voice by making access to his or her representative faster, easier, and surer. Moreover, due to mass communications, legislators now operate in a "fishbowl" political atmosphere in which practically every significant legislative action is duly reported for voter consumption and reaction. The governmental trend during this century, in fact, has increasingly been towards a more "pure democracy" in which congressmen, in effect, poll their district and vote the desires of their constituents rather than following the more representative mode of voting their own convictions, regardless of voter preferences. There is nothing necessarily desirable or irreversible in this trend, but it does indicate that population growth per se need not have the effect of diminishing the voice of the individual constituent.

It is also argued on occasion that population growth results in a greater potential for war, either because of the expansionary attitude that it engenders or the need for additional space and resources that it creates. But, even though population in the United States and Europe grew the fastest during the nineteenth century, this period saw no major worldwide wars. Conversely, as population growth declined sharply in the early part of this century, two world wars erupted.

"The theory that over-population causes war is attractive at first sight,"[43] comments Sauvy. But demographic depression, he adds, can also be a cause of war.[44] For "storms are not caused by high atmospheric pressure as such but by differences in pressure between two neighboring zones. Similarly, wars are not due to the unrest of compressed populations, but to differences of pressure. . . ."[45] Amongst the bones of discontent of the present day, the desire to reduce real or supposed over-population takes second place to ideological and political tensions."[46]

Finally, the Commission on Population Growth and the American Future warns that it is "troubled by [its] assessment of the readiness and capability of government to deal with problems associated with population growth and change. . . ."[47] The commission goes on to argue that "slowing down the rate of population growth would ease the problems facing government in the years ahead. . . ."[48]

One must reread these statements several times to comprehend their full import. For what the commission is, in effect, saying is that government is no longer capable of serving a growing population. Therefore, the American people will simply have to reduce their numbers in the future for the benefit of government.

But the conclusion that a growing population will outstrip the capabilities of federal, state, and local governments to provide services is in no way a rationale for reduced population growth. It is instead a mandate for more productive and progressive people in government and for more efficient and effective governmental operation. The idea that people must be eliminated to make things easier for government is not only a convenient "out" for inept politicians and bureaucrats and outdated government agencies, but a rather grotesque socialistic perversion of the American political promise. For, as Rousas J. Rushdoony puts it, socialism "has a poor record when it comes to eliminating problems; its answer adds up to eliminating people. In fact, one of socialism's major and chronic problems is simply *people*. . . . Socialism always faces over-population; a free economy does not."[49]

Conclusion

Population growth is a major factor enabling the United States to not only maintain but improve its status as an independent political power in the world. At the same time, this growth is resulting in a population size and diversity which is conducive to maximum political freedom and personal liberty internally.

By contrast, a decline to zero population growth would seriously impair the country's capability to maintain national independence because it would result in a pressure vacuum into which the Soviet Union (which is concerned about *increasing,* not decreasing, its population) would not hesitate to enter by force of arms if necessary. The differential pressure that is already building up in this regard is vividly captured by Patrick Buchanan, who reports that a revised CIA estimate indicates that the

Russians may be allocating between 14 and 17 per cent of their gross national product to their armed forces. The United States, grudgingly, spends about 6 per cent. If U.S. defense expenditures were raised to match the middle level of the Russian effort—say, 15 per cent of GNP—the U.S. defense budget would have to be raised from almost $100 billion to about $250 billion. . . . The Soviets now have twice as many surface combat ships and submarines afloat as the U.S. They are ahead 2-to-1 in armored vehicles and heavy mortars, 3-to-1 in artillery pieces, 4-to-1 in tanks and 5-to-1 in interceptor aircraft. They have dispersed their factories in the heartland of the Eurasian land mass, trained their populace in civil defense, and deployed 10,000 surface-to-air missiles to defend their country from western attack. In the U.S., civil defense is a joke: There are no surface-to-air missiles covering the North American continent. While the U.S. is strenuously working its way back up toward a full 16 divisions, the CIA estimates that the Soviet Union now has 168 divisions on active duty. There is no conceivable combination of potential threats to Soviet interests to justify that magnitude of military power. The Russians have constructed the most powerful military machine in the history of man.[50]

Moreover, a decline to a stationary American population would inevitably result in growing governmental regulation, increasing restrictions on economic liberty, and an eventual erosion of political freedom, all due to massive but misguided state attempts to achieve by fiat and force the economic and social advancement that would be lacking as a result of the absence of normal growth processes.

As Colin Clark sums up, population limitation is "bad economics and bad politics. While not the only cause, population limitation has been a frequent and potent cause of claims by the state to regulate economic life, the dependence of the individual upon state welfare services, excessive taxation, and deterioration of the value of money. Those people on the other hand, who courageously and intelligently face the challenge of population increase, will be rewarded by economic, political and cultural progress to an extent beyond any limits that we can now foresee."[51]

7

THE FACTS OF U.S. POPULATION GROWTH

Population growth has resulted in unprecedented material advancement, social development, and political progress for the American people. But there is nothing automatic or inevitable about population growth. In fact, the exact opposite is the case.

Throughout history population growth has been the exception rather than the rule. As Ronald Freedman, professor of sociology and associate director of the Population Studies Center at the University of Michigan, and Bernard Berelson, president of the Population Council, point out, over the milleniums until very recent times, the "human population increased at a very low rate. From the time of the agricultural and urban revolution about 5,000 years ago the population increase probably never reached as much as .1 percent a year for any long period until the 17th century."[1]

This extremely slow growth was due to the fact that in the past fertility just about matched mortality; birth rates were nearly equal to death rates. Population growth only occurs, of course, when birth rates are greater than death rates, when there are more births than deaths. And what population growth did occur in the past was primarily due not to an increase in fertility, or birth rates, but to a decrease in mortality, or death rates. But, for every death rate decrease in the past, the human population made a corresponding reduction in birth rates, resulting in the infinitesimally slow population growth that has occurred for more than 99 percent of human history.

In prehistoric times, for example, birth and death rates were both very high. The United Nations estimates that the rates ranged from fifty to as much as eighty per 1000 population.[2] And we know that the rates must have been approximately equal because there were only an estimated 5 to 10 million people in the world as recently as 10,000 years ago, or approximately 8000 B.C.

During the premodern period—from 8000 B.C. to about A.D. 1650—death rates dropped and birth rates followed, with both rates fluctuating between forty and fifty per 1000 people, according to United Nations estimates.[3] Once again, birth and death rates on the average must have hovered fairly close together, because the rate of growth was practically imperceptible during this period, and the number of people over the 10,000-year period increased to only about 300 million in A.D. 1 and to 470–545 million in 1650.[4]

During the modern era (1650 to the present), death rates dramatically plunged, from around forty to as few as nine per 1000, due primarily to revolutionary advances in medicine, hygienics, and sanitation. Birth rates followed this descent, but at a slower pace. Because of the very sudden and sustained drop in death rates and the time lag before birth rates followed, population growth has been very rapid in the past three centuries.

However, due to the continuing decline in birth rates that has followed the drop in death rates, the rate of world population growth has today reached its peak. In advanced nations the process of slowing population growth is already well on its way. And the same process is now beginning to take place in developing countries, too. Figure 1 shows trends of birth and death rates in advanced and developing nations between 1750 and 1970 and how these rates are expected to perform between now and 2000. The gaps between the birth and death rates represent the rate of population growth per 1000 people due to natural increase (excluding immigration and emigration).

As the graphs show, population growth speeded up in the advanced countries during the years 1750–1800. It reached its zenith in the first half of this century, following which it began to subside. It spurted forward again in the fifties, but is now once again slowing down, as the gap between birth and death rates continues to narrow.

In developing countries, rapid population growth did not begin until the early 1900s and became very swift in the years after World War II. Growth has been much more rapid in developing countries than in advanced nations because (1) the death rates made a much steeper descent, and (2) the time lag before birth rates declined was more extended. However, here, too, the rate of population growth is beginning to decrease, as birth and death rates draw closer together.

For example, more current estimates than are presented in the graphs—which are based on population statistics collected only through 1970—indicate that birth rates are actually falling faster than shown. This is particularly true for the advanced nations, a number of which are now experiencing near-zero population growth. But it is also true for developing countries, where birth rates are dropping earlier than expected. The Population Reference Bureau, for example, reports that world birth rates dropped significantly between 1965 and 1974, from an average of 34 per 1000 people to 30 per 1000—a rate of

Figure 1. Birth, Death, and Growth Rates (per 1000 population), 1750–2000

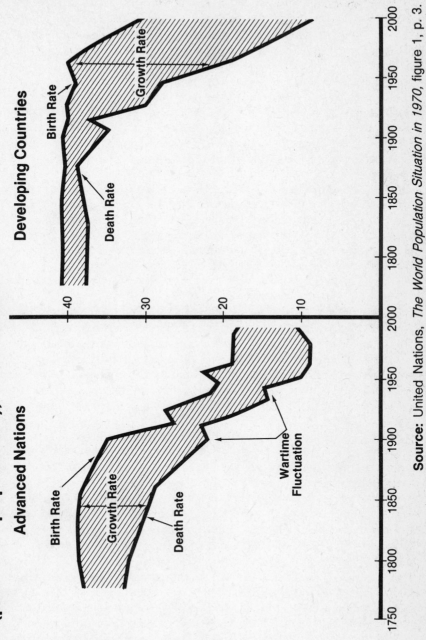

Source: United Nations, *The World Population Situation in 1970*, figure 1, p. 3.

153

decline that for the first time in many years was greater than the decline in death rates.[5]

At the same time, death rates in both advanced and developing countries will increase in the future as population growth slows down. This is not because of any greater general incidence of death, but simply because populations become older as their growth slows down. Death rates increase because there is an increased proportion of older people in relation to the total population. The graph for the advanced nations actually shows an initial increase in the death rate for this reason. But the advanced-nation death rate will increase even further in the future, and the same death rate increase will also eventually take place in developing countries. In the future, as the gap between birth and death rates narrows, a continuing slowdown in population growth can be expected.

Here in the United States, birth and death rates have followed the basic pattern established by advanced nations as a whole, as is shown in Figure 2. In the early nineteenth century, the U.S. death rate had already dropped from that of previous times to an estimated rate of a little over thirty per 1000 population. At the same time, the birth rate was still very high, at fifty-five per 1000 population, resulting in a rate of population growth due to natural increase (birth rate minus death rate) of more than twenty per 1000 population, or in excess of 2 percent a year.

During the next two centuries, the death rate continued to drop, reaching a level of 8.9 in 1976. But the birth rate dropped even faster, declining from 55 to a low of only 14.7 per 1000 population in 1976, resulting in a population growth rate due to natural increase of only 5.8 per 1000 population, or 0.58 percent a year. Meanwhile, as Figure 2 also shows, average population growth per decade due to immigration varied from a high of 9.5 per 1000 population, or 0.95 percent, in 1820–30 to zero in the thirties and 0.19 percent in the seventies.

Thus, U.S. population grew as a result of both natural increase and immigration from 4 million to well over 200 million from 1790 to 1970. Yet, throughout this time, the rate of population growth has decreased, as is shown in the table on page 156.[6]

In the decade 1790–1800, for example, U.S. population increased at an average annual rate of 3 percent. The growth rate then decreased gradually throughout the nineteenth century, to an average of 1.9 percent a year during the decade 1900–10. In 1910–20, there was a sharp drop to an average annual rate of 1.4 percent, followed by a slight increase to 1.5 percent in 1920–30, and then a precipitous decline in 1930–40 to 0.7 percent. The rate of average annual population growth recovered to 1.7 percent in 1950–60, but then dropped again to 1.2 percent in 1960–70 and to a projected rate of only about 0.7 to 0.8 percent in the decade of the seventies.

Thus, from the standpoint of U.S. as well as world population, birth and

154

Figure 2. U.S. Birth, Death, and Immigration Rates (per 1000 population), 1820–1974

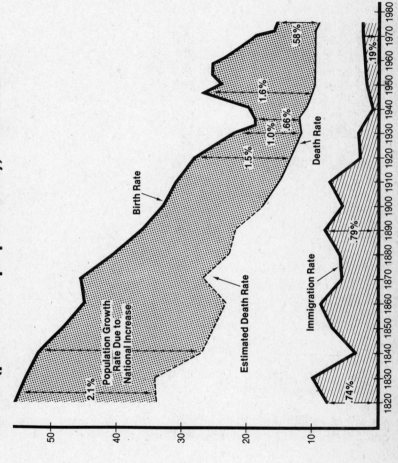

Decade	Total Population	Average Annual Rate of Population Growth
— 1790	3,929,214	—
1790–1800	5,308,483	3.0%
1800–1810	7,239,881	3.1
1810–1820	9,638,453	2.9
1820–1830	12,866,020	2.9
1830–1840	17,069,453	2.8
1840–1850	23,191,876	3.1
1850–1860	31,443,321	3.0
1860–1870	39,818,449	2.4
1870–1880	50,155,783	2.3
1880–1890	62,947,714	2.2
1890–1900	75,994,575	1.9
1900–1910	91,972,266	1.9
1910–1920	105,710,620	1.4
1920–1930	122,775,046	1.5
1930–1940	131,669,275	0.7
1940–1950	151,325,798	1.4
1950–1960	179,323,175	1.7
1960–1970	203,235,298	1.2

death rates are once again converging to produce the extremely slow growth that has characterized human populations overall since the beginning of history. This does not mean that certain societies at certain times in the past have not experienced rapid population growth or decline. Undoubtedly, there have been many rises and falls of particular human populations throughout history. But it does mean that, in the long term, birth rates were adjusted to death rates, resulting in what for all practical purposes was zero population growth.

This constant adjustment of birth rates to death rates over milleniums of human experience suggests that, in the long run, human populations basically opt in favor of survival and the status quo versus growth and change. Just as survival is the strongest drive for individual human beings, so also it is the strongest drive for human populations. If we go back in time to the prehistoric era, for example, when people were completely exposed to all the possible ravages of death, we may assume that they had everything they could do simply to maintain their existing populations. Their societies operated at maximum fertility, but they still were just able to replace themselves due to high mortality. Birth and death rates were approximately the same, with the result that there was literally a life-and-death struggle for bare population survival. The people reproduced at maximum rates simply to hold their own.[7] Truly, theirs was a society where, in the immortal words of Lewis Carroll, it took "all the running you can do, to keep in the same place." Consequently, because of the strength of the survival instinct, we can be sure that primitive cultures developed the goal of high fertility as an integral part of their people's lives, since it was absolutely vital to the continuing existence of their societies.

However, since population growth has all but imperceptibly occurred throughout history, something must have happened to cause death rates to decline. Here, of course, we are reduced to pure conjecture. But it is conjecture based on knowledge of how population growth has occurred in more recent times.

Take, for example, the discovery of fire. Fire that keeps people warm during cold weather might also have the effect of reducing disease and, thus, death. Likewise, a fire burning through the night might scare away predatory animals that otherwise would kill sleeping humans. The discovery of fire could have had the effect of reducing death rates and causing population to grow.

Population would grow because existing birth rates would be higher than the reduced death rates. And the effect of this population growth would be to cause, indeed, force, change. The change might involve simply extending existing facilities, for example, occupying more caves and hunting in ever wider areas. Or it might involve developing new types of housing and new methods of food production. For example, the pressure of population growth could have caused cave people to eventually forsake their caves—there are, after all, only so many caves conveniently located to hunting grounds—and build houses in the trees or on the ground. And undoubtedly it was population pressure that caused peoples of the past to switch from hunting and fishing to more productive and dependable agricultural methods of food production.

But, in any case, population growth creates the need for change. And, even though the change is for the better, it initially involves the costs of extra work and increased investment. It also brings costs of a socioeconomic, political, and cultural nature. For it unsettles those who want to do things the "way we've always done them"; it causes shifts in the social, economic, and political power structure; and it results in new cultural values that overturn and replace the old.

Thus, even as population growth begins to occur, strong societal forces are set in motion in opposition to the resulting changes. Societies undergoing population growth throughout history have undoubtedly varied widely in their degree of acceptance or rejection of the changes caused by that growth. The United States of the eighteenth and nineteenth centuries seems to have for the most part welcomed population growth and the progressive changes that accompanied it. On the other hand, France during the nineteenth century for all practical purposes rejected population growth, with the result that it tended to stagnate due to lack of growth's modernizing influence.

But the overall lesson of history is that, in the long run, society is basically conservative, preferring the known present to the unknown future, the status quo to any proposed change, regardless of how beneficial it may ultimately prove. Thus, over the long term, human populations have adjusted their birth rates to almost coincide with their death rates, insuring population survival, while providing a small population surplus as insurance against man-made or natural catastrophes. Kingsley Davis, for example, cites the case of India, where "during the two thousand years that intervened between the ancient and the modern period . . . population . . . must have remained virtually stationary. . . . In 'normal' times . . . the customs governing fertility would provide a birth rate slightly higher than the usual death rate. This would build up a population surplus as a sort of demographic insurance against catastrophe. Inevitably, however, the catastrophe would come in the form of warfare, famine, or epidemic, and the increase of population would suddenly be wiped out."[8]

Following a decline in death rates, human populations eventually also lower their birth rates. But population growth occurs during this process because there is usually a time gap between the two rate declines. This time gap occurs because a society that, in order to insure population survival, has for hundreds or even thousands of years inculcated a certain birth rate as an integral part of its culture cannot immediately adjust this rate when there is a decline in the death rate. There will inevitably be a "cultural lag," during which the birth rate remains at the same level, while the death rate decreases to a lower level. While this "cultural lag" is in effect, population grows as a result of more births than deaths. This population growth, in turn, creates a need for change. Insofar as the culture accepts this need and makes the changes necessary to accommodate more people, improvements are generated that benefit all members of society.

However, at the same time that population growth is promoting improvements through change, it is also activating counterforces opposed to the change. The liberating advancement brought about by increasing numbers of people generates a conservative resistance to the resulting change. At the same time that population growth creates a need for change, it also creates pressure for a decrease in the birth rate. This pressure is not immediately felt by the members of the society because the change is gradual. But, over time, it becomes increasingly more pronounced, resulting in a reduction in fertility on the part of the society's members. Eventually, the pressure for reduction in the birth rate created by population growth is relieved only by bringing it once again in line with the death rate, resulting in the normal state of population that has existed for the most part throughout history. This is the population that is stationary or growing only enough to provide minimum safeguards against decline or disaster.

Birth rate declines in growing populations begin in a society's upper class because they are better educated and therefore more knowledgeable concerning birth- and death-rate trends. They are also less tradition-bound and thus quicker to change their fertility practices. In addition, the upper class has the least to gain and the most to lose from the continuing change that results from population growth.

By contrast, lower classes not only are less knowledgeable concerning population trends and less free of cultural direction, but have the most to gain and the least to lose as a result of the progressive change induced by population growth. As a result, their birth rates tend to remain higher longer.

However, as change results in improvement in their conditions, lower classes also eventually adopt a more conservative attitude. For, as their lot improves, they become increasingly more concerned with protecting what they have gained than with achieving additional gains. Consequently, their opposition to the change wrought by population growth also increases, and adjustments to lower birth rates are accordingly made.

Thus, population growth carries within itself the seeds of its own cessation. In effect, it comes with its own cultural self-governor, an essentially natural check that comes into play through millions upon millions of individual voluntary decisions and that eventually has its way in relation to any population increase through an adjustment in human motivation.

The operation of this built-in growth regulator can be observed not only in population cycles of the past, but in today's pattern of population advance in both advanced nations and developing countries. It is a pattern in which a death-rate drop results in an increase of population, following which the birth rate declines, resulting in a decrease and eventual leveling out of population growth. This is what has happened in the past, and it is what is happening today. For, although all human populations instinctively understand and appreciate the importance of protecting against the debilitating effects of depopulation, few have the perseverance, stamina, and courage to indefinitely face the future changes created by population growth with faith instead of fear.

The "Population Bomb" Argument

In the 1960s, the subject of population was brought to the attention of the American public with a jolt. This happened when the media were filled with cries of alarm that population was a "bomb" that was going to go off and wipe us all out unless something was done soon.

Former United Nations Secretary General U Thant put it this way:

It took mankind all of recorded time until the middle of the last century to achieve a population of 1 billion. Yet it took less than a hundred years to add the second billion, and only 30 years to add the third. At today's rate of increase, there will be 4 billion people by 1975 and nearly 7 billion by the year 2000. This unprecedented

...crease presents us with a situation unique in human affairs and a problem that grows more urgent with each passing day.[9]

U Thant was sounding a clarion call to action in this statement. Yet his statement was relatively calm compared to the apocalyptic pronouncements of other observers of the world population scene. The old *Life* magazine, for example, reported in an editorial that "a British scientist recently calculated that with the population of the world now about 3 billion and doubling every 37 years, we will reach the ultimate terrestrial limit of 60 million billion humans in somewhat less than 1,000 years. At that stage, people will be jammed together so tightly that the earth itself will glow orange-red from the heat."[10]

But, as if this were not enough, some commentators were so overwhelmed by world population growth that they took off on flights of pure fantasy. *Newsweek,* for example, reported that the "current rate of growth, continued in 600 years, would leave every inhabitant of the world with only 1 square yard to live on. By the year 3500, the weight of human bodies on the earth's surface would equal the weight of the world itself. By the year 6000, the solid mass of humanity would be expanding outward into space at the speed of light."[11]

Meanwhile, Robert Cook, president of the Population Reference Bureau, told us that "present population growth rates present an obviously and unavoidably lethal threat to all that civilization has achieved unless something is done to reduce them."[12] Former Secretary of the Interior Stewart Udall observed that "if the world continues unchecked on the course we are on . . . man himself can become increasingly an endangered species."[13] Robert and Leona Rienow, authors of *Man Against His Environment,* declared that the "rate of human overbreeding today has become not only monstrous and abnormal; it is a positive extermination mechanism which no amount of science can ward off."[14] And Paul Ehrlich, whose *Population Bomb* perhaps epitomized the population explosion mentality of the period, bluntly stated that growing numbers of people were like "cancer" because "a cancer is an uncontrolled multiplication of cells," and "the population explosion is an uncontrolled multiplication of people."[15]

Nor, of course, was the United States excluded from the population explosion syndrome. Sociologists Lincoln and Alice Day, for example, informed us that "a rate that has averaged 1.7 percent since the end of World War II has been adding more than 2,700,000 to our population *each year,* a number about equal to the population of the whole San Francisco–Oakland urban area, and nearly half a million larger than the entire Boston metropolitan area. Less than one hundred years at this rate and our number would be one billion—a third of the present population of the entire world."[16]

All of these commentators presented a picture of uncontrolled, runaway, exploding population growth leading to an eventual blow-up of civilization, if

160

not the end of humanity. However, this picture of population-caused catastrophe is not a new one. It is as old as history. There have always been people in every society who have looked into the future and forecast disaster due to population growth.

More important, the picture is not an accurate one. It is based on a false view of the nature of population growth, a view derived from myopic misconceptions rather than valid knowledge of the dynamics of population growth in the real world.

Our current Cassandras deal in misconceptions because they labor under the spell of the master misconceiver, Thomas Robert Malthus. It was Malthus' basic belief that population growth, unless "checked," would always increase faster than any material progress or increase in "subsistence," with the result that most people would always be poor or living at the level of subsistence. As he put it, the "power of population is indefinitely greater than the power in earth to produce subsistence for man. Population, when unchecked, increases in geometrical ratio. Subsistence increases only in an arithmetical ratio. This implies a strong and constantly operating check on population from the difficulty of subsistence."[17]

That Malthus' theory has a certain simplistic attraction that is difficult to resist cannot be denied. It operates on an animalistic level of pure biology. Malthus, in effect, tells us, that the "unchecked" human sex drive always operates like an instinctive biological force, constantly causing population to grow, grow, grow. And the miserly earth yields up meager fruits that never provide more than a fraction of the food required to feed the hungry hordes. It is the dramatic but tragic story of the irresistible force of population growth meeting the immovable object of inadequate food production and—BOOM!—population growth is "checked," but only at the expense of great and continuing human misery.

This Malthusian drama of despair has captured the imagination of generation after generation of population experts, including our present crop of doomsayers. However, there is one thing wrong with the scenario. It is exactly the opposite of what has happened in the past or what can be expected to happen in the future.

Far from outdistancing material progress in the past, population growth has lagged far behind, as is evidenced by the continuing rapid increase in per capita income that has occurred in the United States and other advanced countries since Malthus formulated his population principle. The United States in particular was an ideal country in which to test Malthus' theory of the supposed geometric increase of an "unchecked" population, for nowhere were the "checks" on population growth fewer than in the United States. Or, as Malthus himself observed, nowhere were the "means of subsistence . . . more ample, the manners of the people more pure, and consequently the checks to marriage fewer. . . ."[18]

161

Yet, instead of accelerating in response to the absence of Malthusian "checks," the rate of population growth in the United States declined, prompting observers such as Richard A. Easterlin of the University of Pennsylvania's economics department to point out that

from Malthus to Paul Ehrlich, there have been those who see the growth in man's numbers driving him inexorably, like lemmings to the sea, towards misery and death. A basic premise of this view is that human reproductive behavior does not voluntarily respond to environmental conditions. Instead, man, following his natural instincts, will breed without restraint and population will grow until environmental limits force a halt through higher mortality.

Nowhere, I think, is this view called into more doubt than by American historical experience. Here, if anywhere, environmental constraints on population growth at the start of the nineteenth century appeared to be at a minimum. Certainly this is what Thomas R. Malthus himself thought. . . . [Yet] the astounding thing is that from about 1810 on, American fertility started to decline. And this, shortly after a vast expansion of natural resources had been accomplished through the Louisiana Purchase! While the data are not perfect, by 1860, for the white population, the ratio of children under five to women 20–44 years old (the fertility measure most generally available) had fallen by a third from its 1810 level, and by 1910, by over a half. Put differently, in 1790 almost half of the free families contained five or more persons; by 1900, the proportion of families with five or more persons had fallen to less than a third. How can one reconcile this dramatic reduction in fertility with the seemingly abundant state of natural resources throughout much of this period?[19]

How, indeed, except to conclude that the Malthusian vision of growing numbers of people constantly pressing against the means of subsistence is false. Malthus lived at a time when population was growing rapidly, and he therefore could easily have gotten the mistaken impression that population growth is like a bomb that explodes whenever subsistence is expanded. But there is nothing in the population history of the last several centuries or, for that matter, in all population history to suggest that Malthus' views are anything more than an utter misconception of population dynamics.

For example, Malthus believed that peoples of the past had always lived at the thin edge of subsistence because population constantly expanded to use up available food supplies. But cities, towns, and villages have existed far back into antiquity, and these are signs of not food scarcity but an agricultural surplus. For a food surplus is necessary to make it possible for people to leave farming communities and live in denser settlements where they are dependent on the food production of others for their subsistence.

The same thing can be said with equal if not greater force in relation to the many civilizations that have existed over the milleniums. People living in a semistarving state do not build pyramids, temples, coliseums, roads, aqueducts, and all of the thousands of other artifacts that are known to have been created by civilizations of the past.

But if history provides little evidence for the idea that lack of subsistence has acted as a "check" on population growth, it provides even less for the notion that population growth has ever proceeded "unchecked" in the past. Since population growth is the result of a difference between birth rates, or fertility, and death rates, or mortality, a population in which growth is "unchecked" would at all times exhibit maximum fertility. Yet there are few societies where fertility has even approached, much less been at, its theoretical maximum since the beginning of human history.

Called fecundity, theoretical maximum fertility is defined as the maximum physiological capacity of the human female to conceive. However, as W. D. Borrie points out, assuming "that a woman's fertile years lie between ages 15 and 49, that is, a period of thirty-five years, and that she was married throughout the whole of this period, it might be quite possible for her to have up to twenty conceptions; but this is much above the *average* figure known to have existed in any community."[20]

According to Alfred Sauvy, the theoretical maximum number of children that can be achieved by a population on the *average* is ten to twelve per family.[21] But, as Colin Clark notes, this theoretical maximum is also "hardly ever obtained."[22] For, as Borrie comments, the "highest known *average* number of births to women by the end of their child-bearing years is about ten. This seems to have been the level attained by the early settlers in French Canada in the seventeenth century. The nearest modern approach to this is found in the Cocos Islands with a total of about 8.8 children, or the anabaptist Hutterites of North America whose fertility in 1946–50 also implied an average of about eight children by the end of the child-bearing period."[23] And, currently, the average number of births per woman is five to six in developing countries and two to three in advanced nations.

So, when Malthus discussed the "power of *unchecked* population," he was actually hypothesizing about something that has rarely, if ever, actually existed in practice. In fact, he as much as admitted this when he made the point that even in the United States, where population was growing faster than anywhere else in the world and where "checks" to population growth were at an absolute minimum, the rate of increase was "short of the utmost power of population."[24]

To say that population growth was "unchecked" or "uncontrolled" in the past is to say that fertility, or the birth rate, has always been maintained at maximum physiological capacity. Since population growth has been infinitesimally slow throughout history, this necessarily implies that the death rate was at equally high levels. But this has not been the case. As the death rate has dropped, the birth rate has declined along with it. Population growth thus has been and is today fundamentally not a function of "uncontrollable" biological forces but of socially determined cultural norms.

This is not to deny that famines, plagues, and wars have taken their toll of human life in the past, reducing population levels in the process. But it is to say that these human miseries have not been the determining factor in the rate of population growth throughout history.

Population growth is determined not biologically, as Malthus thought, but culturally. Whether population grows or declines depends on each culture's most profound beliefs concerning the value of human life and of increasing numbers of people. Cultural factors, not blind biological forces, basically determine whether population grows or declines. And, throughout 99 percent of history, the cultures of the world have in the long run embraced an almost stationary rather than a significantly growing population. Human population growth throughout history has always tended toward zero, not infinity. Growth is the exception, not the rule, of population. And the recurring problem throughout history has been not to stop population growth but to keep it going or at least to prevent a decline.

Most cultures possess the "gut" knowledge that survival is threatened by a population decline. But it takes adventuresomeness, the courage to face the unknown, the willingness to change settled ways, to cause population to grow. There have been cultures that consciously set about to increase population growth—particularly pioneering cultures that recognized the obvious need for more people to conquer the wilderness and idealistic cultures that were highly motivated to expand population and thus give their cultural ideals wider currency. There have been other populations that have lost the will to live and effectively committed suicide by permitting depopulation and eventual extinction.

But the vast majority of societies have settled in the middle of the road, doing whatever was necessary to prevent population decline but not actively encouraging population growth. Even societies that in one period may have positively promoted population growth eventually lost their pioneering spirit or cultural idealism and retrogressed to a stationary population state in another period.

Overall, world population growth has been extremely slow throughout history, with population increasing only enough to provide a safeguard against the threat of decline. And, where population growth has occurred, it has been the result for the most part of an indirect rather than a direct cause. Societies did not grow in population as a direct result of booming birth rates, as Malthus thought. Rather, population growth was presented to them in the form of lower death rates resulting indirectly from seemingly unrelated improvements in medical, sanitary, and hygienic conditions.

According to Anthony Flew, it is possible that Malthus envisioned himself as "the Newton of the moral (i.e., human) sciences." It is thus probable that he patterned his principle of population on Newton's first law of motion, which states that "every body continues in its state of rest or uniform motion in a right line unless it is compelled to change that state by forces impressed on it."[25] Flew suggests that, since the first law of motion generates the notion of a force, the principle of population gives rise to the Malthusian concept of a

164

check. But this is to pick the wrong aspect of Newton's law on which to base a population principle. For the normal condition of population is not one of "uniform motion" but a "state of rest."

Conclusion

Throughout history, peoples of all nations have instinctively understood and appreciated the vital human and societal need to at least replace themselves. From a parental viewpoint, this means having at least two children who grow to adulthood and continue the reproductive cycle.

When death rates are high, this may require having an average of seven or eight children, since with high death rates it is probable that five or six of the children will die before reaching adulthood. On the other hand, when death rates are low, an average of a little more than two children may be sufficient to achieve population replacement.

Population growth has primarily occurred not as a result of booming birth rates but dropping death rates. And, when death rates have dropped, resulting in population growth, birth rates have normally followed after a time lag during which society has gradually adjusted its cultural reproductive norms to the new minimum required for population survival. This process of adjustment between dropping death rates and declining birth rates is what demographers today call the demographic transition. Currently, as Donald J. Bogue, professor of sociology and director of the Community and Family Study Center at the University of Chicago, points out, the "entire world is in its grip; there is no major population on earth that has not entered upon or already passed through the early stages of this process. As yet there are only two or three major populations on earth that may be said to have entirely completed it."[26]

World population as a whole, for example, is about in the middle of the demographic transition. This means that there will continue to be substantial world population growth through the end of this century and into the next. The current world population growth rate of 2 percent is too high, and changes in the rate of population growth happen too slowly for there to be any other outcome. However, it also means that, although world population growth will continue, it will continue at a decelerating rate and eventually return to a normal near-equilibrium state at some point in the future. It would be idle to attempt to predict *exact* figures for this future world population. Most such pinpointed predictions are notoriously inaccurate.

However, *based on broad trends of past and present world population growth,* it is possible to suggest that world population will return to an extremely slow growth rate about the time it reaches the neighborhood of 10 billion people, which should be approximately the middle of the next century. As is shown in Figure 3, this population projection roughly falls between low

Figure 3. World Population Growth, 1750–2050

(Dotted line indicates estimate)

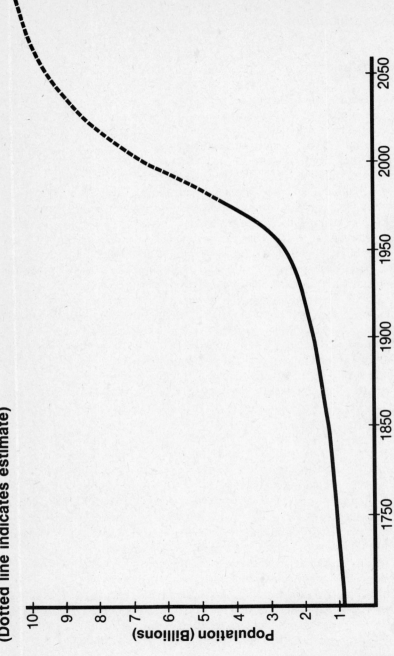

Figure 4. U.S. Population Growth, 1800–2050
(Dotted line indicates estimate)

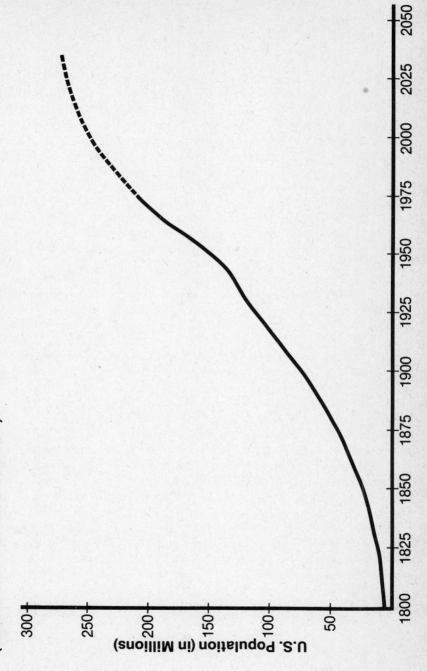

U.S. Population (in Millions)

and medium population growth projections developed by the United Nations.[27]

In contrast to the world situation, the United States is now nearing the end of its demographic transition. Once again, it is necessary to point out that exact population projections have no scientific validity because no one really knows what the future holds for birth- and death-rate trends in any particular case. But, *assuming present fertility and mortality trends continue,* it is likely that U.S. population growth will continue to slow down and then begin to flatten out around the end of the century, at a level of 250 to 275 million people, as is shown in Figure 4.[28]

Thus, contrary to the views of "population explosionists" such as Lincoln and Alice Day, who could tell us as late as 1965 that we were "experiencing one of the most rapid rates of sustained population growth in the history of man,"[29] we are, in fact, facing not a "population bomb" but a "population bust," in which the birth rate descended to a low of 14.7 in 1976,[30] a rate which is even lower than the Depression rates of the thirties.

This "birth dearth," as sociologist Ben Wattenberg calls it,[31] is ushering in a new demographic situation that is unique in the population history of the United States and, for that matter, the world. In the past, population growth has primarily been a result of a declining death rate rather than an increasing birth rate. But the death rate today is about as low as it can go. Any further decrease will be achieved primarily as a result of an extension in average lifetime. But, even should such an extension occur, it would have relatively little effect on total population growth, for it would simply mean that people in their sixties and seventies would live longer. This will be a welcome development to the elderly but, since these folks are long past their reproductive prime, no new population growth will occur.

The decline in the death rate that, in fact, has always had the most positive impact on population growth rates of the past has, of course, been the reduction in mortality of female infants. This is because girl babies who live instead of die grow up to have babies of their own, who in turn have babies of their own, resulting in multiplying population growth. But this growth-inducing factor has now also run its course, since more than 97 percent of the girls that are born today live to be 45 years old; that is, they live to the end of their reproductive period.

In the middle of the Depression of the thirties, a significant increase in the U.S. birth rate began, extending into the mid-fifties. But this was also a time when the death rate was still dropping. In the future, it will be the birth rate alone that will determine what, if any, population growth occurs. No longer will the United States be able to "back into" population growth via death-rate reductions. Increased fertility will be the key—the only key—to future population growth. Growth will be totally dependent on direct procreative action rather than indirect reproductive reaction. It is thus a totally new and different population situation that will confront the United States in the years ahead.

168

8

THE IDEOLOGY OF POPULATION CONTROL

Population growth has resulted in manifest material, social, and political benefits for the American people. Yet, since the country was founded, the rate of population growth has been in a long-term decline. This is a normal development, which has taken place in all advanced countries and is now taking hold in developing countries as well. It is a result of society's putting on the "cultural brakes," so to speak, to slow down population growth.

All human societies appreciate the absolute necessity of at least replacing themselves in order to prevent the disaster of depopulation. But few can maintain the drive and energy to maintain population growth over time. Population growth enables people to improve their lot, but it also brings change. And society's basically conservative instincts in favor of the status quo eventually overcome human desires for the improvements induced by change.

There are a number of ways in which societies apply cultural limitations to population growth. In premodern times, when society was more hierarchical, these took the form of laws and customs such as the eldest son delaying marriage until his father died in order to gain his inheritance, regulations by which peasants often had to seek the manorial lord's permission to marry, and edicts forbidding marriage of paupers.[1] In addition, many societies have had customs which forbade or restricted intercourse for long periods after the birth of a child. As W. D. Borrie sums it up, throughout history there have been "social customs, religious practices, economic forces and many other factors . . . which always keep reproductive performance below physiological capacity."[2]

By comparison, in today's more democratic times, the cultural and social forces limiting population growth rely more on human motivation than customs and laws. There are probably as many reasons advanced for modern fertility decline as there are people who have studied the issue, but the major causes include:

- The abolition of work and the establishment of compulsory education for children, which result in increased child-rearing costs and the delay if not elimination of the time when children can begin to contribute to the support of the family.
- Modern child-rearing practices, which require more parental attention. The child used to bring himself up, as Sauvy says, but now he is "the centre of much attention. He has acquired more value and more importance and his birth has become a kind of event, about which people think twice."[3] In addition, it could be added that parents who follow "democratic" practices of family management might think twice about having more than two children in order not to be "outvoted" at family council meetings.
- The emancipation of women, which results in an increasing variety of nonmaternal interests and careers for women to pursue.
- Opportunities for social advancement, which create an incentive for parents to have smaller families so they can better prepare their children to take advantage of the opportunities.
- The development of education, increase in the living standard, greater consumption possibilities, and growth of cities, all of which have the effect of tremendously broadening people's interests and activities, thus resulting in a decreasing emphasis on child-bearing as a source of satisfaction and enjoyment.

And underlying all of these factors is the critical one of the drop in mortality, which removes the incentive as well as the necessity to maintain high fertility in order to insure population survival.

Thus, the slowdown in population growth in the modern era has come about not due to any overall plan but, rather, as Borrie points out, to the "personal decisions of millions of human beings."[4] Or, in the words of John Maier, M.D., associate director for the medical and natural sciences of the Rockefeller Foundation, beginning "in Europe and North America, and today throughout the industrialized world, low rates of population growth have been achieved over the years solely on the basis of the personal decision and initiative of individuals who wanted better lives, better education, and better opportunities for their children. . . . This was done without any national policy directed at limiting rates of population growth; indeed, in those countries where there was at various times an official policy, it was in the direction of increasing the rate of population growth."[5]

As University of Pennsylvania economist Richard A. Easterlin comments, it is "worth noting that the fertility declines of the past were accomplished

170

entirely by voluntary action on the part of the population. To some extent marriage was deferred. But also there were declines in fertility within marriage. These developments took place in a situation where not only was there no public policy to help those interested in fertility limitation, but attitudes, and even laws in many states, were hostile to the practice or even discussion of contraception or other fertility control practices."[6]

This is not to say that contraception and other fertility controls were not practiced. Contraception, abortion, and infanticide, of course, are as old as history. But it is to say that these practices have had for the most part a negligible effect on fertility reductions over time in most areas of the world. These reductions have taken place primarily as a result of positive economic and social advancements and resultant changes in human motivation and incentive rather than negative fertility controls. This is the basic point made by even the antigrowth Population Reference Bureau, Inc., when it states that with "all the recent public discussion of pills and IUD's ("loops"), it must be pointed out that the recent decline in the birth rate is not necessarily due to the new contraceptive devices and oral contraceptives. Commenting on this misinterpretation by some authors, Mr. Robert C. Cook, president of the Population Reference Bureau, stated: 'The all-time low in 1932–33 occurred at a time when the new contraceptives did not exist. I believe this demonstrates that the decline is due, not to contraceptive advances, but to a realization on the part of younger married couples in America that rearing children in this complicated and expensive world presents big problems. People in the United States are reducing their fertility for a variety of reasons. One of the most important, I am sure, is to do a good job of raising and educating the children they choose to have.'"[7]

Arthur J. Dyck, Mary B. Saltonstall Professor of Population Ethics at Harvard University's School of Public Health, reports that

developmentalists believe that very minimal changes in the welfare of population units—families, villages, or other social groups—such as more education, reduction in infant mortality, better knowledge of nutrition, better health care and the like, would already, with or without resort to modern contraceptives, greatly reduce birth rates in less affluent nations and among less affluent groups in countries like the United States. It is interesting to note that John Wyon found that in certain areas of India where the Green Revolution has increased income and food production, birth rates are going down but without increased resort to modern contraceptives. With higher incomes, these Indian villagers are seeking more education for their children, can more readily keep their children alive, and their children in turn, as they seek more goods and more education, are delaying marriage, and hence also delaying and reducing child bearing. Delayed marriage is an extremely important variable in reducing birth rates. It is probably a major reason why birth rates in the United States continue to decline despite the increasing number of women of reproductive age.[8]

171

And the University of Chicago's Philip Hauser states concerning fertility reductions in Taiwan, South Korea, Hong Kong, and Singapore that "motivation and incentive were generated by rising education and higher levels of living that initiated fertility decline and preceded any effective family planning programs. Such programs, no doubt, helped to accelerate the decline of the birth rate. I have yet to learn of any nation in which a family planning program has initiated a decline in fertility, that is, I have yet to learn where 'restrictive behavior' has spread with 'speed' in a population still mired in illiteracy and poverty and characterized by traditional behavior."[9]

Basically, human fertility is a function of motivation rather than contraceptive and other fertility controls. If motivation is lacking, no amount of contraceptive technology will have any effect on fertility. Conversely, if motivation is present, people and societies will find a way to reduce fertility regardless of contraceptive availability.

Motivation is the key to reduced fertility, and this motivation increases as mortality is reduced and people improve their living standards. Consequently, the most effective birth control from the standpoint of human welfare is the free will of individual couples in a society where they are provided with the opportunity to advance themselves and their children.

This process of people having fewer children as they become better able to afford more children is oftentimes considered a paradox. But it is a paradox only to those who view it through the blinders of Malthusianism. For, as Easterlin says, both "theory and the empirical research done so far on historical American fertility suggest that human fertility responds voluntarily to environmental conditions."[10] And, as people's living conditions become better, their improving "environment" motivates them to have smaller families.

The so-called population problem therefore consists of not "controlling" population growth but helping people to improve their conditions in life. But this positive, humane, and realistic view is not shared by those who profess the ideology of population control.

The Population Control Movement

"My report is on population control. People are everywhere. . . . Some people say there are too many of us, but no one wants to leave. . . ."

These words of a little girl making a school report in the *Peanuts* cartoon strip succinctly sum up the basic problem raised by population control. The thesis of population control is that there are too many people. The problem is that "no one wants to leave."

The population control movement has been a factor in American life at least since the early part of this century. "Well-to-do white people," comments author James Ridgeway, "have had a passion for population control since the eugenics movement of the early 1900s."[11] Margaret Sanger of "planned parenthood" fame was the key figure in this early eugenics movement. She is known as the patroness of birth control, but as sociologist Richard LaPiere has observed, she was "motivated by the then popular eugenic thesis that the high birth rate of the lower classes was a threat to the biological quality of the population."[12]

During the thirties, the population control movement lost some of its thrust with the rapid decline in fertility and fears of depopulation. But in the fifties, when population growth increased not only in the United States but in the developing countries of the world, it quickly reactivated itself under the aegis of John D. Rockefeller III. Ridgeway tells the story of how the

Neo-Malthusian line achieved increased importance when the Rockefellers put money into the population-control movement by financing the Population Council, Planned Parenthood and the Population Reference Bureau. In 1957, an ad hoc committee of population experts from the Council, the Rockefeller Fund, Conservation Foundation and Planned Parenthood published a scheme for controlling populations called "Population: An International Dilemma." The report said population was the key to stability in both rich and poor nations. The idea was to persuade educated people of the population dangers. Birth control itself would grow out of the dictates of family planning. The committee believed population was a problem in the United States. "Excessive fertility by families with meager resources must be recognized as one of the potent forces in the perpetuation of slums, ill-health, inadequate education, and even delinquency."[13]

According to Phyllis Tilson Piotrow, the first large foundations to make grants in the population field were the Rockefeller Foundation and the Carnegie Foundation.[14] These foundations were joined by the Ford Foundation, which, for example, gave 80 percent of all its population grants to Rockefeller's Population Council during the fifties.[15]

Throughout this time and up to the present day, there has been an explosion in the number of organizations promoting population control, including such groups as Zero Population Growth, the Population Crisis Committee, the Association for Voluntary Sterilization, Friends of the Earth, the Hugh Moore Fund, the Population Institute, Planned Parenthood–World Population, Compulsory Birth Control for All Americans, Inc., the Coalition for a National Population Policy, and the Council on Population and Environment, among others. Long-standing conservation groups have also joined the population control movement, with the Sierra Club, for example, whose "members are drawn from the same social and economic classes that populate the Social Register,"[15] publishing in conjunction with Ballantine Books Paul Ehrlich's overpopulation tome, *The Population Bomb.*[17]

Why this vast increase in interest in controlling population? One reason,

173

according to Dudley Kirk, Morrison Professor of Population Studies at Stanford University's Food Research Institute, is that the

> upper-middle class that forms the chief constituency of the ZPG movement has experienced invasion of its residential and recreational areas, an invasion that it understandably continues to interpret as a population explosion. Indeed for members of this class there *was* a population explosion. First, it had more of a "baby boom" in the 1950s than did the rest of the population, reflected in great pressure on schools and other facilities in the suburbs. Second, and even more important, this group formerly had close to a monopoly of the better residential areas in the suburbs, the universities, the better beaches, access to the national parks (i.e. owned autos), and so on. What is seen as urban sprawl is the result of the growing affluence of the mass of the American people, who now have sufficient income to buy homes in the suburbs, to go to the universities, to travel, and to go to the favored recreational areas such as our wilderness and our national parks.[18]

Or, as James Ridgeway puts it in a world context, the

> Neo-Malthusians insist in arguing that population programs mean economic betterment for the family. In many poor countries, where wealth is concentrated in the hands of a very few or held externally through multinational corporations, that would necessitate redistribution. But there is little evidence to indicate that population-control programs result in income redistribution. It can work the opposite way around. Population control can be a means for rulers to control the populace. And when the issue is considered in terms of modern technology, population control can become a way to narrow and increase the wealth of a few individuals and corporations.[19]

But it is not only social scientists who have perceived this elitist aspect of population control. Minorities themselves, the people most affected by population control programs, have also been quick to react. According to the Rev. Jesse Jackson, for example, the fact that "this issue should surface simultaneously with the emergence of blacks and other non-whites as a meaningful force in the nation and the world appears more than coincidental."[20] The black leader goes on to state that "birth control as a national policy simply marshals sophisticated methods to remove and control the weak, the poor, quite likely the black and other minorities, whose relative increase in population threatens the WASPs in this nation." And he assails birth control as "a form of genocide . . . the destruction of the black people."[21]

In the words of a black social worker serving as a program coordinator for comprehensive family planning in the Berkeley City Health Department, the "current issue of population, in my mind, displaces an emerging American conscience for human dignity and eradication of poverty and hunger. I see population control or overpopulation as a political issue which diagnoses our society ills as one of too many people with problems by reducing the people as opposed to reducing the problems. In my opinion, when we attempt to solve problems by getting rid of people or potential people who will have these problems, like welfare recipients and those who will be poor or hungry, that's genocide. And I join with many people in making this charge against the move toward population control."[22]

Meanwhile, Mrs. Freddie Mae Brown stated at the First National Congress on Optimum Population and Environment that "whites are scared of us blacks getting control. Otherwise, all their population control programs wouldn't be directed at the ghettos. You've got Planned Parenthood ladies calling on us twice a day, but nobody is knocking on doors in suburbia and the rural areas."[23]

The population control movement basically follows the ideology of Malthusianism, which, as Sauvy comments, is "an emotional state of mind at least as much as a rational argument. . . .[24] faced with two quantities that need adjusting, it tends to lower the highest instead of boosting the lowest. . . .[25] If you put on gloves that are too small, you will find that your fingers cannot reach the end of them. A Malthusian attitude will whisper to you that they are too large and you may order an even smaller pair. But if you are a non-Malthusian you will order a larger pair and may then get your fingers into the ends."[26]

The ideology of Malthusianism has created an intellectual bias in most studies of population that no less an authority than Simon Kuznets has noted, commenting that

there is no excuse for the consistent bias in the literature in the field, in which the clearly observable limits of *existing* resources tend to overshadow completely the dimly discernible potentials of the new discoveries, inventions, and innovations that the future may bring. Perhaps only those who are alarmed rush into print whereas those who are less concerned with the would-be dangers are likely to be mute. And, to be sure, what exists can be observed; what is yet to come can only be surmised; and scholars naturally tend to dwell on the observable and tangible, and are wary of pies in the skies. Yet it must be recognized that we are concerned here with processes which have been vitally affected by additions to knowledge, unforeseen and undreamed of (except by Jules Verne, H. G. Wells, and others of their ilk); and that scientific caution should not extend to the exclusion of a dominant factor because it is difficult to grasp and fit into a model with a determinate, and hence limit-bound, outcome.[27]

An example of what this bias means in practice is provided in the reports published by the Commission on Population Growth and the American Future. Allen C. Kelley, chairman of the Department of Economics at Duke University, performed the research for the commission's lead economic report. In his report, Kelley states that his research "was initiated with the hypothesis that a diminished rate of population growth, even lower than prevailing rates in the United States, would be strongly beneficial to the long-term economic advance of the average American."[28]

Admittedly, to conduct any scientific research, a hypothesis is helpful. But why not a hypothesis that population growth is beneficial to economic advancement? In response to a query on this point, Kelley responded that "the hypothesis of the negative relationship between population and economic growth" was used because "almost everyone begins from this premise."[29]

But it would be exceedingly difficult to come up with a strongly positive view of the effect of population growth on economic development proceeding from a negative hypothesis concerning their relationship. Thus, if "almost everyone" proceeds from this negative hypothesis, it should not be surprising to find that the vast bulk of economic research tends to favor diminished or zero population growth.

It should be noted, though, that Kelley is a notable exception to this rule. For, as he says, the "mass of literature seems to 'confirm' it [the negative hypothesis], but . . . in my reading of the literature, I found little hard evidence in support of the negative association. Actually, as you may perceive, I am somewhat of an eclectic on the matter, which, incidentally, places me strongly in the minority."[30]

The Malthusian bias against population growth is most fully revealed in the report of the Commission of Population Growth and the American Future, which was headed by John D. Rockefeller III. President Richard M. Nixon laid the basis for the commission's formation with this statement in 1969: "One of the most serious challenges to human destiny in the last third of this century will be the growth of the population. Whether man's response to that challenge will be a cause for pride or for despair in the year 2000 will depend very much on what we do today. If we now begin our work in an appropriate manner, and if we continue to devote a considerable amount of attention and energy to this problem, then mankind will be able to surmount this challenge as it has surmounted so many during the long march of civilization."[31] In this statement, Nixon viewed population growth as both a "challenge"—something which calls us to new heights of accomplishment—and a "problem"—something to be eliminated.

In 1970, Congress passed an act to establish the Commission on Population Growth and the American Future: "Be it enacted by the Senate and House of Representatives of the United States of America in Congress assembled, that the Commission on Population Growth and the American Future is hereby established to conduct and sponsor such studies and research and make such recommendations as may be necessary to provide information and education to all levels of government in the United States, and to people, regarding a broad range of problems associated with population growth and their implications for America's future."[32]

Note here that population growth now no longer presents a "challenge" but a "broad range of problems." The act passed by Congress required the Commission on Population Growth and the American Future to "conduct an inquiry into the following aspects of population growth in the United States and its foreseeable social consequences," including specifically:

1) the probable course of population growth, internal migration, and related demographic developments between now and the year 2000;
2) the resources in the public sector of the economy that will be required to deal with the anticipated growth in population;
3) the ways in which population growth may affect the activities of Federal, State, and local government;
4) the impact of population growth on environmental pollution and on the depletion of natural resources; and
5) the various means appropriate to the ethical values and principles of this society by which our Nation can achieve a population level properly suited for its environmental, natural resources, and other needs.[33]

One might expect that the objectives of a commission of this type would be to objectively examine the pros and cons of population growth as it affects the future of the country. The inquiry begins on this note, with information-gathering and the determination of resource requirements in (1) and (2), respectively. It continues in the same vein, with inquiries into the effects of population growth on government, pollution, and natural resources in (3) and (4). But, in (5), we are suddenly presented not with an inquiry into population growth but a conclusion concerning population growth, namely, the Malthusian conclusion that it is necessary for the nation to achieve a "population level properly suited for its environmental, natural resources and other needs." In other words, rather than inquiring what can be done to develop resources and control the environment to meet population needs, the commission is specifically instructed to determine how best to control population to meet environmental and resource needs.

Prior to publication of its final report, the commission issued an interim report. This report maintains the facade of an objective inquiry into population growth. But in the body of the report we suddenly find near-zero population growth proclaimed as a "national objective." Discussing so-called unwanted births, the report states that there is "some evidence (from the 1965 National Fertility Study) that the elimination of unwanted births would result in fertility levels ultimately commensurate with *near-zero growth.* If this conclusion is valid for 1970 (the 1970 National Fertility Study now underway will provide the basis for such a judgment), the policy implications can hardly be overestimated because the *national objective* could be attained by enabling individuals to achieve their own preferences [emphasis added]."[34] The final

177

report of the Commission on Population Growth and the American Future, which makes the sweeping generalization that "no substantial benefits would result from continued growth of the nation's population,"[35] is thus anticlimactic.

Population control programs begin on a purely voluntary "family planning" basis, involving improving the means and extending the availability of birth control and contraceptive services. People are free to use or not use these services as they wish. For many in the population control movement, this voluntary "family planning" approach is as far as they wish to go.

However, there are others who do not believe that family planning is sufficient to achieve the desired population level. This is due to a belief that people will not have the "right" number of children if they are permitted to have the number of children they want. For example, Dr. Roger O. Egeberg, former HEW assistant secretary for health and scientific affairs, stated that we

talk about family planning and we champion the principles of free choice. But what does freedom of choice in family planning imply in the present state of society? It implies enormous population growth for the simple reason that the typical American family, if it can, will elect to have three children, not two. Thus, family planning, in the present state of things, will lead to intractable population growth . . . to 300 million Americans by the year 2000. . . .[36]

According to Judith Blake, chairman of the Department of Demography at Berkeley, the "principal cause of . . . [population] growth in the United States [is] the reproduction behavior of the majority of Americans who, under present conditions, want families of more than three children and thereby generate a growth rate far in excess of that required for population stability."[37] If this is the case, voluntary measures may not be sufficient. Socioeconomic controls or even compulsion may be necessary, for as Kingsley Davis puts it, with

indirect measures (that is, measures that leave people free to make their own reproductive decisions but which alter the conditions affecting those decisions), one hopes that compulsory measures will not become necessary. It can be argued that over-reproduction—that is, the bearing of more than four children—is a worse crime than most and should be outlawed. One thinks of the possibility of raising the minimum age of marriage, of imposing stiff penalties for illegitimate pregnancy, of compulsory sterilization after a fifth birth.[38]

University of California biologist Garrett Hardin is even more specific on the need for compulsion, stating that

birth control is not population control. Individual goals, not community needs, motivate individual actions. In every nation women want more children than the community needs. How can we reduce reproduction? Persuasion must be tried first. Tomorrow's mothers must be educated to seek careers other than multiple motherhood. Community nurseries are needed to free women for careers outside the home. Mild coercion may soon be accepted—for example, tax rewards for reproductive nonproliferation. But in the long run a purely voluntary system selects for its own failure: noncooperators outbreed cooperators. So what restraints shall we employ? A policeman under every bed? Jail sentences? Compulsory abortion? Infanticide? . . . Memories of Nazi Germany rise and obscure our vision. We need not titillate our minds with such horrors, for we already have at hand an acceptable technology: sterilization. . . . It should be easy to limit a woman's reproduction by sterilizing her at the birth of her nth child. Is this a shocking idea? If so, try this "thought-experiment": let n = 20. . . . Many who want no third child would fight resolutely for the freedom to have that which they do not want. But what is freedom? Hegel said that "Freedom is the recognition of necessity." People need to recognize that population control is needed to protect the quality of life for our children.[39]

Hardin goes on to suggest that there is an irreconcilable conflict between population control and the right of parenthood, which should be resolved in favor of population control for

the "right" to breed implies *ownership* of children. This concept is no longer tenable. Society pays an even larger share of the cost of raising and educating children. The idea of ownership is surely affected by the thrust of the saying that "He who pays the piper calls the tune." On a biological level the idea of ownership of children has not been defensible for almost a century, not since August Weismann drew his celebrated diagram of the relationship of germ plasm to somatoplasm. Biologically, all that I give "my" child is a set of chromosomes. Are they *my* chromosomes? Sequestered in the germinal area long before *my* birth, "my" gonadal chromosomes have lived a life of their own, beyond my control. Mutation has altered them. In reproduction, "my" germ plasm is assembled in a new combination and mixed with another assortment with a similar history. "My" child's germ plasm is not *mine;* it is really only part of the community's store. I was merely the temporary custodian of part of it. If parenthood is a right, population control is impossible. If parenthood is only a privilege, and if parents see themselves as trustees of the germ plasm and guardians of the rights of future generations, then there is hope for mankind.[40]

In an article entitled "The Tragedy of the Commons," Hardin compares American society of today to a "commons" full of cattle in which each herdsman attempts to

increase his herd without limit—in a world that is limited. Ruin is the destination to which all men rush, each pursuing his own best interest in a society that believes in the freedom of the commons. *Freedom in a commons brings ruin to all. . . .* our society is deeply committed to the welfare state, and hence confronted with another aspect of the tragedy of the commons. In a welfare state, how shall we deal with the family, the religion, the race or the class (or indeed any distinguishable and cohesive group) that adopts overbreeding as a policy to secure its own aggrandizement? To couple the concept of freedom to breed with the belief that everyone born has an equal right to the commons is to lock the world into a tragic course of action. . . . [We must have] mutual coercion, mutually agreed upon by the majority of the people affected. . . . The only way we can preserve and nurture other and more precious freedoms is by relinquishing the freedom to breed, and that very soon.[41]

As a means of encouraging the limitation of reproduction, or freedom to, as Hardin calls it, "breed," as well as postponement of marriage, Kingsley Davis suggests a

greater rewarding of nonfamilial than of familial roles. . . . For instance, the government could pay people to permit themselves to be sterilized; all costs of abortion could be paid by the government; a substantial fee could be charged for a marriage license; a "child-tax" could be levied; and there could be a requirement that illegitimate pregnancies be aborted. Less sensationally, governments could simply reverse some existing policies that encourage childbearing. They could, for example, cease taxing single persons more than married ones; stop giving parents special tax exemptions; abandon income-tax policy that discriminates against couples when the wife works; reduce paid maternity leaves; reduce family allowances; stop awarding public housing on the basis of family size; [and] stop granting fellowships and other educational aids (including special allowances for wives and children) to married students.[42]

In any deliberate effort to control the birth rate, Davis contends, the government also has "two powerful instruments—its command over economic planning and its authority (real or potential) over education. The first determines (as far as policy can) the economic conditions and circumstances affecting the lives of all citizens; the second provides the knowledge and attitudes necessary to implement the plans. The economic system largely determines who shall work, what can be bought, what rearing children will cost, how much individuals can spend. The schools define family roles and develop vocational and recreational interests; they could, if it were desired, redefine the sex roles, develop interests that transcend the home, and transmit realistic (as opposed to moralistic) knowledge concerning marriage, sexual behavior, and population problems."[43]

Planned Parenthood–World Population lists a number of what it calls "examples of other proposed measures to reduce U. S. fertility," including increased homosexuality; chronic economic depression; requiring women to work and providing few child-care facilities; compulsory abortion of out-of-wedlock pregnancies; compulsory sterilization of all who have two children—except for a few who would be allowed to have three; confining childbearing to only a limited number of adults; and stock certificate-type permits for children.[44]

180

Martha K. Willing, treasurer of Population Dynamics, carries these "proposals" one step further, with a plan in which "after the third child is born, both mother and father will have to present themselves at the hospital to undergo sterilization procedures. If the couple does not appear, or if only one appears, there will be no birth certificate issued to the third child, but instead a third-child paper. The mother can be tattooed or marked to signify a third birth to any subsequent doctor. Instead of the missing parent, the child can be sterilized on the spot, insuring that this undue share of the gene pool will not be carried forward." But, apparently wishing to cushion the sensibilities of anyone who might consider infant sterilization too harsh, Willing points out that such sterilization would be "so distasteful that extremely few parents would carry a third child past three months. Of these, even fewer would refuse sterilization after the third child is born. So it would be a rare child that was in fact sterilized under this scheme."[45]

Dr. Edgar Chasteen, board member of Zero Population Growth, has what appears to be an even more efficient population control plan. "The completely effective and reversible contraceptive necessary for a policy of compulsory birth control is not yet available," he says. "Medical science is experimenting, however, with a shot and a time capsule that would inhibit fertility indefinitely. Within a few years, such contraceptives will be as available and as pleasant as the sugar-cube polio vaccine. This will make it possible to innoculate all males and females against fertility as they reach puberty. After marriage, this process could be reversed by another shot or pill designed to restore fertility temporarily."[46]

In addition to these various proposals for preventing people from being born, there are others for eliminating people who are living but are defective, old, or mentally ill. Nobel Laureate James D. Watson, for example, believes that a child should not be given legal status until three days after its birth, so that should it be born with defects previously undetected within the womb, the "doctor could allow the child to die if the parents so chose and save a lot of misery and suffering."[47] And Robert H. Williams, a Seattle M.D., states that

law and policies should be changed to deal realistically with present and future problems related to imminent overpopulation and the quality of people's lives. . . . We should increase our activities immediately, and to a major degree, in dealing with population control, selective abortion, problems of mentation, aging, suicide and negative euthanasia. It seems unwise to attempt to bring about major changes permitting positive euthanasia until we have made major progress in changing laws and policies pertaining to negative euthanasia. We must exercise great wisdom, not only in attempting to ascertain what is right but what are the most intelligent routes to pursue in establishing the most appropriate laws and public policies concerned with the quality and quantity of life, both generated and terminated.[48]

For as Paul Ehrlich says, the "population explosion is an uncontrolled multiplication of people. Treating only the symptoms of cancer may make the victim more comfortable at first, but eventually he dies—often horribly. A similar fate awaits a world with a population explosion if only the symptoms are treated. We must shift our efforts from treatment of the symptoms to the cutting out of the cancer. The operation will demand many apparently brutal and heartless decisions. The pain may be intense. But the disease is so far advanced that only with radical surgery does the patient have a chance of survival."[49]

Population Control Means People Elimination

Population explosionists such as Paul Ehrlich believe that population growth must be stopped or civilization is doomed to destruction. As the front cover blurb of Ehrlich's *Population Bomb,* puts it: "Population control or race to oblivion?"

When anyone questions the need to *immediately* check U.S. population growth, as Julian L. Simon of the department of economics at the University of Illinois points out, the standard alarmist response is "a series of calculations about how after a certain number of doublings of population, there will be only standing room, or a solid mass of human bodies, on earth or in the U.S. This apparently shows that population growth must stop *sometime.* "

But Simon goes on to note that "of course population growth must stop sometime, just like any other growth process must stop sometime. But the question is—must growth stop *now?* And the standing-room-only sort of argument is quite inapplicable at this point in time."

Population alarmists assume that "if we do something *now* we will inevitably continue to do the same in the future. But one need not believe that if people decide to have more children *now,* they will also continue indefinitely to have them at the same rate. By analogy, because a man decides to have another bite of pie today does not mean that we should worry that he will eat himself to death. If he is like most people, he will stop after he recognizes a reasonable limit. But many seem to have a different model of people and fertility, that of the drunkard: if he takes one drink, he's down the road to hell."

Furthermore, Simon notes, population alarmists seem to think that "people (especially poor people) have babies without rational thought, and without wanting them. It is wrong, however, to think that 'primitive' people breed prolifically and without rational control." For the "quickest and surest route to [a reduced birth rate] is . . . by further increasing life expectancy, and especially by reducing child mortality. Recent empirical studies have shown that when child mortality falls, the birth rate falls, too. And the best way to reduce child mortality is by better nutrition."

182

So, Simon comments, until mortality falls "very low, parents will continue to have more children than they want, on the average, because of the conservative but rational desire to err on the high side rather than the low side. That is, parents are more willing to chance having *too many* children rather than *too few*, too many sons rather than none. Recent analyses have shown that if people really do behave in this fashion, the effect of a fall to a very low mortality rate could have a terrific effect on the birth rate in poor countries, in exactly the direction the population-control enthusiasts wish."

But some Westerners, Simon sums up, have the "opposite view with respect to death control. They would *lessen* the emphasis on increasing life expectancy. As Ehrlich put it, '. . . we should see that the majority of federal support of biomedical research goes into the broad areas of population regulation, environmental sciences and behavioral sciences, rather than into shortsighted programs of death control.' But I am sure that to postpone the drop in mortality will *not* achieve what population-control extremists want as well as will perfect death control—and it is morally abhorrent, too, at least to me."[50]

The population control approach thus is not only counterproductive but morally repugnant. But, unfortunately, postponing efforts to save people's lives is the least offensive and violent aim of the population control, or "Stop the world—I want *them* to get off," mentality. For this mentality is based on a single-minded ideological view that humanity will "breed" itself into extinction unless population is controlled *now*. It thus attacks increasing numbers of people as if they were cancerous cells that must be cut away at any cost. It offers the velvet glove of "voluntarism," but behind it lurks the mailed fist of coercion, buttressed by such "humanitarian" measures as compulsory sterilization, euthanasia of the mentally and physically defective, the abortion of babies before birth, and infanticide after birth.

Underneath all neo-Malthusian writing and thinking, states distinguished psychiatrist Fredric Wertham, lies hidden a "suggestion of death and violence. This manifests itself in many different ways. However, concealed under a cover of moralisms, the whole idea includes a depreciation and devaluation of human life. Death rates and birthrates are discussed in conjunction, with the same highhandedness. A high birthrate is an unmitigated evil and the sole cause of further evils. A high death rate is a boon."

It is a dehumanization to speak of the procreation of people, Wertham goes on to say, as "barnyard activity or rabbitlike behavior. The superfluous people, and especially their parents, are regarded as really guilty. The equation is simple: poverty is equal to superfluousness, superfluousness is equal to a crime. The consequence is punishment. You may have the right to exist, but you lose the right to procreate. If someone in authority tells us that we have no right to procreate, it is only one step further for him to tell us we have no right to live. As William Hazlitt summarized the Malthusian theory: 'The poor have no right to live any longer than the rich will let them.' The overpopulation theory lends itself to abuse as justification for letting people die, for hidden violence."

And, although the avowed motive may be to bring about a better life, Wertham points out, controlling the size of a whole nation comes "perilously close to forcible elimination. The theoreticians of the Nazi 'population politics,' like the German-Swiss psychiatrist Professor Ernst Ruedin, were steeped in Malthusianism. A recent communication to a West German magazine states that the menace of overpopulation shows how sensible and beneficial for all mankind Hitler's 'population politics' could have been. It is strange how few people realize the close connections—psychological, social, and political—between the very term 'population explosion' and the extermination of populations."[51]

Wertham also tells the story of the so-called "euthanasia" movement in Germany, where euthanasia had not the ancient and legitimate meaning of "mitigation and relief of pain and suffering of the death agony" but the murderous meaning of "putting of a person to death painlessly." According to Wertham, from the "very beginning—that is, before the outbreak of war and before any written expression by Hitler—it was officially known to leading professors of psychiatry and directors of mental hospitals that under the designation of 'euthanasia' a program was about to be carried through by them and with their help to kill mental patients in the whole of Germany. The object was 'the destruction of life devoid of value.' That definition was flexible enough for a summary proceeding of extermination of patients."[52]

Wertham recounts how a book called *The Release of the Destruction of Life Devoid of Value* was most influential in the German euthanasia movement. Published in 1920, the book was written by two prominent scientists, the jurist, Karl Binding, and the psychiatrist, Alfred Hoche. Binding and Hoche, Wertham relates, speak "of 'absolutely worthless human beings'; they plead for 'the killing of those who cannot be rescued and whose death is urgently necessary'; they refer to those who are below the level of beasts and who have 'neither the will to live nor to die'; they write about those who are 'mentally completely dead' and who 'represent a foreign body in human society'. . . . These ideas were expressed in 1920. Surely Hoche and Binding had not heard of Hitler at that time, nor did Hitler read this book. It is not without significance that at this time, when Hitler was just starting his career, the 'life devoid of value' slogan was launched from a different source. Evidently there is such a thing as a spirit of the times which emanates from the depths of economic-historical processes."

"This little book," Wertham sums up, "influenced—or at any rate crystallized—the thinking of a whole generation. Considering how violence-stimulating the ideas in it are, it is significant that both authors were eminent men who played a role as intellectual leaders in a special historical period. This illustrates the proposition that violence does not usually come from the uncontrolled instincts of the under-educated, but frequently is a rationalized policy from above."[53]

Sterilization and abortion were also a significant part of German life before Hitler arrived on the scene. Kenneth M. Mitzner, founder of Mobilization for the Unnamed and president of the League Against Neo-Hitlerism, tells how the

abortion movement began before 1900 and had significant support in intellectual circles by 1911. An overpopulation psychology began to develop at about the same time. After Germany's defeat in World War I, there was a complete collapse of social and ethical values. Abortion, strongly promoted by certain intellectual groups, became rampant, although still illegal. . . . By the time Hitler came upon the scene even as a bit player, German society was saturated with the anti-life mentality. Hitler just perfected the techniques. . . . Hitler opposed abortion for "Aryans." [But] abortion for non-Aryans was promoted and even forced. In the Rusha case (Nuremberg), the abortions performed on Russian and Polish forced laborers were judged to be crimes against humanity. It is interesting that some Nazi doctors balked at doing abortions beyond 20 weeks but many New York doctors do not.

Mitzner goes back "a little further in history to revolutionary France in 1795 and the man who, as far as we can determine, was the first in the modern western world to promote abortion as a means of population control. . .:

'This state will forever be poor, if its population surpasses the means by which it can subsist. . . . Do you not prune the tree when it has overmany branches? . . . but it is not at the moment that man reaches maturity one must destroy him in order to reduce population. It is unjust to cut short the days of a well-shaped person; it is not unjust, I say, to prevent the arrival in the world of a being who will certainly be useless to it. The penalty against child-bearing mothers (in Europe) is an unexampled atrocity. Who then has a greater right to dispose of the fruit than she who carries it in her womb?' "

Does anyone really believe, asks Mitzner, that "France was over-populated in 1795? Does anyone really believe that the Marquis de Sade (after whom 'sadism' is named) made these statements because of a humanitarian concern for the welfare of society?"[54]

The basic principle of the abortion movement is "precisely the principle that underlay the Nazi extermination of the Jews," states Charles E. Rice of the Notre Dame Law School.

It is the principle that an innocent human being can be killed if his existence is inconvenient or uncomfortable to others or if those others deem him unfit to live. The unborn child is in fact a human being from the moment of his conception. This

185

could easily be demonstrated at length. Even if you somehow do not believe that the child in the womb is a living human being, you ought at least to give him the benefit of the doubt. If an innocent human being can be killed because he is too young, that is, he has not lived nine months from his conception, there is no reason in principle why he cannot be killed because he is too old. Or too retarded. Or too black. Or too politically undesirable. The philosophy is Nazi Germany's. And this nation is adopting it.[55]

Once we permit the killing of the unborn, points out R. A. Gallop of the University of Manitoba, there will be "no stopping point, no age limit. We are setting off a chain reaction which will eventually make us the victims. . . . A doctor who will take money for killing innocent children in the womb, will kill anyone for an appropriate fee. This is the terrible nightmare we are creating for the future!"[56]

For man's civilized belief that the road to social maturity is the conversion of the unwanted into the wanted is discarded by doomsday prophets who call for heartless and drastic measures to curb their manufactured overpopulation crisis, comments Herbert Ratner, nationally known medical authority. Here, we should not be misled, states Ratner, by "the hue and cry of automatic liberals who fervently proclaim against the Vietnam War and capital punishment—against the killing of strangers. When it comes to the killing of our most intimate neighbors, these same automatic liberals fiercely plump for parricide in their espousal of abortion on demand. To seek liberty and happiness through the exclusion of life is a peculiar abridgement of the dictum for all, the right to life, liberty and the pursuit of happiness."[57]

The population control movement, as its name implies, is thus concerned not so much with solving problems as it is with controlling people. As Milton Himmelfarb, director of research and information services of the American Jewish Committee, states, the "political motivation in question is, I believe, an authoritarianism so intense that it is hardly to be distinguished from totalitarianism. This hypothesis explains why the alarm about population was sounded when the American population was *not* growing alarmingly: If you want emergency powers—authoritarian, even totalitarian powers—you must first persuade people that there is an emergency."[58]

Or, as Herbert Ratner puts it, the "true interest" of population control propaganda emanating from voluntary and official agencies and foundations is "not in the happiness of a person already here, but in the control of present population for the sake of a blueprinted future, a future which increasingly sounds more and more like a blueprinted future for an animal colony rather than a human society."[59]

Considering the ultimate control that would exist if the state had the right to determine who was to be born, Samuel McCracken of Reed College observes that "I can imagine no multiplication of state power more noxious in itself and more destructive of freedom than granting the state the right to license existence. Lest this seem an overwrought way of looking at the issue, consider the world envisioned by compulsory schemes of the sort Chasteen explicitly supports and to which Ehrlich's scheme inevitably leads. The granting to the state of the power to control the production of citizens is bound to alter the relation between it and them, no matter what theory of government one holds." And, McCracken sums up, the theory of government under which the state is granted a veto over creation is the "one which O'Brien in *1984* described to Winston Smith in the basement of the Ministry of Love. And between that theory and the doctrine of compulsory population control there is no conflict at all."[60]

But, if population controllers appear totally insensitive to the destruction of political freedom and morality that would ultimately result from their programs, they also seem completely oblivious to the human and societal problems immediately caused by their proposals. As James Ridgeway points out, for example, Ehrlich's proposals would lead to "a greater use of technology in the form of the pill, coil, etc., administered to women, without any great concern for the woman's health. Just as pesticides can break down the environment by killing fish and aquatic plants, so can birth-control instruments break down the environment by causing harmful physical and psychological effects in women."[61]

For example, adverse effects such as the following have been observed with varying incidences in women taking birth control pills: nausea, vomiting, gastro-intestinal symptoms, breast tenderness, breast enlargement, breast secretions, breakthrough bleeding, vaginal spotting, suppression of menses, changes in menstrual flow, increase in cervical erosions, increased cervical secretions, yeast vulvo-vaginitis, loss of scalp hair, skin pigmentation and discoloration, urticaria, erythema nodosum, erythema multiforma, hemorrhagic eruption, allergic rash, itching, acne, jaundice, leg cramps, edema, increased weight, elevated blood pressure, mental depression, suppression of lactation, thrombophlebitis, pulmonary embolism, cerebral vascular accidents, and vision impairment.[62] As Herbert Ratner comments, it is "safe to say that The Pill is the most dangerous drug ever introduced for use by the healthy in respect to lethality and major complications. It is certainly the most talented drug ever introduced in its ability to produce diverse and varied disease phenomena and systematic abnormalities in normal women. . . . Finally, we are ignorant of The Pill's long range effects, particularly as a contributing cause of cancer."[63]

Meanwhile, legalized abortion is resulting in not only millions of infant deaths but a "surprising" number of maternal deaths and near deaths, according to Matthew J. Bulfin, M.D. According to Bulfin, 87 percent of all obstetricians who viewed an exhibit on abortion and filled out a questionnaire stated that they had hospitalized patients with significant complications following legal abortions. "As the vast majority of abortions are done for social reasons," Bulfin reports, "the deaths and near deaths that do occur from the operation are especially tragic. Some of the most catastrophic type complications following legal abortions occur in young teen-age girls."[64]

It is consequences such as these that perhaps prompt an ecological writer such as Frederick Elder to observe that

anthropocentric man, even though placing man in the center of things, does not deal with his species in a spirit of reverence. He will build a pinball machine of a world without ever asking whether such a project violates something in man. . . . He will quickly agree to abortion on demand as an answer to the population question without ever pausing to reflect upon the fact that abortion on demand marks the same kind of narrow-answer approach that has brought humanity to the brink of ecological disaster in the first place. . . . With reverence for life as criterion for judgment, it can be asked whether solving the population problem by abortion is on any higher ethical plane than solving it by means of forced starvation or nuclear weapons.[65]

Or, as Richard Neuhaus, pastor of Brooklyn's Lutheran Church of St. John the Evangelist, puts it, those who "consider all people (except themselves, presumably) flies in the ointment of nature's pristine holiness, and those eager to subordinate the claims of the poor to their own sense of privileged security, are quick to pick up the makings and fashion from them a cloak of morality in which to clothe their surgically final solution of the problem presented by the cancerous growth of inconvenient people. Theologians and other people who think deep thoughts should be told that ideas such as the political rights of trees, nature's equality with man, and our need to revise our notion of respect for human life should not be left lying around where mad men can get at them."[66]

Norman Podhoretz, editor of *Commentary* magazine, tells about participating in a

conference in Washington called to explore the question of whether mongoloid infants should be permitted to live. Of course the organizers of the conference phrased the problem in considerably less brutal terms than I have just done, but that was essentially what we had come together—geneticists, biologists, medical men, writers, philosophers, and theologians—to discuss. Setting out for Washington, I had expected that there would be very little disagreement on the main point. To my amazement, however, I discovered that a substantial body of sentiment—substantial less in numbers than in the eminence of those, especially from the scientific community, who constituted it—was by no means willing to grant mongoloids an undisputed right to live. Such creatures, they argued, are an intolerable burden to their parents, to society, and to themselves.

188

Podhoretz relates that "one very distinguished scientist, for example, told me he saw no reason why anyone who accepted abortion should balk at infanticide, particularly when the infant in question was known to be defective whereas the fetus to be aborted might be normal and sound. Hearing this, I was reminded of the old Catholic argument of the 'slippery slope,' according to which the legitimation of abortion would set off just such a downward moral momentum as was implicit in the distinguished scientist's position."

Podhoretz responded to the scientist that "anyone who sees no difference between a fetus and a newborn baby ought to be condemning abortion as murder and not applauding infanticide as enlightened. Certainly, I said, mongoloids are defective, but so are many other kinds of people. Some are blind, some are deaf, some are halt, some are lame, and some have missing limbs; some are given to madness and some are the prey of disease. If mongoloids can be put to death, why not these, and if these, why not anyone who fails of absolute perfection?"

It is clear, Podhoretz goes on to say, that

the ethos out of which ideas like these emerge has infected the population control movement. . . . It is this which leads me to suspect that we may be dealing here not merely with an effort to control the size of the population but with an effort to control its character; not merely with an effort to control the quality of life but with an effort to control the quality of the human "stock" itself.

The last time such an effort was made, of course, was by the Nazis, and so horrible were the consequences that many people assumed it would never be tried again. Evidently, however, it has taken only twenty-five years for the eugenic dream to return—and now that it is back, it is back in force, purged of its crackpot racism, bolstered by an infinitely greater store of knowledge than was ever available to the Nazi scientists in those primitive days before the discovery of DNA and RNA and the "cracking" of the genetic code, and armed in the righteousness of a promise to eliminate all hereditary disorders and to save the world at last from human imperfection itself.

If this is truly what we are faced with in the ideology of population control, we all have reason to tremble. "Use every man after his desert," said Hamlet, "and who should 'scape whipping?" *A fortiori*, then: Let only the perfect live, and who should 'scape killing? Who, that is, but the framers of the definition of what "perfection" means? And even they in the end would devour themselves, so full of murderous hatred is the fantasy of human perfection for the reality of human life and for the imperfections to which the flesh must always be heir no matter what the geneticists or anyone else may ever contrive to do.[67]

Conclusion

The ideology of population control is concerned not so much with population as with *control*. The so-called population problem is simply a smoke screen used to conceal the real motive of gaining absolute control over not only the lives but the procreation of people. The population control ideology is thus totally repugnant to American political principles of equality and justice and totally destructive of the Judeo-Christian moral heritage on which the United States was founded.

The population control movement preaches "quality," not equality, with the missing e signifying the elimination of those who fail to measure up to an arbitrarily and ideologically defined "quality of life." Under this dispensation, all Americans become not individual human beings with an equal and inalienable right to life but biological specimens whose right to life is dependent on whatever current definition of "quality" happens to be politically in vogue.

Population control operates not on the basic rule of justice that a person is innocent until proven guilty, but on the perverted principle that people can be denied the right to life for supposed "problems" that have not as yet even occurred much less been proven to have been caused by those to be eliminated. Under this approach, all Americans are declared "guilty" without a trial and exposed to potential elimination at any time, since there is no way of ever proving that they will *not* cause "problems" in the future.

The population control movement clothes itself in moralisms to justify its substitution of "quality of life" for the sanctity of life. But it simultaneously attempts to destroy the right to life, the sacredness of the family, the inviolability of the person, the right to parenthood, the primacy of heterosexual relations, and every other moral principle of a civilized, humane, and progressive society.

However, the development of the population control movement should not come as a surprise. For it is, in fact, the logical outcome as well as the final gasp of the liberal Welfare State of today. Supposedly, the basic purpose of the Welfare State is to succor those who cannot take care of themselves, the poor, the elderly, the handicapped. But Garrett Hardin tells us that because of the inevitable "tragedy of the commons" in which the "freedom to breed" inexorably conflicts with equal rights to the common welfare, this Welfare State goal will bring ruin. So, to save its own skin, the Welfare State begins practicing not welfare but "wombfare," destroying rather than nurturing its young.

However, the "tragedy of the commons" is not a justification for population control. It is rather a call for the elimination of the Welfare State. This is because the Welfare State is in the long run a way not of helping people but controlling them. And population control is the last desperate act and ultimate weapon of a Welfare State whose lust for power and instinct for survival knows no political or moral limits.

190

What population control boils down to is a blatant and brutal attempt to solve problems not by alleviating the conditions that cause them, but by eliminating the people who have the problems. But the idea of eliminating problems by getting rid of people is not new. The concept has been with us always.

Nor should anyone think they are outside the pale of population control ideology. Hardcore population controllers effectively exclude no one from their overpopulation syndrome. They do not like the poor because their "quality of life" is inferior. They do not like the middle class because they have most of the babies. And they do not like the rich because they consume too many resources.

But where the state promotes contraception, sterilization, abortion, infanticide, and euthanasia on demand or *command,* we find not only fewer people but the depravity of a Nazi Germany or the dissolution of society such as in the latter stages of the Roman Empire. For these population control "tools of the trade" are not a medium for increasing human happiness but a method of committing national suicide. As Malcolm Muggeridge observes, in the

birth pill, quasi-divine invention, a little death wish in itself, may be seen the crowning glory of the pursuit of happiness through sex. To adapt a famous saying by Voltaire, if the pill had not been invented it would have been necessary for it to exist. . . . With the pill, the procreative process has at last been sanctified with sterility. Aphrodite sinking into the sea, unmenstrual, and forever sterile; unending, infertile orgasm—a death-wish formula if ever there was one. Add the possibility, even probability, that in the long run the pill will prove to be a scourge compared with which afflictions like the Black Death seem like an influenza epidemic. . . . This neat compact death wish, so easily swallowed, is for export as well as home consumption. Under the auspices of the World Health Organization and other enlightened agencies, earnest colporteurs of contraception carry the good news to darkest Africa; awesome lady missionaries of family planning take their coils and caps and pills, as traders once did colored beads, to the teeming populations of Asia and Latin America. Only among the Western educated, however, do they find any appreciable number of clients. In the countryside their product has few takers. The result is that it is the new bourgeoisie, the residents of *Oh! Calcutta* rather than of Calcutta proper, who take to the pill. The others continue to procreate regardless, leaving the apostles of the liberal mind to the self-genocide they have chosen. Truly, God is not mocked.[68]

191

9
THE AMERICAN POPULATION CHALLENGE

Population continues to grow in the United States today. But there is no "population explosion." The explosion is in population control propaganda that threatens to undermine and destroy the basic rights of life, liberty, and equality that form the moral and legal foundation of the country.

It is not simply that hardcore population controllers want to determine how many people there are in the land. Nor is it just that they want to regulate the number of births. What they want is power over life and death. They want the power to decide who lives and who dies.

To gain this godlike power, they are willing to pervert and overturn practically every value of a humane society—values that it has taken thousands of years of trial and error and bitter experience to slowly and painstakingly develop.

The right to life, the sanctity of human life, the right to have children, the inviolability of the family, government as servant rather than master: none of these values is sacred to the population controllers. They are just a few of the basics that the populationists consider totally expendable in their drive to achieve the power of life and death over all of us.

The population controllers know best how to build a "good" society. And, of course, their definition of a good society is one in which they decide who lives and who dies. And the penalty for not "fitting" in their "good" society is not ostracism or imprisonment; it is death.

The population controllers have a vision of a utopia in which everybody will be just like them—intelligent, farseeing, perfect. Meanwhile, those who do not fit this utopian pattern will be permanently excluded; they will be contracepted right out of existence, or sliced, sucked, scalded or smothered to death if they happen to make it as an unborn child in their mother's womb, or dipped in a bucket of saline solution if they should have the temerity to be born, or perhaps gassed at a later date if it should turn out after their birth that they have physical, mental, emotional, ideological, or other "defects" that disqualify them for existence in the population-controlled utopia of the future.

All of this will, of course, be done for the people's own good, because the anguish of living as an imperfect human in a utopia of perfect beings would be too much for them to bear. Nor will people be able to successfully protest that they would prefer to have their life with its "defects," because the population controllers, of course, will know better what is best for them, aside from the fact that such a plea would, in effect, be prima facie evidence of a "defective" understanding of what is required to live in a utopia.

The population control movement thus presents not merely an economic, social, and political crisis but a profoundly moral challenge to America. For the ideology of population control is ultimately a moral aberration resulting from man's turning away from God and attempting to become godlike himself. It is in many cases, in fact, precisely those who are most vociferous in proclaiming the "death of God" who are also most vehement in promoting death for the American population.

Norman Podhoretz recognizes the moral challenge presented by population control when he points out that "God, according to the Bible, commands us to be fruitful and to multiply. This too is entailed in the choice of life over death. Being imperfect, which is to say mortal, we cannot choose to live forever. But we can choose the longest possible life—all the life there is for mortal man to live—if we accept our rightful place in the chain of the generations. If we honor our fathers and our mothers, our days (so it is specifically written in the Ten Commandments themselves) will be lengthened upon the earth. And if we are fruitful and we multiply, our days will be further lengthened through our issue on the earth. To choose life is therefore also to choose the breeding of life. Thus, according to the Bible, saith the Lord."

By contrast, Podhoretz observes, the "Devil, if he exists, does not command us to be fruitful and to multiply. If he exists, he exists for the purpose of tempting or seducing as many of God's creatures as he can into a refusal to choose the breeding of life. He is nothing, we know, if not cunning. The Bible suggests that he lures us into suicide through playing on our fantasies of eternal life which spring in turn from our fear of death. *Lo mot t'mutun,* says the serpent to Eve in a statement so emphatic that, if accurately translated, it would have to read: "You shall not surely die dead.'"

With just such cunning manipulation of the laws of the human organism, Podhoretz concludes, does the

Devil lure us away from fertility and into the service of sterility. As he seduces into suicide not with the praise of death but with the dream of an escape from death,

194

so he seduces into sterility not with denunciations of the generative act but with the promise of sexual riches and sexual delights free of all troublesome consequentiality: onanism and sodomy, copulation without end and without issue. Above all, without issue; without issue above all.

Would he not, if he existed, be pleased with the size and condition of his American flock? Could even he with all his cunning have ever dreamed that so many would come to preach sterility and even to sterilize their very own selves in the name of a greater piety toward nature, a greater sense of responsibility to the future, and a greater reverence for life?[1]

Or, as Malcolm Muggeridge comments, when

men turn away from God, Pascal tells us, they must either imagine they are gods themselves or, aware of the disastrousness and absurdity of such a pretension, revert to being animals and seek their satisfaction in their own carnality. Megalomania or erotomania—the two great sicknesses of the age; the clenched fist or the phallus, Nietzsche or D. H. Lawrence, Hitler or Hugh Hefner. . . . How I envy the historian who, looking back across the centuries at the decline and fall of our Western civilization, as Gibbon did on that of Rome, will remark on how, as we systematically destroyed or allowed to be destroyed, all the values and restraints of the Christian way of life which we had inherited, we remained convinced that each innovation, each new assault on marital fidelity, on the sanctity of the home and the responsibilities of parenthood, was bound to be conducive to our well-being and enlightenment. . . . In the light of these antics, it is difficult to resist the conclusion that Western man, having wearied of the struggle by himself, has decided to abolish himself. Creating his own boredom out of his own affluence, his own impotence out of his own erotomania, his own vulnerability out of his own strength; himself blowing the trumpet that brings the walls of his own city tumbling down. Convincing himself that he is too numerous, and laboring accordingly with pill and scalpel and syringe to make himself fewer in order to fall an easier prey to his enemies. Until at last, having educated himself in imbecility and drugged and polluted himself into stupefaction, he keels over, a weary battered old brontosaurus, and becomes extinct.[2]

However, it should come as no surprise that men who lose their faith in God and God's providence also lose faith in themselves and their ability to maintain and expand the human enterprise. It is a curious fact only to those lacking in moral imagination that many of the people who claim that God is dead and man is godlike are the very same people who become increasingly more hysterical over the fact that population continues to grow. They wail in evermore frightening and nightmarish tones concerning the continuing growth of population and the absolute necessity to stop it immediately.

But this is strange. If these folks are so godlike, cannot they provide for increasing numbers of people? Apparently not. For, as soon as they eliminate God and place themselves in God's position, they immediately throw up their hands and immerse themselves in doom and despair. This is not only ironic but illuminatingly reflective of the truth that man without God does become hysterical over his problems, does become despondent over his ability to solve them, does destructively turn inwards on himself and those closest to him.

Thus the response to the challenge of population control must be a profoundly moral one, one which places faith in God and God's providence at the center of things. It must affirm the sanctity of life and the inalienable right to life of all Americans. It must assert the inviolability of parenthood and the family. And it must demand that government be "of, by and for the people" rather than in control of the people.

The first step in affirmation of the sanctity of life and the inalienable right to life is the passage of a human life amendment to the Constitution absolutely prohibiting the taking of innocent human life from the moment of conception until the "spirit doth part." It is one of the tragic ironies of modern times that the Supreme Court of the United States, the highest tribunal of a country that fought a war against the antilife excesses of Nazi totalitarianism, has recently taken away this inalienable right to life from Americans by permissively allowing abortion on demand, while the Supreme Court of Germany, the country where the Nazi attack on life arose, has even more recently magnificently reaffirmed the right to life by absolutely prohibiting abortion on demand, stating that the

life of each individual human being is self-evidently a central value of the order of justice. . . . The right to life is guaranteed to everyone who lives. . . . The security of human existence against encroachments by the state would be incomplete if it did not also embrace the prior step or 'completed' life. . . . Human life represents within the order of the basic law an ultimate value. . . . It is the living foundation of human dignity and the prerequisite for all other fundamental rights.[3]

The inviolability of parenthood and the family remains relatively intact as a traditional American right. But it must be reasserted and defended against all attacks and encroachments of the present and the future. The United Nations is not noted for allegiance to principles, but one that the organization has consistently upheld (in the Universal Declaration of Human Rights) is that the family is the "natural and fundamental unit of society. It follows that any choice and decision with regard to the size of the family must irrevocably rest with the family itself, and cannot be made by anyone else."[4] For it is for the "parents to decide, with full knowledge of the matter, on the number of their children, taking into account their responsibilities toward God, themselves, the children they have already brought into the world and the community to which they belong," states Pope Paul VI in *On the Development of Peoples.* "In all this they must follow the demands of their own conscience enlightened by God's law authentically interpreted, and sustained by confidence in Him."[5] Or, as G. K. Chesterton put it, the "most important things must be left to

196

ordinary men, the mating of the sexes, the rearing of the young, the laws of the state. This is democracy, and in this I have always believed."[6]

Finally, government must be the servant rather than the master of the people. In the United States of America, it is the government that is to be limited by the people, not the people by the government. The federal government is today spending hundreds of millions of dollars attempting to reduce population growth through provision of birth control services and the development of contraceptive technology. This is a business in which the government does not belong. Let the government get out of the birth control business.

But, conversely, this does not mean that government should positively promote increased population growth through programs or subsidies. This would be just as inappropriate as being in the birth control business.

Governments do not have children. People do. And becoming a parent is the most magnificent, unique, and personal thing that any man or woman can do. It is to partake in the creation of new life and the reasons for participation in this act of creation must come from within rather than be imposed from without.

Given the facts, the American people are quite capable of making their own decisions concerning how many children to have—without governmental intervention or interference. Decisions concerning child-bearing revolve around questions of values to which only prospective parents can provide the answers. All kinds of seemingly scientific statistics can be assembled concerning the effects of population growth or the lack of same. But, in the final analysis, these statistics are nothing more than numbers in the nude. To become decent for discussion, they must first be clothed in opinions or values. The decision to have children is based on value judgments that only individuals can make for themselves. Whether children are a joy to have or a burden to bear or both is for people in their role as parents to decide, not government. As Julian Simon puts it, the decision to have children must be made by "individuals and societies on the basis of their values. Science gives no answer to this question."[7]

Consequently, let government do its job of pursuing its traditional goals of freedom, order, and justice. Of course, government can do hardly anything that does not have some effect on child-bearing decisions. The provision of free public schooling, for example, indirectly subsidizes people with children. Yet the justification for public schools rests primarily on the belief that such subsidized education benefits the whole community rather than merely those who receive the schooling. Consequently, this public service and any other governmental program that may have an impact on child-bearing decisions should be justified on the basis of its primary intent and purpose, not in terms of its effects, if any, on population growth. The best government population policy is a neutral policy, or, in effect, no policy at all.

Given the facts of population growth free from population control propaganda and provided the opportunity to discuss and debate these facts in relation to their own personal values and beliefs, the American people are fully capable of making child-bearing decisions that are in the best interests of the country as a whole as well as in their own particular interests. Common sense will be their best guide as to what rate of population growth is most beneficial at any given point in time.

Population growth comes with its own built-in self-regulator, a completely humane and effective mechanism that utilizes changes produced by growth to maximize opportunities for the economic, social, and political advancement of all members of society. A natural balance is thus struck between the rate of population growth and the rate of changes advancing the human condition. This balance is achieved through the individual self-control of each and every member of society. And, because the balance is arrived at freely as a result of the individual, personal decisions of society's members, it provides the optimum adjustment between growth and change from the standpoint of overall welfare.

This is not to say that child-bearing decisions will always be ideal in every case. Nor is it to say that it will always be possible to gauge just how "optimum" the decisions are at any point in time. But it is to say that individual, personal decision-making is not only the best but the only possible approach to childbearing from the standpoint of achieving the greatest total welfare for the American people.

And it is also to say both reason and experience indicate that, should the American people choose continuing population growth, it will be broadly beneficial to them, their children, and their children's children.

For, as such things are measured, America is a relatively young country. As we enter our third century, we are confronted with vast challenges to our way of life and fantastic opportunities to improve our condition of life. Continuing population growth, not mere population survival, will be necessary to surmount these challenges and take advantage of these opportunities if we are to build a better life for all Americans.

To achieve this goal will above all require faith. This is because a human population that has faith welcomes growth as a sign of plenty. This is a population that places great value on human life, that believes each human life is by definition of inestimable quality because it not only comes from God but is a gift of God. This is a population open to life.

By contrast, a human population that lacks faith looks on growth with foreboding. This is a population whose fear of the future causes it to denigrate and deny the inestimable value and quality of each individual human life. In this population, the temporary pleasures of hedonism and indolence become dominant at the expense of the permanent rewards of sacrifice and hard work. This is a population that is closed to life.

Let us tell a tale of two societies, one that accepts population growth, another that rejects it. In the first society, population growth is accepted, and whatever changes are necessary to accommodate additional people are made.

198

We can say about this society that it places a high value on human life because it is willing to make the necessary changes in its cultural, political, and social institutions to make room and provide for more people.

However, in doing whatever is necessary to accommodate more people, the society is also the recipient of unforeseen benefits. The society is provided with an incentive to develop new methods and ways of doing things that are more productive than the old. It inculcates within itself the habit of creatively reacting to human needs and dynamically responding to new challenges as opportunities for improvement instead of problems to be avoided. Most significant of all, the society develops a greater humaneness because its culture becomes evermore grounded in the basic principle of service to others rather than service to self.

In the second society, population growth is rejected, and changes necessary to accommodate additional people are resisted. We can say about this society that it places a low value on human life because it is unwilling to effect the changes necessary to accommodate more people.

In refusing to accept more people, this society suffers unforeseen consequences. It loses the incentive to develop new and more productive ways of doing things. It inculcates the habit of reacting negatively to human needs. It habituates itself to respond destructively to new challenges by eliminating people instead of solving problems. Most significant of all, the society becomes less humane because its culture increasingly becomes based on the principle of service to self rather than to others.

Inevitably, both the creative society that accepts population growth and the destructive society that rejects it will be confronted with crises of one kind or another. It might be thought that the society whose population is growing will face more such crises than the society whose population is stationary. But the opposite is the case. The growing society solves its problems as it goes, while the no-growth society tends to accumulate problems.

When crisis strikes, which society will be better able to surmount it and survive for another day? Because of its past efforts to improve as a result of population growth, the creative society will react positively to the crisis, developing constructive solutions that will enable it to surmount the obstacles in its path. By contrast, the destructive society will have no ingrained habit of positive response to fall back on. Consequently, it will react negatively by eliminating people rather than solving problems. Eventually, the destructive society will succumb to its problems and destroy itself.

The moral is dynamic and clear: In this constantly changing world of ours, growth is not something that can be accepted or rejected without consequences. It is rather an inexorable law of life that applies to human populations as well as individual human beings.

Growing is to be desired and accepted, not feared and rejected. Growing, of course, hurts. But not growing hurts even more.

There is no such thing as not growing, staying the same. Either you go up

199

or you go down. As individual human beings, we know that somebody who stops growing as a person in effect commits suicide. The same is true for a human population that stops growing; it commits cultural suicide. In a changing world, lack of growth is not a sign of stability; it is a sign of death.

Population growth is the basic motivating force of human improvement in the world. There is no greater incentive to improving the lot of human kind than increasing numbers of people, particularly in societies that place a high value on human life and thus make whatever changes are necessary to provide for new human life. But, even in societies that resist change, population growth can provide the pressure necessary to break down the barriers of reaction and help to create a new and better life for all.

Wherever there are people, there are problems. But this is a description of the human condition, not a prescription for population control. Lack of population growth does not eliminate problems; it just makes them worse and more difficult to solve. In free, just, and rightly ordered societies, people solve more problems than they make. More people do more things better. This is the source of improving living standards.

This is not to say that there will be no problems in creating a better way of life for a growing number of Americans in the future; there are immense problems to be solved. But it is to say that it is precisely in solving such problems that a humane, just, and good society is created, a society in which all exist as individual, human beings sharing in the more abundant life provided by growth. As playwright Eugène Ionesco comments, we

are all—as numerous as we may be—unique souls, unique human beings. That is true of all living things. No two cats are alike, no two tigers bear the same markings on their fur. Stand in the street and look at the people! None is like the other. They are all the same and yet so different. The creativity of the Creator is infinite. The only truth is in the individual except when he submerges himself into the mass and loses himself in a totality. Then he is no longer himself and loses his personality and his worth. Similarly, no moment in the life of any person is like that of another. This evening or tomorrow everything can change. In pain and suffering can be found the eternal renewal of that which is good and beautiful in creation. The poor, the moderately well off, the rich, all cling to life. That is, they want to be![8]

And the future is to be viewed with optimism, not pessimism, states Rene Dubos, author and professor emeritus at New York's Rockefeller University, who tells us of his

enormous faith in the resiliency of human beings and of natural systems. Indeed, I take great pleasure in watching people and places rebound after a disaster. I am impressed in particular by the ability of human beings and of whole civilizations to change the course of their social trends, to start on new ventures, and often to take advantage of apparently hopeless situations for developing entirely novel formulas of life. This is what Carl Sandburg had in mind when he wrote in *The People, Yes* that he was "credulous about the destiny of man." In any case, I believe that optimism is essential for action and constitutes the only attitude compatible with sanity. As the French historian Elie Halevy wrote to one of his friends in 1895, "Pessimism is nothing but a state of mind, whereas optimism is a system, the finest and the most philosophical invention of the human mind." Optimism is a creative philosophical attitude, because it encourages taking advantage of personal and social crises for the development of novel and more sensible ways of life.[9]

Nor can we turn the clock back to some "simpler" period as some would seemingly have us do, according to Isaac Asimov, author and formerly an associate professor of biochemistry at the Boston University School of Medicine, who points out that a

double-edged sword of good and evil has hung over human technology from the beginning. The invention of knives and spears increased man's food supply—and improved the art of murder. The discovery of nuclear energy now places all the earth under threat of destruction—yet it also offers the possibility of fusion power as an ultimate solution to man's energy problems. . . . Science and technology are getting a bad press these days. Increasingly scornful of the materialism of our culture, young people speak about returning to a simpler, pre-industrial, pre-scientific day. They fail to realize that the "good old days" were really the horribly bad old days of ignorance, disease, slavery and death. They fancy themselves in Athens, talking to Socrates, listening to the latest play by Sophocles—never as a slave brutalized in the Athenian silver mines. They imagine themselves as medieval knights on armored chargers—never as starving peasants. . . . Yes, science has helped create problems, too—serious ones. And we must labor to solve them—in the only way history tells us problems have been solved: by science. If we were to turn away now, if a noble young generation abandoned the materialism of an industry, what would happen? Without the machinery of that industry, we would inevitably drift back to slavery. . . . In these days of urban decay and energy crisis, there is a constant longing to return to the land and flee back to a simpler way of life. But it can't be done. We have a tiger by the tail and we can't go home again. We never could. . . . We can save, conserve, cut out waste, but what we have we must keep. The only solution, as always in the history of mankind, is to solve problems by still further advances in technology.[10]

Perhaps the view of Herman Kahn, head of the Hudson Institute, can provide as good an insight as any into what the future may hold. Kahn's view is

both optimistic and pessimistic. We would prefer to call it realistic, and I think the emphasis is very much on realism, not on trying to give a sunny view or a dim view. . . . What we're saying basically is that even with bad management and bad luck and a certain amount of evil, we would expect the thing as a whole more likely

201

to come out well, rather than badly. It's remarkable—we argue—how well mankind is likely to be doing, even if it goes badly for a while. A good example of this: Let's assume this is 1900 and I tell you that in the next 75 years, per capita income is to be multiplied by five and the number of people by four and the total gross world product by a factor of 20. You'd say, "Gee that's a very optimistic prediction. You must really think things are going to get well." Well, not quite. There are two world wars, there's the Communist Revolution, there's Hitler, a Great Depression, and there are lots of other problems. What we're saying is that despite all of these problems, the system has enormous vitality, enormous ingenuity, and we know something in 1975 which we didn't know even 10 years ago. We know pretty much how to handle these problems—[although] not necessarily the way they will be handled, because who knows what the future is going to bring.[11]

Population growth causes change, but it is positive change that is beneficial to everyone, particularly those at the bottom of society. Author James Michener perhaps expresses this best when he says that "I like America because the movement upward that I was encouraged to make is open to all. I take pride in celebrating our 200th birthday because the sort of changes I have experienced and fought for remain possible in every aspect of our national life. I am hopeful about our future because I have seen the tremendous energy we can focus on a problem when the prospects look bleakest. America is a nation of incessant change, and I have always believed such a condition was good for people of energy and imagination."[12]

In August, 1975, two California demographers reported the possibility of a new "baby boom," based on 1974 California birth statistics, which are more current than those for the rest of the country. "Examination suggests that the decline in the nation's birth rate is coming to a halt and that an upturn is in the making," stated June Sklar, research demographer, International Population and Urban Research, University of California, Berkeley, and Beth Berkov, demographic analyst, Family Health Services Section, California State Department of Health, Berkeley. "To begin with, the proportion of childless young women is now very high, and there is evidence that they do not desire to remain childless permanently. To reach their reproductive goals, they will have to begin their families soon. Evidence that young women may be starting to make up for lost time is provided in the latest data for California."[13]

Crucial in the future trend of the overall birth rate, according to Sklar and Berkov, are "the large cohorts of women born during the peak baby boom years of the middle and late 1950's. In the next half decade they will enter their 20's. If present reproductive patterns continue, by 1980 their entrance into the prime reproductive ages will raise fertility by 9 percent for the crude birth rate and 2 percent for the general fertility rate; and if they do not continue the present pattern of postponing marriage and childbearing, fertility will rise even more. In sum, our evidence suggests that the American birth rate may have bottomed out and that the country is likely to see a rise in reproduction."[14]

It is of course impossible to know for sure what direction the American birth rate may take in the future, particularly in a time of social, economic, and political uncertainty. But, contrary to the propaganda of population control, it can be said that an increase in the birth rate will prove healthy and beneficial from a profoundly human viewpoint, as well as for the country as a whole.

For as Michael Novak puts it, to

marry, to have children, is to make a political statement hostile to what passes as "liberation" today. It is a statement of flesh, intelligence, and courage. It draws its strength from nature, from tradition, and from the future. Apart from millions of decisions by couples of realistic love, to bring forth children they will nourish, teach, and launch against the void, the human race has no future—no wisdom, no advance, no community, no grace. Only the emptiness of solitary space, the dance of death. It is the destiny of flesh and blood to be familial.[15]

In the United States of America today, this destiny is confronted by a population challenge. But the challenge is not the myth of overpopulation. It is the challenge to grow in people and plenitude and productiveness and power for good—or die the slow but not uncertain death of a nation that had an all-too-fleeting moment of glory, while failing to live up to its ultimate promise and potential for human greatness.

Grow or die! This is the American population challenge.

EPILOGUE

THE UNITED STATES
AND WORLD POPULATION GROWTH

This is a book about population growth in the United States. It is not a book about world population growth. Yet, inevitably, the question will be asked: Yes, but what about India?—and, by extension, what about all of the developing countries where population growth is so rapid and growth rates so high? The tacit assumption behind this question is that, even if population growth is beneficial in an advanced nation such as the United States, surely this cannot be the case in India and other developing countries.

This book does not purport to be about world population growth. Yet some answer, however brief, should be provided to this question, because it affects the United States in several ways. The United States government, for example, is currently taking the position that developing countries should move to reduce their population growth. At the United Nations World Population Conference in 1974, the United States formally proposed that "all countries agree over the next 25 years to convince their populations to adopt a goal of an average of two children per family."[1] Since advanced nations such as the United States are already at or even below this two-child-per-family average, this proposal was primarily directed at developing countries.

But this official U.S. position has raised several questions. One is how can the United States tell other countries to control their population growth unless it also controls its own population growth? It is necessary, it is said, to set a "good example."

Another question is what effect should the existence of rapid population growth in developing countries have on U.S. aid programs to these countries? It has been proposed, for example, that aid should be directly tied to whether or not developing countries are operating family planning and birth control programs to reduce population growth. "It is time we face our real responsibilities," says the University of Kentucky's Wayne H. Davis, who believes that hunger in developing countries cannot be eliminated by feeding hungry people because this simply causes the reproduction of even more hungry people. "Those who call for increased food production in the world are asking only that we make a grave problem still more serious. Responsible people must oppose any food distribution plan that is not tied to a program of birth control and a genuine effort to help the recipients break the poverty cycle."[2]

A more radical proposal is what is called "triage." First advanced by William and Paul Paddock in a book called *Famine—1975,* this concept involves simply cutting off all aid to certain developing countries whose "population growth trend has already passed the agricultural potential. This combined with inadequate leadership and other divisive factors make catastrophic disasters inevitable. These nations form the 'can't-be-saved' group. To send food to them is to throw sand in the ocean."[3]

Garrett Hardin makes a comparable point using the metaphor of a lifeboat. "Metaphorically," he states, "each rich nation amounts to a lifeboat full of comparatively rich people. The poor of the world are in other, much more crowded lifeboats. Continuously, so to speak, the poor fall out of their lifeboats and swim for a while in the water outside, hoping to be admitted to a rich lifeboat, or in some other way to benefit from the 'goodies' on board."[4] What should the passengers on a rich lifeboat do? Hardin's answer, in effect, is to keep the poor people out of the rich lifeboat and do not share any "goodies" with them, because, in his words, "every life saved this year in a poor country diminishes the quality of life for subsequent generations."[5]

Paul Ehrlich also likes the boat metaphor, but he uses it to tell us that there is a bit of self-interest as well as humanitarian concern for the "quality of life" of future generations in controlling populations in developing countries. For "we are going to be sitting on top of the only food surpluses available for distribution, and those surpluses will not be large. In addition, it is not unreasonable to expect our level of affluence to continue to increase over the next few years as the situation in the rest of the world grows ever more desperate. Can we guess what effect this growing disparity will have on our 'shipmates' in the UDCs [underdeveloped countries]? Will they starve gracefully, without rocking the boat? Or will they attempt to overwhelm us in order to get what they consider to be their fair share?"[6]

There are a number of things that can be said about these views of world population growth as they affect the position of the United States. The first is that it is exceedingly presumptuous to believe that people in developing countries will all look to the United States for a good example of how many people to have. It is far more likely that they will view America's attempts to control its own population as not a good example but a ludicrous case of softheaded self-delusion. What else can these countries think when they observe a nation

206

with ten times or more their per capita income claiming that it cannot support a fraction of their population growth?

Second, it is downright arrogant for the United States to adopt the posture that it knows best how many people other countries should have. "Does it strike you as ironic that a country with as many unsolved social and practical problems as ours is so ready to tell the rest of the world how many children it ought to have?" asks Jane Jacobs. "The Population Growth Zero campaign tells us some things about our national character, most of them unpleasant. . . . We seem to have a messianic compulsion to settle the problems of the whole world and population control may be another vehicle for that."[7] In other words, the "ugly American" rides again, and as Daniel Callahan, director of the Institute of Society, Ethics and the Life Sciences, tells us, he is "no less ugly because he employs demographic and agricultural data."[8]

Third, it can be said that the approach of triage, or the lifeboat ethic, is morally obtuse. For, as Callahan points out, there is

no firm evidence to sustain a thesis that any of the poor countries are in so hopeless a condition that they must be written off. It is thus a perfectly moral course to act as *if* each and every country can be saved, and *as if* we can take at least some minor steps to help them (in cooperation with other developed countries). How can we know otherwise? Moreover, if we abandon them, we will all the more surely bring about a self-fulfilling prophecy; their fate will indeed be hopeless if no one comes to their aid. While we surely have obligations to future generations, our more immediate objective is toward those now alive. There is no moral justification for making them the fodder for a higher quality of life of those yet to be born, or even for the maintenance of the present quality of life. . . . If we are to worry about our duty to posterity, it would not hurt to ask what kind of moral legacy we should bequeath. One in which we won our own survival at the cost of outright cruelty and callousness would be tawdry and vile. We may fail in our efforts to help poor countries, and everything Dr. Hardin predicts may come true. But an adoption of his course, or that of triage, seems to me to portend a far greater evil.[9]

Finally, but most important, we may ask if the people who preach triage and the lifeboat ethic are not simply looking through the wrong end of the telescope, as Malthus did. For their views are based on the typical Malthusian misconceptions that people "breed" without limit and population growth hinders rather than helps economic development and food production.

These views are misconceptions because they are not grounded in real-world developments. In respect to the first, for example, Goran Ohlin, professor of economics at Uppsala University, Sweden, observes that "population alarmists tend to assume that population growth will always be excessive unless the 'egoistic' desire to have children is checked. Little is to be hoped for from the fertility transition—it is as if it had never occurred or, at any rate, will not occur again. But, in fact, it is already under way in many developing

207

countries and I think I only share a common impression when I find it overwhelmingly probable that it will occur everywhere. Population growth will slow down whether or not governments try to do anything about it."[10]

In respect to the second view concerning the negative effect of high population growth on human development in less developed countries (LDCs), the fact is that the exact opposite is the case. For, as University of Pennsylvania economist Richard A. Easterlin comments, the "evidence is that per capita economic growth rates have also been high. An analysis of the recent economic growth of these countries observes that 'the data for 1955–65 are remarkable. The average growth rate of 1.9 percent in the LDC's is certainly higher than the average rate in Western Europe or the United States during the nineteenth century. That the average rate for all non-Communist less developed countries is this high is one of the most striking economic facts of the two postwar decades.'[11] Moreover, it is likely that in most LDC's, per capita output growth in the recent period has been much higher than that in the century or so prior to World War II; we know this to be true of India, for which long period output estimates are available. Thus, higher population growth in LDC's in the postwar period has typically been accompanied by more rapid growth of per capita income."[12]

Julian Simon reports that Simon Kuznets compiled data for twenty-one countries in Asia and Africa, and nineteen countries in Latin America. In the separate samples, and in the forty countries together, he relates, there is "*not* a significant negative correlation between population growth and growth of per capita product; the relationships are actually positive though very weak."

Simon also recounts the work of Jean-Claude Chesnais and Alfred Sauvy, who analysed the relationship between demographic and economic growth in the 1960s for various samples of up to seventy-six less developed countries and found mostly slightly positive but nonsignificant correlations.[13]

Economist and demographer Colin Clark grouped by rates of population growth all countries in Asia, Africa, and Latin America covered by the *National Accounts of Less-Developed Countries, 1959–1968,* published by the Organization for Economic Cooperation and Development, and came up with the following result:

Countries with Population Growth of	Number of Countries	Median Growth of Real Product per Head, 1959–61 to 1966–68
Below 2% per year	8	0.6
2–2.4% per year	10	1.5
2.5–2.9% per year	19	1.6
Over 3% per year	23	2.4

"The result is quite clear, and the opposite of what most people expect," concluded Clark. "The developing countries with the highest rate of population growth also have the highest rates of growth of production *per head.*"[14]

Using population and per capita GNP growth-rate data for the period 1960–70 published in the *1972 World Bank Atlas* by the International Bank for Reconstruction and Development, the author performed a similar analysis for eighty-seven developing countries with over one million population. Weighted in terms of population size, the results are shown in the table below:

	Population Growth Rate, 1960–70			
	Less than 2%	2–2.4%	2.5–2.9%	3+%
Number of countries	11	21	28	27
Population (millions)	71	1632	569	273
GNP per capita growth rate, 1960–70, weighted in terms of population size	2.9%	1.7%	2.6%	3.0%

The table shows a definite positive correlation between population and per capita GNP growth rates for developing countries with population growth rates of 2 percent or more. These countries include all of the major developing nations and more than 97 percent of total population in the less developed world. Countries with population growth rates of less than 2 percent also show a high per capita GNP growth rate, but it should be noted that these are mostly small nations averaging less than 7 million people and including less than 3 percent of total world population.[15]

Furthermore, contrary to the views of the neo-Malthusians, population growth has also stimulated increasing per capita food production in developing countries. For example, both the Food and Agriculture Organization of the United Nations (FAO) and the U.S. Department of Agriculture (USDA) agree that from 1952 to 1972 per capita food production has increased in developing or low-income countries at an annual rate of approximately 0.4 percent. "In view of this," comments D. Gale Johnson, professor of economics, vice president and dean of faculties at the University of Chicago, and former president of the American Farm Economic Association, "the persistence of the idea that the food situation in low-income countries is deteriorating is surprising."[16]

The Preparatory Committee of the World Food Conference held in Rome in 1974 gave its assessment of the growth of food production during the same two-decade period as follows: "The fact that for so long a period food production in the developing countries has kept ahead of a rate of population growth that is unprecedented in world history is a tremendous achievement. Further-

209

more, food production in these countries in 1972 was 20 per cent greater than in 1966, the previous year of widespread bad weather, so that even between the troughs of the longer-term trend production has outpaced population growth."[17]

Furthermore, it is only in the twentieth century, with its high population growth rates, that developing peoples have come to have greater assurance of freedom from hunger. Hunger and famine have been a part of human existence throughout history at every level of population development. But, as the 1974 *Report of the U.N. Symposium on Population and Development* points out, food supplies have become "more certain and famines less frequent in the present century."[18]

As D. Gale Johnson puts it, those

who believe that the food situation of the poorer people of the world has deteriorated during the past quarter-century have no satisfactory explanation for a development unprecedented in recorded history, namely, the dramatic increase in life expectancy in the developing countries. During the 1950s there were a number of developing countries in which life expectancy increased at a rate of approximately one year per year—a rate of increase never achieved in Western Europe or North America. . . . The largest percentage declines in death rates occurred among the young. Infants and children normally suffer first and most from a reduction of food availability. Those of us who decry the high rates of population growth in the developing countries should not forget that the increases in these rates have been due entirely to reductions in death rates and not at all to an increase in birth rates. There has been an enormous reduction in human suffering that has gone largely unrecognized —the pain and grief of hundreds of millions of parents that have been avoided by the reduction in infant and child mortality. Thus, although the rapid growth of population has imposed costs, the benefits that have accrued from the factors causing this growth should not be ignored.[19]

In 1973–74, there was a food crisis, in which famine took lives in the African Sahel, Ethiopia, and parts of India. But, as the Economic Research Service of the U.S. Department of Agriculture reported in 1974, the factors that gave rise to this crisis are

largely transitory and can be corrected by intelligent policies. Very high prices and limited supplies of food and fertilizer are likely to prevail for the next year or two. The developing countries that rely on imported grain and fertilizer will be the most adversely affected. Any serious deterioration in their food production or in general world crop conditions in 1975 or 1976 could have serious consequences requiring additional emergency measures. In the longer term, food prices relative to prices of other goods and services can be expected to fall from current high levels, but may remain somewhat higher than in the late 1960's. Also, many aspects of food production and consumption that prevailed during the two decades prior to 1972 will reappear. During that period, more food was produced per person, food supplies

210

were generally adequate to meet demand, and the life expectancy of the world's population increased significantly. This will continue in most countries and for the world as a whole. But, also as in the past, substantial malnutrition will probably persist among low-income groups in the less prosperous developing countries, and special national and international nutritional programs will be necessary to help those most seriously threatened by food shortages.[20]

In 1975, according to the Agriculture Department's Economic Research Service, developing countries achieved a "sharp 5-percent increase in total agricultural production. More important, the index of per capita output climbed to a new high of 104 after three years in a row when per capita output held at a level equal to the 1961–65 average of 100." During the same year, total agricultural output "fell at least 1 per cent in the developed countries" because the "substantial recovery of U.S. and Canadian production was not enough to offset a sharp drop in the Soviet Union and more modest setbacks in Western and Eastern Europe."[21]

Summing up, the Economic Research Service states that the "availability of inputs—the underlying major determinant of the world's ability to produce more food—does not appear to be an impediment to future increases in production. Perhaps twice as much land is available for food production as is presently being used. The cost of bringing much of this land into production would not be prohibitive. The technology and inputs (such as fertilizer) to greatly expand production either exist or can be developed in both the developed and developing countries. Substantial increases in production capacities are now underway in both developed and developing countries. Trends of the past two decades do not indicate a significant slowing down of yield increases."[22]

And, as is pointed out by Roger Revelle, Richard Saltonstall Professor of Population Policy at Harvard University and director of the Center for Population Studies at Harvard, the "quantity of potentially arable land on the earth is so much larger than the area actually cultivated today, and the possibilities for increasing agricultural production on currently cultivated lands are so great, that the area of the earth's surface that will be devoted to agriculture in the future is chiefly an economic and social variable rather than a physical one."[23]

Furthermore, according to Revelle, in the specific case of India both the need and the possibilities exist for a "sharp acceleration in the rate of modernization of agriculture. The Irrigation Commission of the Government of India has estimated that the irrigated area of 43 million gross cropped hectares in 1973–1974 could just about be doubled during the next 30 years, at a total cost of roughly $14 billion. This would be less than 1 percent of India's current gross national product. If this projected irrigation development can be combined with an optimum utilization of fertilizers, with crop varieties that are

211

highly responsive to fertilizers (the 'miracle,' or high-yield, varieties), with control of plant diseases and pests and with development of the knowledge, skill and human potential of Indian farmers, the problem of India's food supply could recede into the background for the foreseeable future."[24]

Consequently, as James W. Howe and John W. Sewell of the Overseas Development Council state, triage and lifeboat proposals to

> turn our backs on the world's poorest people cannot be lightly dismissed—if only because of the stature of some of those who advocate this course. . . . This willingness to accept so inhumane a course of action may stem in large measure from despair that the task of bettering the human condition is not feasible for some countries. So many have said so much about the crises, the ills, and the awesome magnitude of the overall problems of development that the evidence of human *progress* has been lost from sight altogether. But the shocking thing about the admonitions to let death rates rise is that they are based on needless pessimism. Nothing in the record to date —or even in recent trends—warrants such a conclusion. On the contrary, that record encourages us not to tire, for the goal of meeting every person's basic human needs *is* within reach. Astonishing progress has been registered in the past thirty years. Now is hardly the time to abandon this course.[25]

Nor do current conditions warrant calls for triage or lifeboat ethics on the basis of alerting people to the need for action to alleviate an impending food problem. For prophecies of "inevitable" disaster have a self-fulfilling nature that can cause an opposite reaction. As John Maddox points out, commenting on the dire predictions of doom issued by extreme environmentalists, too often they have expressed "moderate or unsure conclusions in language designed to scare, sometimes with the open declaration that exaggeration is necessary to 'get things done,' but with the result that other people have been alarmed and mystified, not enlightened. . . . The most serious insidious danger in the environmental movement is that it may sap the will of advanced communities to face the problems which no doubt lie ahead."[26] Maddox is discussing the extreme environmentalist movement, but the same point applies with equal if not greater force to those who take a doomsday, or lifeboat, approach to the problems of feeding a growing world population. To put this another way, one would normally not vote for these folks as people with whom you would most like to share a lifeboat.

This is not to say that the United States should serve as Santa Claus to the developing countries of the world. This would not only be unfeasible but counterproductive. The Welfare State approach works no better on an international than on a national level, and there is good reason to believe that the availability of "free" American food aid has actually retarded rather than enhanced agricultural development in recipient developing nations.

It is also not to say that the United States should kowtow to Third World pretensions that we are to blame for their undeveloped status. As former U.S. Ambassador to India and the United Nations Daniel P. Moynihan states, it is time we asserted that "economic growth is governed not by Western or American conspiracies, but by its own laws."[27]

Neither is it to say that we should not point out when appropriate that countries of the Third World are on occasion their own worst enemies. For, as North Carolina State University economics professor E.C. Pasour, Jr., points out, much of the

cause for the current world food crisis can be attributed to the destruction or reduction of private property rights of food producers in countries where the hunger problem is most acute. Numerous examples can be cited where governments have weakened or destroyed economic incentives by confiscating private land, forcing farmers to work on collectivized farms, instituting price controls on food, and other such measures. India provides a good example . . . much of the food crisis in India can be attributed to actions taken by the Indian government affecting incentives of food producers. After her big electoral victory in 1972, Mrs. Gandhi's party reduced the amount of land that could be held by an adult male from 30 irrigated acres to 18 acres. The confiscated acres went to the landless. In addition to the direct effect of land confiscation on incentives, the policy also affected the profitability of tractors and implements. The reduced acreage was not large enough to support the machinery. The government also nationalized the wholesale grain trade, forcing farmers to sell their crops at fixed prices below the market level, whereas previously farmers were permitted to sell half of their grain to wholesalers at the higher market price. The impact of such actions on the quantity of food produced and marketed is predictable. (Black markets and corruption forced the government to rescind this action.) The adverse effect of price controls on output has been confirmed in scores of cases on every continent.

Consequently, Pasour concludes, there is "little doubt about the relationship between economic incentives and food production. A recent USDA study supports this view: 'Among the major impediments to increasing food production in both the developing and planned economies are policies designed to maintain low and stable food prices to consumers.' Thus, it seems paradoxical that population control (including Draconian controls such as compulsory sterilization of population in India and other countries) has received more attention than measures affecting economic incentives and food production in developing countries.[28]

Nor should we be patsies in relation to poor countries that, as Roger Revelle observes, are run by "an elite who could care less about improving the lot of their poor." For, as F. James Levinson of the Massachusetts Institute of Technology notes, it is "no secret that some countries receiving our food aid turn right around and export their own food production for profit."[29]

But the United States should not play the role of Scrooge, the *Christmas Carol* character invented by Dickens to deliver the classic Malthusian line that it is "better to let the poor die so as to reduce surplus population."[30] For, in terms of helping to increase food supplies in the developing world, it seems clear, as Revelle says, that the "American public would be more than happy to supply the technology and expertise to get the job done."[31]

The United States should also remove its Malthusian blinders and demand that, as Donald P. Warwick, chairman of the department of sociology and anthropology at York University in Toronto puts it, the "population field must be more honest." For, as Warwick relates,

> John Caldwell, an established member of the field, compared the population planning movement to "a kind of missionary enterprise where the missionaries are activated more by revealed truth than by a proven one." Measured by the gap between published reports and cocktail party conversations, this is one of the least candid areas of public policy or scholarly research. Reports are strewn with double-talk and double-think. "Population studies" is a euphemism for family planning research; "family planning" a cover for birth control; abortion (itself a euphemism for feticide) is called a "retrospective method of fertility limitation," and so on. Donors claim to be supporting programs aimed at helping couples to attain their own reproductive goals, when in fact most of the money goes for limiting births. Social scientists carry out methodologically dubious Knowledge-Attitude-Practice (KAP) surveys with the frank intention of generating data to show the need for family planning programs, and draw totally unwarranted conclusions from their findings. Private organizations subvert their own priorities and compromise their independence to take advantage of easy population money. Researchers give evidence of suppressing findings which deviate from donor expectations or which would embarrass the host country.[32]

In addition, the United States must recognize and realistically play a role in the vast changes in production and plenitude and power that are presently occurring and will continue to occur in the future, not only in developing countries but throughout the world as a result of population growth. For the world is entering on what space expert G. Harry Stine calls the Third Industrial Revolution, which, in Stine's words, is "astronautics passing from the stage of exploration to the stage of exploitation."[33]

The First Industrial Revolution extended human muscle through chemical energy and mechanical power. The Second Industrial Revolution expanded the human brain through automation and computer technology. Now, in the Third Industrial Revolution, Stine points out, these continually evolving human capabilities will enable us to vastly enlarge our field of operations by "getting into space on a large scale so that we can use the Solar System. Learning how to conduct industrial operations in space will occupy our best technical people for the next century. It will involve developing new industrial operations in orbit in the Earth-Moon system first—in near-Earth orbit, in lunar orbit, and on the Moon itself. Eventually, within fifty years, space industrial systems will grow to encompass most of the Solar System. . . ."[34]

And this will only be the beginning of the Third Industrial Revolution. For, as science writer Adrian Berry relates, we "have on Earth almost unlimited deuterium for our energy and a growing plastics technology for our industrial raw materials. We have solar energy in the still longer term, with all the benefits to come from mining the moon and exploiting the asteroids and planets. And, in the thousands of years to come, we shall exploit the energies to be found in hundreds of thousands of stars. Even the terrific but still mysterious energy sources of pulsars and quasars may be discovered and put to use." Consequently, Berry comments, it will seem "almost unbelievable to our descendants . . . that the year 1972, when breakthroughs of every kind were being made in space and planetary exploration, should have been marked by an intergovernmental conference in Stockholm attended by delegates from 112 nations with the official slogan of 'Only One Earth.' "[35]

World-renowned cosmologist Sir Fred Hoyle perhaps puts it best when he states that

> I would take to task those governments, those industrialists and economists, who see present-day technology as being more or less the end of the road; a road that started with our remote ancestors swinging about in trees, a road which has taken us precisely to our present-day position, and will take us little or no further. The truth, I believe, is exactly the opposite. The gap between us and the civilizations of the future may be as large as a factor of 10^9. The road is only just beginning. Almost everything remains to be played for.[36]

Thus it is that, far from heading for a rendezvous with ruin, we are moving, as New School for Social Research long-range planner F.M. Esfandiary states, toward an

> age of limitless abundance—abundant energy, food, raw materials. Decades from now this late 20th century will be remembered as a period in which the world shifted from age-old scarcity to a new era of plenty. . . . How absurd the American panic over scarcity when we are entering an age of abundance. . . . How absurd to focus on "finiteness" . . . when our world is transcending finiteness opening up the infinite resources of an infinite universe. . . . How short-sighted the exhortations to no-growth at precisely the time when we urgently need more and more growth. . . . How retrogressive the preachings to lower living standards of the relatively rich to raise conditions of the poor, at a time when we can raise everyone's living conditions by vigorously developing and spreading abundance, not sharing scarcity.[37]

The growth of world population to nearly four billion people has not only proved to be humanity's most tremendous and splendid accomplishment, but has brought with it unprecedented improvement in living conditions, or "quality of life." In the future, population growth will provide us with the way to expand on this achievement. All we need is the will—most important, the good will—to enable growing numbers of people to continue to create peaceful and beneficial human advancement throughout the world—and the universe.

NOTES

Preface

1. Julian L. Simon, "The Welfare Effect of an Additional Child Cannot Be Stated Simply and Unequivocally," *Demography,* February, 1975, p. 102. Simon develops this concept in greater detail in *The Economics of Population Growth* (Princeton, N.J.: Princeton University Press, forthcoming).

Chapter 1

1. R. Buckminster Fuller, "How Little I Know," *Saturday Review,* November 12, 1970, p. 70.

2. Ansley J. Coale, "The History of the Human Population," *Scientific American,* September, 1974, p. 43. It has taken anywhere from one million to 10,000 years to reach our present population level of 4 billion, depending on what date is selected for the arrival of the first human beings. Assuming humans have been on earth for a million years, Coale calculates that the annual rate of growth during the first 990,000 years was only 0.0015 percent. In other words, for every one million people on earth, only fifteen were added each year. As Coale observes: "Thus, whatever the size of the initial human population, the rate of growth during man's first 990,000 (about 99 per cent of his history) was exceedingly small." But, supposing instead of a million years ago, human history began 100,000 years ago. According to the United Nations, a continuous average increase of slightly less than 0.02 percent per year would have produced our present world population from only about two dozen people. This comes out to adding only 200 people for every one million people each year. Even assuming life began with only two people 10,000 years ago, the average annual growth rate necessary to arrive at our present world population of 4 billion would have been only 0.13 percent, requiring the addition of only 1300 people for every one million people, or one person for every 769 existing people each year.

3. Josiah Cox Russell, "Demographic Patterns in History," *Demographic Analyses, Selected Readings,* Joseph J. Spengler and Otis Dudley Duncan, eds. (Glencoe, Ill.: The Free Press of Glencoe, 1956), p. 67.

4. W.D. Borrie, *The Growth and Control of World Population* (London: Weidenfeld and Nicholson, 1970), p. 297.

5. Thomas Robert Malthus, *An Essay on the Principle of Population and a Summary View of the Principle of Population,* Anthony Flew, ed. (Harmondsworth, Middlesex, England: Penguin Books, 1970), pp. 71–72.

6. *Ibid.,* p. 74.

7. R.M. Hartwell, *History and Ideology* (Menlo Park, Calif.: Institute for Humane Studies), p. 1; reprinted from *Modern Age,* Fall, 1974.

8. T. R. Malthus, *An Essay on the Principle of Population,* 5th ed., 3 vols. (London: John Murray, Albemarle Street, 1817), III, pp. 320–21.

Chapter 2

1. U.S. Department of Commerce, *U.S. Economic Growth* (Washington, D.C.: Government Printing Office, 1969), p. 19; U.S. Bureau of Economic Analysis, *Long Term Economic Growth, 1860–1970* (Washington, D.C.: Government Printing Office, 1973), series A2, p. 183.

2. *U.S. Economic Growth,* p. 21; *Long Term Economic Growth, 1860–1970,* series A12, p. 183.

3. Quoted in Alfred Sauvy, *General Theory of Population,* Christophe Campos, trans. (New York: Basic Books, 1969), p. 412.

4. Simon Kuznets, *Economic Growth of Nations* (Cambridge, Mass.: The Belknap Press of Harvard University Press, 1971), p. 35.

5. *Ibid.,* pp. 22–24.

6. Simon Kuznets, "Population Change and Aggregate Output," *Demographic and Economic Change in Developed Countries* (Princeton, N.J.: Princeton University Press for the National Bureau of Economic Research, 1960), p. 324.

7. Sauvy, *General Theory,* p. 298.

8. Elgin Groseclose, "Too Many Mouths to Feed?" *Research Reports,* American Institute for Economic Research, Great Barrington, Mass., December 9, 1968, p. 198; reprinted from *Barron's,* November 18, 1968.

9. Colin Clark, "More people, more dynamism," *Ceres,* November-December, 1973, p. 28.

10. Albert O. Hirschman, *The Strategy of Economic Development* (New Haven, Conn.: Yale University Press, 1959), pp. 176–77.

11. Department of Economic and Social Affairs, *The Determinants and Consequences of Population Trends* (New York: United Nations, 1973), p. 365.

12. Kuznets, "Population Change," p. 328.

13. *Ibid.,* p. 330.

14. James A. Michener, "What's Good About Today's Youth," *U.S. News & World Report,* December 10, 1973, p. 54.

15. Edmund S. Phelps, "Some Macroeconomics of Population Levelling," U.S. Commission on Population Growth and the American Future, *Economic Aspects of Population Change,* Elliott R. Morss and Ritchie H. Reed, eds., vol. II of commission research reports (Washington, D.C.: Government Printing Office, 1972), p. 83.

16. Kuznets, "Population Change," p. 337.

17. Quoted in Colin Clark, *Population Growth: The Advantages* (Santa Ana, Calif: R.L. Sassone, 1972), p. 82.

18. Kuznets, "Population Change," pp. 331–32.

19. Allen C. Kelley, "Demographic Changes and American Economic Development: Past, Present and Future," U.S. Commission on Population Growth and the American Future, *Economic Aspects of Population Change,* Elliott R. Morss and Ritchie H. Reed, eds., vol. II of commission research reports (Washington, D.C.: Government Printing Office, 1972), p. 28.

20. Kuznets, "Population Change," pp. 331–32.

21. Sauvy, *General Theory,* p. 291.

22. *Ibid.,* p. 290–91.

23. Clark, *Population Growth,* p. 85.

24. Kuznets, "Population Change," pp. 326–27.

25. *Ibid.,* p. 327.

26. *Ibid.,* pp. 327–28.

27. Adam Smith, *The Wealth of Nations,* Edwin Cannan, ed. (New Rochelle, N.Y.: Arlington House, n.d.), vol. 1, p. 1.

28. Edwin S. Mills, "Economic Aspects of City Sizes," U.S. Commission on Population Growth and the American Future, *Population Distribution and Policy,* Sara Mills Mazie, ed., vol. V of commission research reports (Washington, D.C.: Government Printing Office, 1972), pp. 389–90.

29. George J. Stigler, "The Division of Labor Is Limited by the Extent of the Market," *The Journal of Political Economy,* June, 1951, p. 192.

30. *Ibid.*, p. 190.

31. Harvey Leibenstein, "The Impact of Population Growth on the American Economy, *Economic Aspects of Population Change*, p. 60.

32. William B. Reddaway, *The Economics of a Declining Population* (London: George Allen and Unwin, 1939), pp. 60–67.

33. Sauvy, *General Theory*, p. 289.

34. *Ibid.*, pp. 194–95.

35. Kuznets, "Population Change," p. 336.

36. *Ibid.*

37. *Ibid.*

38. *Ibid.*

39. U.S. Commission on Population Growth and the American Future, *Population and the American Future* (Washington, D.C.: Government Printing Office, 1972), p. 12.

40. *Ibid.*, p. 41.

41. *Ibid.*

42. U.S. Bureau of the Census, *People of the United States in the 20th Century*, a Census Monograph by Irene B. Taeuber and Conrad Taeuber (Washington, D.C.: Government Printing Office, 1971).

43. *Population and the American Future*, p. 41.

44. *Ibid.*, p. 38.

45. *Ibid.*

46. *Ibid.*

47. *Ibid.*

48. Kelley, "Demographic Changes," pp. 22–23.

49. *Ibid.*, p. 24.

50. Ronald G. Ridker, "Resource and Environmental Consequences of Population Growth in the United States . . . A Summary," U.S. Commission on Population Growth and the American Future, *Population, Resources and the Environment*, Ronald G. Ridker, ed., vol. III of commission research reports (Washington, D.C.: Government Printing Office, 1972), p. 19.

51. *Ibid.*, p. 21.

52. *Economic Aspects of Population Change*, p. 4.

53. *Ibid.*, pp. 4–5.

54. J.M. Keynes, "Some Economic Consequences of a Declining Population," *The Eugenics Review*, vol. XXIX, no. 1, April, 1937, p. 17.

55. Quoted in Kenneth Smith, *The Malthusian Controversy* (London: Routledge & Kegan Paul, 1951), pp. 161–62.

56. Ludwig von Mises, *Human Action*, 3rd ed. (Chicago: Henry Regnery Company, 1966), p. 142.

57. Kuznets, "Population Change," p. 339.

58. Dudley Kirk, "The Influence of Business Cycles on Marriage and Birth Rates, *Demographic and Economic Change in Developed Countries*, p. 254.

59. Alfred Sauvy, *General Theory*, pp. 298–99.

Chapter 3

1. Joseph L. Fisher, "Population and Natural Resources," *The Economics of Environmental Problems*, Frank C. Emerson, ed. (Ann Arbor, Mich.: University of Michigan, 1973), p. 3.

2. *Ibid.*, pp. 3–4.

3. Melvin Kranzberg, "Can Technological Progress Continue to Provide for the Future?," *The Economic Growth Controversy* (White Plains, N.Y.: International Arts and Sciences Press, 1973), p. 71.

4. U.S. Commission on Population Growth and the American Future, *Population, Resources and the Environment*, Ronald K. Ridker, ed., vol. III of commission research reports (Washington, D.C.: Government Printing Office, 1972), p. 81.

5. Karl Brandt, "Is Overpopulation a False Cry? Why a Professor Thinks It Is," *The National Observer*, July 15, 1963, p. 12.

6. Harrison Brown, James Bonner, and John Weir, *The Next Hundred Years* (New York: Viking Press, 1957), p. 115.

7. United Nations, *Report of the Symposium on Population, Resources and Environment* (New York: United Nations, 1974), p. 6.

8. James Boyd, "Minerals and How We Use Them," *The Mineral Position of the United States, 1975–2000* (Madison, Wisc.: University of Wisconsin Press, 1973), p. 3.

9. *Report of the Symposium on Population, Resources and Environment*, pp. 16–17.

10. *The Determinants and Consequences of Population Trends*, p. 369.

11. *Report of the Symposium on Population, Resources and Environment,* p. 17.

12. *The Determinants and Consequences of Population Trends,* p. 390.

13. *Ibid.,* pp. 390–91.

14. Boyd, "Minerals and How We Use Them," p. 6.

15. H.J. Barnett and C. Morse, *Scarcity and Growth* (Baltimore: The John Hopkins Press, 1963), p. 10.

16. Hans H. Landsberg, Leonard L. Fischman, and Joseph L. Fisher, *Resources in America's Future* (Baltimore: The Johns Hopkins Press, 1963), p. 335.

17. Marion Clawson, *America's Land & Its Uses* (Baltimore: The Johns Hopkins Press, 1972), p. 100.

18. R. Buckminster Fuller, *Utopia or Oblivion: The Prospects for Humanity* (New York: Bantam Books, 1969), p. 4.

19. Frank Austin Smith, "Waste Material Recovery and Reuse," *Population, Resources and the Environment,* p. 67.

20. Leonard L. Fischman and Hans H. Landsberg, "Adequacy of Nonfuel Minerals and Forest Resources," *Population, Resources and the Environment,* p. 90.

21. John D. Morgan, Jr., "Future Use of Minerals: The Questions of Demand," *The Mineral Position of the United States, 1975–2000,* pp. 54, 65.

22. *Population, Resources and the Environment,* p. 73.

23. V.E. McKelvey, "Mineral Resource Estimates and Public Policy," *Summary of United States Mineral Resources* (Washington, D.C.: U.S. Department of the Interior, 1973), pp. 17–18.

24. Donald A. Brobst and Walden P. Pratt, "Introduction," *Summary of United States Mineral Resources,* pp. 2–3.

25. The National Commission on Materials Policy, *Material Needs and the Environment: Today and Tomorrow* (Washington, D.C.: Government Printing Office, 1973), p. 5-3.

26. *Ibid.,* pp. 5–6.

27. U.S. Department of the Interior, *Mineral Resources: Potentials and Problems* (Washington, D.C.: U.S. Department of Interior, 1974), p. 14.

28. U.S. Department of the Interior, *Geological Estimates of Underground Recoverable Oil and Gas Resources in the United States* (Washington, D.C.: U.S. Department of Interior, 1975), p. 2.

29. *Mineral Resources: Potentials and Problems,* p. 15.

30. *Ibid.,* p. 14.

31. *Geological Estimates of Underground Recoverable Oil and Gas Resources in the United States,* p. 2.

32. David A. Loehwing, "Man-Made Shortage," *Barron's,* October 18, 1971, p. 7.

33. *Mineral Resources: Potentials and Problems,* p. 14.

34. *Ibid.,* p. 16.

35. U.S. Department of the Interior, *Nuclear Energy Resources* (Washington, D.C.: Government Printing Office, 1973), pp. 2, 5.

36. *Mineral Resources: Potentials and Problems,* pp. 14, 17.

37. *Ibid.,* p. 18.

38. *Ibid.,* p. 17.

39. M. King Hubbert, "The Energy Resources of the Earth," *Energy and Power* (San Francisco: W.H. Freeman and Company, 1971), p. 40.

40. M. King Hubbert, "Energy Resources," *Resources and Man* (San Francisco: W.H. Freeman and Company, 1969), p. 206.

41. Chauncey Starr, "Energy and Power," *Energy and Power* (San Francisco: W.H. Freeman and Company, 1971), p. 3.

42. Tom Pickens, "What we can do to keep the world from going dark," *Chicago Tribune,* April 13, 1975.

43. James H. Winchester, "Here Comes the Hydrogen Era," *Reader's Digest,* December, 1973, p. 144.

44. Freeman J. Dyson, "Energy in the Universe," *Energy and Power* (San Francisco, W.H. Freeman and Company, 1971), p. 27

45. Vincent E. McKelvey, "U.S. Mineral Potential," *The Mineral Position of the United States, 1975–2000* (Madison, Wisc.: University of Wisconsin Press, 1973), pp. 81–82.

46. *Material Needs and the Environment: Today and Tomorrow,* table 4.B.1, pp. 4B-8–4B-9.

47. *Ibid.;* see also *Mineral Resources: Potentials and Problems,* p. 14.

48. Landsberg, Fischman, and Fisher, *Resources in America's Future,* p. 479.

49. *Population, Resources and the Environment,* pp. 91–92.

50. *Ibid.,* p. 94.

51. *Mineral Resources: Potentials and Problems,* p. 12.

52. *Population, Resources and the Environment,* p. 93.

53. Wilfred Beckerman, *Two Cheers for the Affluent Society* (New York: Saint Martin's Press, 1974), p. 178.

54. *Ibid.,* p. 175.

55. Clawson, *America's Land and Its Uses,* p. 3.

56. *Ibid.,* p. 2.

57. Economic Research Service, U.S. Department of Agriculture, *Our Land and Water Resources* (Washington, D.C.: Government Printing Office, 1974), p. 1.

58. *Ibid.,* pp. 2–3.

59. *Ibid.,* pp. 43–44.

60. *Population, Resources and the Environment,* p. 228.

61. *Our Land and Water Resources,* pp. 44–45.

62. *Ibid.,* p. 45.

63. Clawson, *America's Land and Its Uses,* pp. 140–41.

64. *Our Land and Water Resources,* p. 45.

65. *Ibid.,* pp. 12, 45.

66. *Ibid.,* p. 45.

67. Ridker, "Resource and Environmental Consequences of Population Growth in the United States . . . A Summary," *Population, Resources and the Environment,* p. 28.

68. Beckerman, *Two Cheers,* p. 173.

69. *Ibid.*

70. Preston Cloud, "Resources, Population and Quality of Life," *Is There an Optimum Level of Population?,* S. Fred Singer, ed. (New York: McGraw-Hill, 1971), p. 8.

71. World Bank, *Report on the Limits to Growth* (Washington, D.C.: International Bank for Reconstruction and Development, 1972), p. 37.

72. B. Delworth Gardner, "Natural Resources and Human Survival," *Population, Resources and the Future: Non-Malthusian Prospects,* Howard M. Bahr, Bruce A. Chadwick, Darwin L. Thomas, eds. (Provo, Utah: Brigham Young University Press, 1972), p. 87.

73. Cloud, "Resources, Population and Quality of Life," pp. 15–16.

74. Harrison Brown, "Comments on the Use and Depletion of Natural Resources," *Is There an Optimum Level of Population?*, p. 33.

75. Preston Cloud, "Mineral Resources in Fact and Fancy," *Toward a Steady-State Economy*, Herman E. Daly, ed. (San Francisco: W.H. Freeman and Company, 1973), p. 71.

76. *Report on the Limits to Growth*, pp. 43–45.

77. *Ibid.*, pp. 6–7.

78. *Ibid.*, pp. 34–35.

79. Barbara Ward, "The end of a epoch," *The Economist*, May 27, 1972, quoted in Beckerman, *Two Cheers*, p. 178.

80. Beckerman, *Two Cheers*, p. 189.

81. *Report on the Limits to Growth*, pp. 37–39.

82. *Ibid.*, pp. 8–9.

83. Joseph Egelhof, "2176: He thinks we'll make it but not without some trouble," *Chicago Tribune*, January 5, 1976.

84. John Stuart Mill, *Principles of Political Economy* (1848), book IV, chapter VI, quoted in Beckerman, *Two Cheers*, p. 172.

85. Allen Kneese and Ronald Ridker, "Predicament of Mankind," *Washington Post*, March 2, 1972, quoted in *Report on the Limits to Growth*, p. 76.

86. *Report on the Limits to Growth*, p. 9.

87. Harlan Draeger, "Call for action to avert U.S. raw materials crisis," *Chicago Daily News*, July 21, 1975.

88. *Population, Resources and the Environment*, p. 82.

89. Ben J. Wattenberg, "Out of gas? Man's wits will save us," *Chicago Daily News*, March 31, 1975.

90. "The Raw Material," *Manas*, vol. XXVIII, no. 9, February 26, 1975.

91. Bahr, Chadwick, and Thomas, eds., *Population, Resources and the Future: Non-Malthusian Prospects*, pp. 37–38.

Chapter 4

1. Miguel Ozorio de Almeida, *International Conciliation* (New York), January, 1972, no. 586, p. 43, quoted in Beckerman, *Two Cheers*, pp. 101–2.

2. *Ibid.*, p. 102.

3. *Ibid.*, p. 55.

4. *Ibid.*

5. John Maddox, *The Doomsday Syndrome* (New York: McGraw-Hill, 1972), p. 118.

6. Beckerman, *Two Cheers,* p. 56.

7. *Ibid.*

8. Melvin J. Grayson and Thomas R. Shepard, Jr., *The Disaster Lobby* (Chicago: Follett, 1973), pp. 48–49.

9. *Ibid.*, p. 49.

10. *Ibid.*, p. 64.

11. Beckerman, *Two Cheers,* p. 112.

12. *Ibid.*, p. 106.

13. Anthony Downs, "Up and Down with Ecology—The 'Issue-Attention Cycle,'" *Population, Environment, and the Quality of Life,* Parker G. Marden and Dennis Hodgson, eds. (New York: John Wiley & Sons, 1975), p. 203–4.

14. Peter F. Drucker, "Saving the Crusade," *Harper's Magazine,* January, 1972, p. 66.

15. *Ibid.*

16. *Ibid.*, p. 67.

17. *Ibid.*, p. 68.

18. *Ibid.*, p. 66.

19. *Ibid.*, p. 68.

20. Walter W. Heller, "Coming to Terms with Growth and the Environment," *Population, Environment and the Quality of Life,* p. 209.

21. *Ibid.*, p. 211.

22. *Ibid.*, p. 212.

23. *Ibid.*, p. 213.

24. Joseph L. Fisher, "Population and Natural Resources," *The Economics of Environmental Problems,* Frank Emerson, ed. (Ann Arbor: University of Michigan, 1973), p. 11.

25. Barry Commoner, "The Environmental Cost of Economic Growth," *Population, Resources and the Environment,* p. 341.

26. Ronald G. Ridker, "Resource and Environmental Consequences of Population Growth in the United States . . . A Summary," *Population, Resources and the Environment*, p. 26.

27. *Ibid.*, p. 19.

28. Ben Wattenberg, "The Nonsense Explosion: Overpopulation as a Crisis Issue," *Population, Environment and the Quality of Life*, p. 21.

29. William T. Pecora, *Nature . . . An Environmental Yardstick* (Washington, D.C.: Government Printing Office, 1973), p. 7.

30. *Ibid.*, pp. 6–7.

31. *Ibid.*, p. 6.

32. *Ibid.*, pp. 8–9.

33. *Ibid.*, pp. 10–11.

34. *Ibid.*, p. 11.

35. *Ibid.*, p. 6.

36. *Ibid.*, p. 9.

37. *Ibid.*, p. 6.

38. *Ibid.*, p. 11.

39. *Ibid.*, p. 13.

40. Beckerman, *Two Cheers*, p. 112.

41. *Ibid.*, p. 98.

42. *Ibid.*, p. 112.

43. Maddox, *The Doomsday Syndrome*, p. 120.

44. Agricultural Research Service, U.S. Department of Agriculture, *Managing Our Environment* (Washington, D.C.: Government Printing Office, 1972), pp. 24–25.

45. Council on Environmental Quality, *The Fifth Annual Report of the Council on Environmental Quality* (Washington, D.C.: Government Printing Office, 1974), pp. 257–58. This report is hereinafter cited as *Fifth Annual Report*.

46. *Ibid.*, pp. 261–62.

47. *Ibid.*, pp. 267–68.

48. *Ibid.*, pp. 274–76.

49. Dan Miller, "Pollution by cars shrinking despite air standards delay," *Chicago Daily News,* March 28, 1975.

50. *Fifth Annual Report,* pp. 279–80.

51. *Ibid.,* pp. 282–88.

52. Casey Bukro, "Fishing in downtown Detroit? It's done now," *Chicago Tribune,* September 29, 1975.

53. Roul Tunley, "Fresh Start for the Great Lakes," *Reader's Digest,* December, 1974, p. 217.

54. Jerald terHorst, "The resurrection of the lakes," *Chicago Tribune,* August 15, 1975.

55. *Fifth Annual Report,* p. 140.

56. Monroe Anderson, "Complete reuse of sewage now possible: expert," *Chicago Tribune,* May 8, 1975.

57. *Fifth Annual Report,* pp. 147–48.

58. *Ibid.,* pp. 167–70.

59. *Ibid.,* pp. 131–37.

60. John Chamberlain, "The way to get rid of our waste," *Chicago Sun-Times,* October 25, 1973.

61. Peter J. Bernstein, "Garbage a hot item for Dutch," *Chicago Daily News,* April 18, 1974.

62. *Managing Our Environment,* pp. 6, 14.

63. *Ibid.,* p. 6.

64. *Fifth Annual Report,* pp. 318–20.

65. *Managing Our Environment,* pp. 13, 31.

66. *Fifth Annual Report,* pp. 138–39, 151–56.

67. *Ibid.,* pp. 162–67.

68. Gary Farmer, *Unready Kilowatts* (La Salle, Ill.: Open Court, 1975), pp. 109–10.

69. *Managing the Environment,* pp. 3–5.

70. Eugene Guccione, "The Government's Energy Crisis," *The Freeman,* September, 1975, pp. 546–47.

71. *Fifth Annual Report,* pp. 181, 324–26.

72. *Ibid.,* pp. 190–202.

73. Maddox, *The Doomsday Syndrome,* p. 152.

74. *Ibid.,* p. 118.

75. Paul R. Ehrlich and John P. Holdren, "Impact of Population Growth," *Population, Resources and the Environment,* pp. 369–76.

76. *Ibid.,* p. 376.

77. *The Lincoln Library of Essential Information* (Columbus, Ohio: The Frontier Press Company, 1970), p. 895.

78. *Ibid.*

79. *Ibid.*

80. *Ibid.,* p. 893.

81. *Ibid.,* p. 894.

82. Hans F. Sennholz, "Controlling Pollution," *The Freeman,* February, 1973, p. 77.

83. *Ibid.*

84. *Ibid.*

85. Jerome Rothenberg, "Evaluating Public Policy Approaches," *The Economics of Environmental Problems,* p. 81.

86. Barry Commoner, "The Environmental Cost of Economic Growth," *Population, Resources and the Environment,* p. 362.

87. Kenneth E. Boulding, "The Economics of the Coming Spaceship Earth," *Environmental Quality in a Growing Economy,* Henry Jarrett, ed. (Baltimore: The Johns Hopkins Press, 1966), p. 9.

88. Donella H. Meadows, Dennis L. Meadows, Jorgen Randers, and William W. Behrens III, *The Limits to Growth* (New York: Universe Books, 1972).

89. *Report on the Limits to Growth* p. 11.

90. *Ibid.,* p. 16.

91. *Ibid.,* p. 14.

92. *Ibid.,* p. 15.

93. Grayson and Shepard, *The Disaster Lobby,* p. 52.

94. Maddox, *The Doomsday Syndrome,* pp. 143–44.

95. *Ibid.,* p. 140.

96. *Ibid.,* pp. 145–46.

97. *Ibid.,* p. 158.

98. Drucker, "Saving the Crusade," p. 79.

Chapter 5

1. Downs, "Up and Down with Ecology—The 'Issue-Attention Cycle,'" p. 204.

2. Milton Friedman, "Economic Myths and Public Opinion," *The Alternative: An American Spectator,* January, 1976, p. 5.

3. *Long Term Economic Growth, 1860–1970,* series A-42, pp. 188–89.

4. Beckerman, *Two Cheers,* pp. 70–71.

5. Heller, "Coming to Terms with Growth and the Environment," *Population, Environment, and the Quality of Life,* p. 214.

6. *Ibid.*

7. A.W. Sametz, "Production of goods and services: the measurement of economic growth," *Indicators of Social Change: Concepts and Measurement,* E.B. Sheldon and W.E. Moore, eds. (New York: Russell Sage Foundation, 1968), p. 83, table 2, quoted in Beckerman, *Two Cheers,* p. 73.

8. Beckerman, *Two Cheers,* p. 73.

9. William Nordhaus and James Tobin, "Is Growth Obsolete?" (paper presented at the National Bureau of Economic Research Colloquium on Economic Growth, San Francisco, December 10, 1970, and published by the NBER in its 1972 proceedings), quoted in Heller, "Coming to Terms with Growth and the Environment," p. 215.

10. Heller, "Coming to Terms with Growth and the Environment," p. 212.

11. *Ibid.*

12. U.S. Bureau of the Census, "Money Income in 1973 of Families and Persons in the United States," *Current Population Reports,* series P-60, no. 97 (Washington, D.C.: Government Printing Office, 1975), table 22, p. 43.

13. Coale, "Man and His Environment," *Population, Environment and the Quality of Life,* p. 147.

14. Tax Foundation, "Monthly Tax Features," September, 1973.

15. Robert T. Gray, "Will the Social Security Bubble Burst?," *Reader's Digest,* May, 1975, p. 150.

16. *Ibid.,* p. 149.

17. American Institute for Economic Research, "View from an Alp II," *Economic Education Bulletin,* November, 1972, p. 2.

18. Gray, "Will the Social Security Bubble Burst?," pp. 148–49.

19. U.S. Bureau of the Census, *Statistical Abstract of the United States: 1972* (Washington, D.C., 1972), table 78, p. 57.

20. *Ibid.,* table 89, p. 65.

21. *Ibid.,* table 101, p. 70.

22. *Ibid.,* table 108, p. 74.

23. U.S. Bureau of the Census, *Historical Statistics of the United States, Colonial Times to 1957* (Washington, D.C., 1960), series H233, p. 207.

24. U.S. Bureau of the Census, "Educational Attainment in the United States: March, 1973 and 1974," *Current Population Reports* (Washington, D.C.: Government Printing Office, 1974), table A, p. 1.

25. *Ibid.,* table 7, p. 68.

26. *Ibid.,* table C, p. 5.

27. Roger A. Freeman, *The Growth of American Government* (Stanford, Calif.: Hoover Institution Press, 1975), p. 15.

28. Donald Zochert, "Enrollment drop jolts area schools," *Chicago Daily News,* March 3, 1974.

29. U.S. Bureau of the Census, *Census of Population and Housing: 1970, General Demographic Trends for Metropolitan Areas, 1960 to 1970,* Final Report PHC (2)-1 United States (Washington, D.C.: Government Printing Office, 1971), pp. 15–16.

30. "Our Buying Power—A Progress Report," *Reader's Digest,* November, 1975, p. 137.

31. *Long Term Economic Growth, 1860–1970,* Series B5-B8, pp. 212–13.

32. Clawson, *America's Land & Its Uses,* p. 82.

33. Heller, "Coming to Terms with Growth and the Environment," p. 213.

34. Coale, "Man and His Environment," p. 147.

35. Jane Jacobs, *The Death and Life of Great American Cities* (New York: Vintage Books, 1961), p. 200.

36. *Ibid.,* pp. 218–19.

37. Edwin S. Mills, "Economic Aspects of City Sizes," U.S. Commission on Population Growth and the American Future, *Population, Distribution and Policy,* Sara Mills Mazie, ed., vol. V of commission research reports (Washington, D.C.: Government Printing Office, 1972), p. 390.

38. Peter A. Morrison, "Dimensions of the Population Problem in the United States," *Population, Distribution and Policy,* p. 24.

39. U.S. Bureau of the Census, "Social and Economic Characteristics of the Metropolitan and Nonmetropolitan Population: 1974 and 1970," *Current Population Reports,* series P-23, no. 55 (Washington, D.C.: Government Printing Office, 1975), table P, p. 15.

40. *Ibid.,* table Q, p. 14.

41. *Ibid.,* table L, p. 10.

42. Advisory Commission on Intergovernmental Relations, *Urban and Rural America: Policies for Future Growth* (Washington, D.C.: Government Printing Office, 1968), p. 23.

43. *Census of Population and Housing,* table G, p. 16.

44. Edwin S. Mills, "Economic Aspects of City Size," *Population, Distribution and Policy,* pp. 393–94.

45. Philip M. Hauser, "Urbanization: An Overview," *The Study of Urbanization,* Philip M. Hauser and Leo F. Schnore, eds. (New York: John Wiley & Sons, 1965), p. 12.

46. Charles L. Leven, "Changing Sizes, Forms, and Functions of Urban Areas," *Population, Distribution and Policy,* p. 405.

47. Morrison, "Dimensions of the Population Problem in the United States," p. 8.

48. *Ibid.,* table 1.

49. *Census of Population and Housing,* table E, p. 12.

50. *Ibid.,* table 11, p. 1-47.

51. "Social and Economic Characteristics of the Metropolitan and Nonmetropolitan Population: 1974 and 1970," *Current Population Reports,* table E, p. 5.

52. U.S. Bureau of the Census, "Estimates of the Population of New York Counties and Metropolitan Areas: July 1, 1973 and 1974," *Current Population Reports,* series P-24, no. 599 (Washington, D.C.: U.S. Government Printing Office, 1975), table 2, p. 5.

53. U.S. Bureau of the Census, "1973 Population and 1972 Per Capita Income Estimates for Counties, Incorporated Places, and Selected Minor Civil Divisions in Illinois," *Current Population Reports,* series P-25, no. 588 (Washington, D.C.: Government Printing Office, 1975), table 1, p. 6.

54. U.S. Bureau of the Census, "1973 Population and 1972 Per Capita Income Estimates for Counties and Incorporated Places in California," *Current Population Reports,* series P-25, no. 550 (Washington, D.C.: Government Printing Office, 1975), table 1, p. 3.

55. *Census of Population and Housing,* table E, p. 12.

56. "Social and Economic Characteristics of the Metropolitan and Nonmetropolitan Population: 1974 and 1970," *Current Population Reports,* table E, p. 5.

57. *Census of Population and Housing,* table 1, p. 23.

58. "Social and Economic Characteristics of the Metropolitan and Nonmetropolitan Population: 1974 and 1970," *Current Population Reports,* table E, p. 5.

59. Population Reference Bureau, *Intercom,* August-September, 1975, p. 1.

60. Ben J. Wattenberg and Richard M. Scammon, *This U.S.A.* (Garden City, N.Y.: Doubleday, 1965), pp. 86–87.

61. Stanford Research Institute, *City Size and the Quality of Life* (Washington, D.C.: Government Printing Office, 1974), p. 10.

62. *Ibid.,* p. 30.

63. John E. Polich, "Old Suburbs Losing People," *Detroit Free Press,"* July 22, 1975.

64. Richard L. Thomas, "Our cities' budgets approach their limit," *Chicago Tribune,* February 1, 1976.

65. *Ibid.*

66. Sara Mills Mazie and Steve Rawlings, "Public Attitude Toward Population Distribution Issues," *Population, Distribution and Policy,* p. 604.

67. Peter G. Koltnow, *Changes in Mobility in American Cities,* adapted from a report presented at International Road Federation, VI World Conference, Montreal, Canada, October 8, 1970 (Washington, D.C.: Highway Users Federation for Safety and Mobility, 1970), p. 2.

68. *Ibid.,* p. 3.

69. *Ibid.,* pp. 6–7.

70. "Traveltime: A Measure of Highway Performance," report prepared by Travel and Facilities Branch, Urban Planning Division, Bureau of Roads, Federal Highway Administration, U.S. Department of Transportation, Washington, D.C., January, 1970, pp. ii, iii.

71. Koltnow, *Changes in Mobility in American Cities,* p. 6.

72. William D. Hart, *Public Financial Support for Transit* (Washington, D.C.: Highway Users Federation, 1973), pp. 2–3.

73. Jonathan L. Freedman, *Crowding and Behavior* (New York: Viking Press, 1975), p. 1.

74. John B. Calhoun, "Population Density and Social Pathology," *Scientific American,* February, 1962, p. 148.

75. Freedman, *Crowding and Behavior,* p. 42.

76. *Ibid.,* p. 77.

77. *Ibid.,* p. 78.

78. *Ibid.,* p. 62.

79. *Ibid.*

80. *Ibid.,* pp. 67–68.

81. *Ibid.,* pp. 89–90.

82. *Ibid.,* p. 93.

83. *Ibid.,* pp. 107–8.

84. *Ibid.,* pp. 56–57.

85. Kingsley Davis, "The Urbanization of the Human Population," *Scientific American,* September, 1965, p. 53.

86. Robert B. Zajonc, "Dumber by the Dozen," *Psychology Today,* January, 1975, p. 37.

87. E. James Lieberman, "The case for small families," *The New York Times Magazine,* March 8, 1970.

88. Kenneth W. Terhune, *A Review of the Actual and Expected Consequences of Family Size* (Washington, D.C.: Government Printing Office, 1974), p. 5.

89. *Ibid.,* pp. 6–7.

90. *Ibid.,* p. 51.

91. *Ibid.,* pp. 98–99.

92. *Ibid.,* p. 191.

93. Leticia Kent, "More Babies Needed, Not Fewer," *Vogue,* August 15, 1970, p. 87.

94. Alvin Toffler, *Future Shock* (New York: Random House, 1970), p. 1.

95. *Ibid.,* p. 2.

96. Wattenberg and Scammon, *This U.S.A.,* pp. 112–17.

97. Kingsley Davis, "The American Family in Relation to Demographic Change," U.S. Commission on Population Growth and the American Future, *Demographic and Social Aspects of Population Growth*, Charles F. Westoff and Robert Parke, Jr., eds., vol. I of commission research reports (Washington, D.C.: Government Printing Office, 1972), p. 241.

98. Eliot Janeway, "Technological, Social Reforms Termed Solution to Crowding," *Chicago Tribune*, August 16, 1974.

99. Wattenberg and Scammon, *This U.S.A.*, p. 88.

Chapter 6

1. Colin Clark, "Do Population and Freedom Grow Together?," *Fortune*, December, 1960, p. 136.

2. Alexander Hamilton, James Madison, John Hay, *The Federalist Papers* (New York: New American Library, 1961), p. 77.

3. *Ibid.*, p. 78.

4. *Ibid.*, pp. 82–83.

5. Freeman, *The Growth of American Government*, table 46, p. 205.

6. *Ibid.*

7. *Ibid.*

8. *Ibid.*

9. Clark, "Do Population and Freedom Grow Together?," p. 20.

10. *Ibid.*

11. *Ibid.*

12. Caspar W. Weinberger, "The Day of Reckoning Is Here," *Reader's Digest*, November, 1975, p. 94.

13. Tax Foundation, *Monthly Tax Features*, May, 1975.

14. Clark, "Do Population and Freedom Grow Together?," pp. 14, 20.

15. Freeman, *The Growth of American Government*, p. 109.

16. *Ibid.*, p. 1.

17. *Ibid.*, pp. 3–4.

18. *Ibid.*, p. 32.

19. *Ibid.* pp. 8–9.

20. "Russia winning arms race, U.S. warned in Congress report," *Chicago Tribune,* February 2, 1976.

21. Quoted in *Ibid.*

22. Quoted in Bill Anderson, "The nuclear power issue will test Rumsfeld's strength," *Chicago Tribune,* February 12, 1976.

23. "2 experts claim Russia catching up on U.S. arms," *Chicago Tribune,* February 4, 1976.

24. *Ibid.*

25. A.F.K. Organski, Bruce Bueno de Mesquita, and Alan Lamborn, "The Effective Population in International Politics," U.S. Commission on Population Growth and the American Future, *Governance and Population: The Governmental Implications of Population Change,* A.E. Keir Nash, ed., vol. IV of commission research reports (Washington, D.C.: Government Printing Office, 1972), p. 238.

26. *Ibid.,* p. 239.

27. *Ibid.,* p. 240.

28. *Ibid.,* tables 1 and 2, p. 239.

29. *Ibid.,* table 3, p. 241.

30. *Ibid.,* p. 242.

31. *Ibid.,* p. 238.

32. Murray L. Weidenbaum, *Government-Mandated Price Increases* (Washington, D.C.: American Enterprise Institute for Public Policy Research, 1975), fig. 1, p. 40, and p. 41.

33. *Ibid.,* p. 19.

34. *Ibid.,* p. 3.

35. *Ibid.,* p. 21.

36. *Ibid.*

37. *Ibid.*

38. *Ibid.,* p. 33.

39. *Ibid.,* p. 36.

40. *Population and the American Future,* p. 56.

41. *Ibid.*

42. *Ibid.*, p. 58.

43. Sauvy, *General Theory*, p. 516.

44. *Ibid.*, p. 519.

45. *Ibid.*, p. 521.

46. *Ibid.*, p. 523.

47. *Population and the American Future*, p. 54.

48. *Ibid.*, p. 60.

49. Rousas J. Rushdoony, *The Myth of Overpopulation* (Nutley, N.J.: Craig Press, 1971), p. 10.

50. Patrick Buchanan, "Red army stays in the green," *Chicago Tribune*, February 19, 1976.

51. Clark, "Do Population and Freedom Grow Together?," p. 20.

Chapter 7

1. Ronald Freedman and Bernard Berelson, "The Human Population," *Scientific American*, September, 1974, p. 31.

2. Department of Economic and Social Affairs, *The World Population Situation in 1970* (New York: United Nations, 1971), p. 6.

3. *Ibid.*

4. United Nations, *The Determinants and Consequences of Population Trends* (New York: United Nations, 1973), table II.1, p. 10.

5. *World Population Growth and Response* (Washington, D.C.: Population Reference Bureau, Inc., 1976), pp. 2–3.

6. U.S. Bureau of the Census, *Statistical Abstract of the United States, 1972* (Washington, D.C.: Government Printing Office, 1972), table 1, p. 5.

7. Colin Clark, *Population Growth and Land Use* (London and Basingstoke: Macmillan, 1968), pp. 46–48. We, of course, have no records of the fertility and mortality of primitive humans. But we do have some idea of the age at death of primitive peoples as a result of excavations of ancient burial grounds. In addition, we have fertility and mortality records for contemporary primitive tribes, such as the East African Samburu, who are thought be similar to people of prehistoric ages. Using data from these sources, Clark developed a survival profile showing how high fertility is exactly matched by high mortality in primitive cultures, resulting in stationary populations.

8. Kingsley Davis, *The Population of India and Pakistan* (Princeton, N.J.: Princeton University Press, 1951), p. 24, quoted in William Petersen, *Population* (Toronto: Macmillan, 1969), p. 394.

9. "Declaration on Population," issued by United Nations Secretary General U Thant on Human Rights Day, December 10, 1966.

10. "Population Explosion and Anti-Babyism," *Life,* April 23, 1965, p. 6.

11. "How Many Babies Is Too Many?," *Newsweek,* July 25, 1962, p. 27.

12. Robert Cook, *Population Crisis* (Washington, D.C.: Socio-Dynamics Publications, 1970), p. xviii.

13. Stewart Udall, *Population Crisis* (Washington, D.C.: Socio-Dynamics Publications, 1970), p. xviii.

14. Robert Rienow with Leona Train Rienow, *Man Against His Environment* (New York: Ballantine Books, 1970), p. 15.

15. Paul R. Ehrlich, *The Population Bomb* (New York: Ballantine Books, 1968), p. 166.

16. Lincoln H. Day and Alice Taylor Day, *Too Many Americans* (New York: Dell, Inc., 1965), p. 5.

17. Malthus, *An Essay on the Principle of Population,* p. 71.

18. *Ibid.,* p. 74.

19. Richard A. Easterlin, "Does Human Fertility Adjust to the Environment?," *American Economic Review Papers and Proceedings,* May, 1971, pp. 399–400.

20. W.D. Borrie, *The Growth and Control of World Population* (London: Weidenfeld and Nicolson, 1970), p. 29.

21. Clark, *Population Growth and Land Use,* p. 22.

22. *Ibid.,* p. 28.

23. Borrie, *The Growth and Control of World Population,* p. 29.

24. Malthus, *An Essay on the Principle of Population,* p. 74.

25. *Ibid.,* p. 32.

26. Donald J. Bogue, *Principles of Demography* (New York: John Wiley and Sons, 1969), pp. 55–56.

27. *The World Population Situation in 1970,* p. 10.

28. U.S. Bureau of the Census, "Projections of the Population of the United States: 1975 to 2050," *Current Population Reports,* series P-25, no. 601 (Washington, D.C.: Government Printing Office, 1975).

29. Day and Day, *Too Many Americans*, p. 1.

30. U.S. Department of Health, Education and Welfare, *Monthly Vital Statistics Report, Births, Marriages, Divorces and Deaths for February, 1976*, vol. 25, no. 2, April 30, 1976, p. 1.

31. Ben J. Wattenberg, *The Demography of the 1970's: The Birth Dearth and What It Means* (New York: Family Circle, 1971), p. 1.

Chapter 8

1. Borrie, *The Growth and Control of World Population*, p. 54.

2. *Ibid.*, p. 29.

3. Sauvy, *General Theory*, p. 363.

4. Borrie, *The Growth and Control of World Population*, p. 70.

5. John Maier, "The Numbers of Man," *Some Aspects of Population Stabilization* (New York: Rockefeller Foundation, n.d.), p. 10.

6. Richard A. Easterlin, "Does Human Fertility Adjust to the Environment?," *American Economic Review Papers and Proceedings*, May, 1971, p. 406.

7. "U.S. Birth Rate Hits New Low," *Population Profile*, Population Reference Bureau, Inc., February 26, 1968, p. 3.

8. Arthur J. Dyck, "Population and National Responsibility: An Ethical Analysis of the Report of the Commission on Population Growth and the American Future," speech delivered at the American Society of Christian Ethics, January, 1973.

9. "Comment by Philip M. Hauser, University of Chicago," *Demography*, October-December, 1970, p. 453.

10. Easterlin, "Does Human Fertility Adjust to the Environment?," p. 407.

11. James Ridgeway, *The Politics of Ecology* (New York: E.P. Dutton and Co., 1970), p. 181.

12. Quoted in Joseph H. Fichter, "ZPG: A Bourgeois Conspiracy?," *America*, August 19, 1972, p. 88.

13. Ridgeway, "The Politics of Ecology," pp. 183–84.

14. Phyllis Tilson Piotrow, *World Population Crisis: The United States Response* (New York: Praeger, 1973), p. 8.

15. *Ibid.*, p. 15.

16. A. Lawrence Chickering, "Land Use Controls and Low Income Groups: Why Are There No Poor People in the Sierra Club?," *No Land Is an Island* (San Francisco: Institute for Contemporary Studies, 1975), p. 87.

17. Ridgeway, *The Politics of Ecology*, p. 188.

18. Dudley Kirk, "The Misunderstood Challenge of Population Change," speech presented at American Institute of Architects Convention, May 8, 1973, San Francisco.

19. Ridgeway, *The Politics of Ecology*, p. 189.

20. Fichter, "ZPG: A Bourgeois Conspiracy?," p. 89.

21. *Catholic Currents*, July 5, 1971, p. 8.

22. Victor G. Rosenblum, "Life, Law and Process: Aspects of Coercion in Liberation's Guise," *Child & Family*, vol. 9, no. 4, 1970, p. 339.

23. *The First National Congress on Optimum Population and Environment* (Washington, D.C.: Population Reference Bureau, Inc., 1970), p. 6.

24. Sauvy, *General Theory*, p. 390.

25. *Ibid.*, p. 391.

26. *Ibid.*, p. 394.

27. Simon Kuznets, "Population Change and Aggregate Output," *Demographic and Economic Change in Developed Countries* (Princeton, N.J.: Princeton University Press, 1960), p. 339.

28. Allen C. Kelley, "Demographic Changes and American Economic Development: Past, Present and Future," U.S. Commission on Population Growth and the American Future, *Economic Aspects of Population Change*, Elliott R. Morss and Ritchie H. Reed, eds., vol. II of commission research reports (Washington, D.C.: Government Printing Office, 1972), p. 31.

29. Letter, Allen C. Kelley, chairman, Department of Economics, Duke University, Nov. 30, 1973.

30. *Ibid.*

31. *Population Growth and the American Future*, p. 3.

32. Public Law 91–213, 91st Congress, S. 2701, March 16, 1970.

33. *Ibid.*

34. U.S. Commission on Population Growth and the American Future, *Population Growth & America's Future, An Interim Report* (Washington, D.C.: Government Printing Office, 1971), p. 26.

35. *Population Growth and the American Future*, p. 12.

36. James Reston, " 'Family Planning' or 'Population Control'?," *Reader's Digest*, December, 1970, p. 163.

37. Judith Blake, "Population Policy for Americans: Is the Government Being Misled?," *Science*, May 2, 1969, p. 528.

38. Kingsley Davis, "Will Family Planning Solve the Population Problem?," The Victor-Bostrum Fund Report for the International Planned Parenthood Federation, report no. 10, Fall, 1968, p. 16, quoted in *U.S. Population Growth and Family Planning: A Review of the Literature* (New York: Planned Parenthood–World Population), p. viii.

39. Garrett Hardin, "Parenthood: Right or Privilege?," *Science*, July 31, 1970, p. 427.

40. *Ibid.*

41. Garrett Hardin, "The Tragedy of the Commons," *Population, Evolution, and Birth Control*, Garrett Hardin, comp. (San Francisco: W.H. Freeman and Company, 1969), pp. 367–81.

42. Davis, "Will Family Planning Solve the Population Problem?"

43. *Ibid.*

44. *U.S. Population Growth and Family Planning: A Review of the Literature*, p. viii.

45. Martha K. Willing, *Beyond Conception: Our Children's Children* (Boston: Gambit, 1971), p. 174.

46. Edgar Chasteen, "The Case for Compulsory Birth Control, *The American Population Debate*, Daniel Callahan, ed. (Garden City, N.Y.: Doubleday, 1971), p. 278.

47. *Catholic Currents*, July 1, 1973.

48. Robert H. Williams, "Number, Types and Duration of Human Lives," *Northwest Medicine*, July, 1970, pp. 495–96.

49. Ehrlich, *The Population Bomb*, pp. 166–67.

50. Julian L. Simon, "Science Does Not Show That There Is Overpopulation in the U.S.—Or Elsewhere," *Population: A Clash of Prophets*, Edward Pohlman, ed. (New York: New American Library, 1973), pp. 52–54.

51. Fredric Wertham, *A Sign for Cain* (New York: Macmillan Company, 1966), pp. 106–8.

52. *Ibid.*, p. 156.

53. *Ibid.*, pp. 161–62.

54. Kenneth M. Mitzner, "Solution to a Non-Problem," *Life in America*, July-August, 1971, p. 8.

55. Charles E. Rice, "Abortion: The Need for Political Action," mimeographed manuscript, September 22, 1970.

56. R.A. Gallop, "The Logic of Abortion," mimeographed manuscript, September 5, 1971.

57. Herbert Ratner, "Overpopulation: The False Culprit," *Child & Family*, Summer, 1969, p. 195.

58. Milton Himmelfarb, *Population Control: For & Against* (New York: Hart Publishing Company, 1973), p. 200.

59. Herbert Ratner, "Child Spacing: III. Nature's Prescription," *Child & Family,* vol. 9, no. 2, 1970.

60. Samuel McCracken, "The Population Controllers," *Commentary,* May, 1972, p. 51.

61. Ridgeway, *The Politics of Ecology,* p. 191.

62. Herbert Ratner, "The Pill," *Child & Family,* Winter, 1968, p. 79.

63. *Ibid.,* p. 88.

64. Matthew J. Bulfin, "Deaths and Near Deaths with Legal Abortions," report presented at the American College of Obstetricians and Gynecologists Convention, Disney World, Florida, October 28, 1975, pp. 1–3.

65. Quoted in Richard Neuhaus, *In Defense of People* (New York: Macmillan, 1971), p. 196.

66. *Ibid.,* p. 200.

67. Norman Podhoretz, "Beyond ZPG," *Commentary,* May, 1972, pp. 6, 8.

68. Malcolm Muggeridge, "The Decade of the Great Liberal Death Wish," *Child & Family,* vol. 10, no. 3, 1971, pp. 238–39.

Chapter 9

1. Norman Podhoretz, "Speak of the Devil," *Commentary,* April, 1971, p. 6.

2. Malcolm Muggeridge, "Albion Agonistes," *The Alternative: An American Spectator,* February, 1976, p. 11.

3. "German Decision Translated," *Illinois Right to Life Newsletter,* January-February, 1976, p. 1.

4. U Thant, *International Planned Parenthood News,* February, 1968, p. 3.

5. Pope Paul VI, *On the Development of Peoples* (Paterson, N.J.: Association for International Development, 1967), pp. 26–27.

6. *Modern Age,* Spring, 1975, p. 154.

7. Simon, "Science Does Not Show That There Is Overpopulation in the U.S.—or Elsewhere," p. 61.

8. Eugène Ionesco, "The Inalienable Right to Live," *Atlas World Press Review,* May, 1975, pp. 23–25.

9. René Dubos, "Optimism—The Creative Attitude," *Reader's Digest,* April, 1974, p. 63.

10. Isaac Asimov, "There's No Way to Go But Ahead," *Reader's Digest,* November, 1975, pp. 201–4.

11. Egelhof, "2176: He thinks we'll make it—but not without some trouble."

12. James A. Michener, "What America Means to Me," *Reader's Digest,* February, 1976, p. 172.

13. June Sklar and Beth Berkov, "The American Birth Rate: Evidences of a Coming Rise," *Science,* August 29, 1975, p. 693.

14. *Ibid.,* p. 699.

15. Michael Novak, "The Family Out of Favor," *Harper's,* April, 1976, p. 46.

Epilogue

1. "U.S. urging world 2-child limit as population curb," *Chicago Tribune,* August 21, 1974.

2. Wayne H. Davis, "Thoughts on Feeding the Hungry," *The Arizona Republic,* June 11, 1970, reprinted by Hugh Moore Fund, 60 East 42nd Street, New York, N.Y.

3. William Paddock and Paul Paddock, *Famine—1975* (Boston: Little, Brown & Company, 1967), pp. 205–29.

4. Quoted in Daniel Callahan, "Doing Well by Doing Good," *The Hastings Center Report* (Institute of Society, Ethics and the Life Sciences, 623 Warburton Avenue, Hastings-on-Hudson, N.Y.), December, 1974, p. 2.

5. Quoted in *ibid.,* p. 3.

6. Ehrlich, *The Population Bomb,* pp. 132–33.

7. Kent, "More Babies Needed," p. 87.

8. Daniel Callahan, "Doing Well by Doing Good," p. 3.

9. *Ibid.,* pp. 3–4.

10. Goran Ohlin, "The New Breed of Malthusians," *Family Planning Perspectives,* Summer, 1974, p. 158.

11. Everett E. Hagen and Oli Hawrylyshyn, "Analysis of World Income and Growth, 1955–1965," *Economic Development and Cultural Change,* October, 1969, p. 46.

12. Richard A. Easterlin, "Comment," U.S. Commission on Population Growth and the American Future, *Economic Aspects of Population Change,* Elliott R. Morss and Richie H. Reed, eds., vol. II of commission research reports (Washington, D.C.: Government Printing Office, 1972).

13. Julian L. Simon, "Population growth produces better economic performance in the long run than does a stationary population," *The Courier,* May, 1974, p. 23.

14. Himmelfarb, *Population Control: For & Against,* p. 103.

15. *World Bank Atlas* (Washington, D.C.: International Bank for Reconstruction and Development, 1972), pp. 4–5.

16. D. Gale Johnson, *World Food Problems and Prospects* (Washington, D.C.: American Enterprise Institute for Public Policy Research, 1975), p. 14.

17. *Ibid.,* pp. 15, 17.

18. *Report of the Symposium on Population and Development* (Bucharest, Romania: United Nations, 1974), p. 6.

19. Johnson, *World Food Problems and Prospects,* pp. 18–19.

20. Economic Research Service, U.S. Department of Agriculture, *The World Food Situation and Prospects to 1985* (Washington, D.C.: Government Printing Office, 1974), pp. v–vi.

21. Economic Research Service, U.S. Department of Agriculture, *World Agricultural Situation* (Washington, D.C.: Government Printing Office, 1975), p. 3.

22. *The World Food Situation and Prospects to 1985,* p. vii.

23. Roger Revelle, "Food and Population," *Scientific American,* September, 1974, p. 169.

24. *Ibid.,* p. 170.

25. James W. Howe and the staff of the Overseas Development Council, *The U.S. and World Development: Agenda for Action 1975* (New York: Praeger, 1975), p. 71.

26. Maddox, *The Doomsday Syndrome,* p. vi. A textbook example of Maddox' point is the publication of the Club of Rome's report, *The Limits to Growth.* Published in 1972, the report warned that mankind would strangle itself on its own growth in just a hundred years. But, in 1976, Dr. Aurelio Peccei, the club's founder, announced that the report was meant to "shock." Now we have "used that 'shock,' " he stated, "to start a dialogue," the subject of which according to one scientist at a club meeting is not "whether to grow" but rather "how to grow." (See Michael T. Malloy, "No-Growthers, Once Grim, Try a Smile," *The National Observer,* April 24, 1976.) This is comparable to yelling "Fire!" in a crowded theatre in order to "start a dialogue" on the need for more exit doors.

27. Daniel P. Moynihan, "The United States and the New World Society," *Reader's Digest,* June, 1975, p. 68.

28. E.C. Pasour, Jr., "The World Food Crisis," *The Freeman,* December, 1975, pp. 718–20.

29. Ronald Kotulak, "Poor lands do little to feed their own people," *Chicago Tribune,* March 22, 1976.

30. Randy Engel, *A Pro-Life Report on Population Growth and the American Future* (Export, Pa.: U.S. Coalition for Life, 1972), p. 30.

31. Kotulak, "Poor lands do little to feed their own people."

32. Donald P. Warwick, "The Moral Message of Bucharest," *The Hastings Center Report,* December, 1974, p. 8.

33. G. Harry Stine, *The Third Industrial Revolution* (New York: G.P. Putnam's Sons, 1975), p. 14.

34. *Ibid.,* pp. 25–26.

35. Adrian Berry, *The Next Ten Thousand Years* (New York: E.P. Dutton & Co., 1974), p. 193.

36. Fred Hoyle, *The New Face of Science* (New York: World Publishing Co., 1971), p. 117–18, quoted in *ibid.*

37. F.M. Esfandiary, "Homo Sapiens, the Manna Maker," *The New York Times,* August 9, 1975.

INDEX

Dyck, Arthur J., 171
Dyson, Freeman J., 53

E

Easterlin, Richard A., 162, 170–71, 208
Economic Research Service, 211
Egeberg, Dr. Roger O., 178
Ehrlich, Paul *(Population Bomb)*, 93–95, 96, 124, 160, 162, 173, 182, 183, 187, 206
Elder, Frederick, 188
entrepreneurship, 24–25, 31
entropy, 14
Enviromental Protection Agency, 146
Enviromental Science Service Administration, 98
Esfandiary, F. M., 215
Everett, A. H., 37

F

Federal Aviation Administration, 88
Fischman, Leonard L., 45, 46, 54–55
Fisher, Joseph L., 41–42, 45, 76–77
Flew, Anthony, 164
Ford Foundation, 173
Freedman, Jonathan, 123, 124–27
Freedman, Ronald, 151
Freeman, Roger A., 110, 141–42
Friedman, Milton, 102
Friends of the Earth, 173
Fuller, R. Buckminster, 14, 45

G

Gallop, R. A., 186
Gardner, B. Delworth, 62
Gavin, Hector *(Sanitary Ramblings)*, 72
Gotaas, Harold B., 72–73
Groseclose, Elgin, 21
Gross National Product (GNP), 34, 67, 77; and pollution control, 93; and population growth, 19, 138, 141; and social welfare, 102–3; and the welfare state, 142; growth rates in developing countries, 209; United States compared with France, China, India, and the Soviet Union, 20, 145

H

Hagan, Everett, 25, 26–27
Haider, Donald, 119

Roosevelt, President Theodore, 61
Rothenberg, Jerome, 95–96
Rushdoony, Rousas J., 149
Russell, Josiah Cox, 15

S

Sametz, A.W., 102
Sanger, Margaret, 173
Sauvy, Alfred, 20, 26, 30–31, 39, 148, 163, 170, 175, 208
savings: as a result of a growing population, 25–26
Say, J. B. 26
Scammon, Richard, 118, 131–32, 133
Schlesinger, James, 143
Second Industrial Revolution, 214
Sennholz, Hans F., 95
Sewell, John W., 212
Sierra Club, 173
Simon, Julian L., 10, 182–83, 208
Sklar, June, 202
Smith, Adam, 28, 29
Smith, Frank Austin, 46
Social Security, 107–8
Stanford Research Institute, 118
Starr, Chauncey, 52
Steinbeck, John (Travels with Charley), 132
Stigler, George, 29
Stine, G. Harry, 214
suburban growth, 117–18
Supreme Court of Germany, 196

T

ter Horst, Jerald, 87
Terhune, Kenneth W., 129–30
Thant, U, 159–60
thermodynamics: second law of, 14
Third Industrial Revolution, 214–15
Thomas, Richard L., 119
Tiger, Lionel (Men in Groups), 124
Tobin, James, 103
Toffler, Alvin (Future Shock), 131
traffic congestion: as a result of a growing population, 120–23
Triborough Bridge and Tunnel Authority, 121

World Bank, 62–64, 65, 67, 97
World Food Conference (Preparatory Committee), 209

Z

Zajonc, Robert B., 129
zero economic growth (ZEG), 76
zero population growth (ZPG), 10, 16, 62, 64, 138, 156; advocates of, 9–10, 18, 36, 94, 207; and death rate, 109; and housing, 111; and national independence, 149; and upper-middle class, 174; and upward mobility, 105; and zero technological development, 139; "near zero growth" as a national objective, 177
Zero Population Growth, 173, 181